The
ORVIS
Fly-Fishing Guide

The
ORVIS
Fly-Fishing Guide

Tom Rosenbauer

Illustrations by Georgine MacGarvey

Nick Lyons Books

PRINTED IN THE UNITED STATES OF AMERICA
10 9 8

Designed by Tasha Hall

Library of Congress Cataloging in Publication Data

Rosenbauer, Tom
  The Orvis fly-fishing guide.

  "Nick Lyons books."
  1. Fly fishing.   I. Title.
SH456.R66   1984   799.1'2   83-25898
ISBN 0-941130-91-6
ISBN 0-941130-92-4 (pbk.)

Contents

Acknowledgments

I'd like to thank the following people for showing me new techniques to use, new species to fish for, and some wonderful places to research this book: Spider Andreson, Vern and Mark Bressler, Bill Bryson, Carl Coleman, Leigh Condit, Alan Crossley, John Dembeck, Cooper Gilkes, Chuck Knauf, Ron and Maggie MacMillan, Del Mazza, Tom Shubat, Walter Ungermann, Herb Van Dyke, Wayne Walts, and Ron Zawoyski.

I am indebted to Bob Bachman and Neil Ringler, who have changed the way I look at fish populations and their behavior.

Editorial assistance is priceless, and John Merwin, Richard Wolters, Nick Lyons, and Paul Schullery have been particularly supportive throughout the past few years—particularly Nick, who has given me a writing lesson I'll never forget.

Cook Neilson and Silvio Calabi have provided invaluable help and constructive criticisms with my photography.

Pat Gill is a wizard at transforming my scribblings into typed pages. I still don't know how she does it.

For fishing patiently while I scrambled around them with a camera I'd like to thank the following people: Greg Comar, Bob Gotshall, Dave Linde, Dave Perkins, Rick Rishell, Tony Skilton and Jim Sulham.

John Harder was an endless and patient source of technical information on such things as fly-reel drag systems, special saltwater knots, striped bass fishing, and saltwater flies.

Howard Steere provided much assistance on fly-rod materials and actions.

I've never taken the time to thank my mother and father formally for putting up with a fishing fanatic for a son, for understanding that I visit them on Thanksgiving and not Christmas because the steelhead fishing near their home is better in November.

Finally, my deep thanks to Leigh Perkins and everyone at The Orvis Company for immeasurable amounts of help, support, and friendship.

Introduction

"What one book can I buy to start fly-fishing?"

I must have been asked that question dozens of times, and I've always been hard-pressed to answer it with confidence. I could think of a good book on casting, several on entomology and stream tactics, a couple on saltwater fly-fishing, and none on bass fishing. But there wasn't a broad-based, basic book that sensibly covered all aspects of fly-fishing —none that I could truly recommend.

I wrote *The Orvis Fly-Fishing Guide*, therefore, to fill what I perceived as a real and specific need. This book is for both the soon-to-be fly-fisherman as a starting point and for the reasonably proficient fly-fisherman as a reference. (Even quite capable fly-fishermen may need a refresher course on some specialized aspect of fly fishing, such as salt-water knots, the temperature preferences of bass, or the hatches to expect in Montana in late July.) I have tried to offer a balanced view of all the various elements and kinds of fly-fishing—including tackle selection, casting, flies, presentation, tactics, and a host of other subjects, for all the major game fish in fresh and salt water.

The book is the bare bones of fly fishing; it does not set out to tell *everything*. It will provide a sensible jumping-off point for a pastime that is simple in purpose, often amazingly—and quite wonderfully—complex in execution. Hopefully, THE ORVIS FLY-FISHING GUIDE will be a valuable introduction to fly-fishing: a sport that will give you immense pleasure, the chance to meet some wonderful people along the way, and more than a glimpse of some of the world's most beautiful places.

—Tom Rosenbauer
Manchester, Vermont
November 1983

1
What is
Fly-Fishing?

Fly casting makes it possible to deliver a relatively weightless lure or imitation of a living creature on target, using line weight to develop momentum. That's a fairly dry way of saying that, using a fly rod, you can catch fish with an artificial lure that can't be presented by any other method. It means that you can successfully fool a trout that feeds upon tiny insects measuring less than an eighth of an inch long—or lure a 150-pound tarpon into striking a six-inch feathered lure. Artificial flies are used to catch sunfish, bass, trout, pike, bluefish, shark, bonefish, sailfish, salmon, walleye, and even catfish. The possibilities are endless. Any fish that eats insects, minnows, or crustaceans can be caught with an artificial fly. Even shad, which are plankton feeders, can be angered into striking an artificial fly when they ascend freshwater rivers on their spawning run from the sea.

Fly fishing is most commonly associated with trout and salmon in streams; in fact, in most Atlantic salmon rivers in North America fly-fishing gear is the only kind allowed by law. But the same tackle used for trout can provide endless hours of fascination in a midwestern farm pond, fishing for bluegills. The heart-stopping leap of a smallmouth bass hooked on a fly-rod bug can be experienced on the Potomac River in Washington, D.C. A fisherman who lives in Florida, hundreds of

Fly-fishing is much more than just stream fishing for trout.

miles from the nearest trout stream, can use the same fly-rod outfit to catch largemouth bass one day, baby tarpon and snook in brackish canals the next, bonefish on shallow saltwater flats the next, and bluefish in the open ocean for a grand finale.

Fly-fishing is an ancient pursuit, perhaps practiced first by the Roman poet Martial (A.D. 40–104), who reportedly used a feathered hook to capture a saltwater fish similar to a weakfish. History also documents Aelian, another Roman, as observing Macedonian fisherman catching trout on artificial flies a hundred years later.

Throughout the Middle Ages and into the Renaissance, references are made to the imitation of artificial flies when fishing for trout. The early fly-fishers surely did not think of themselves as sportsmen; they were deceiving trout for more pragmatic reasons. Mayflies and other delicate creatures do not stay on a hook very well, nor do they retain their lifelike qualities after being impaled. The early fly-fishers were merely utilizing a bait that would last for dozens of fish without falling off the hook.

Fly-fishing tackle has changed considerably. The early fly-fishers had no fly lines as we know them today. They fished with long rods—sometimes over twenty feet long—and long leaders. Using a technique called dapping, which suspends the fly over the fish, they would tease him into striking. Any distance required was obtained from the long rods they used. Reels were nonexistent, and the line was tied to the end of the rod.

Today's "flies" may imitate anything fish would think of eating, from their own eggs to frogs, insects, mice, leeches, crabs, moths, minnows, and even snails. Rods from space-age fibers and reels constructed of the latest lightweight metallic alloys cast floating fly lines made by an ingenious process in which tiny glass bubbles (called microspheres) are homogenized into a plastic line coating. Fur and feathers are being replaced to some extent by synthetics, although many fly-tiers prefer the traditional materials. But the principle is still the same: a relatively weightless lure is delivered to the fish via a long, flexible rod and a weighted line. And fly-fishermen are still searching for the perfect imitation, the fly that will catch a fish on every cast. Let's hope the end of that rainbow will never be reached.

Flies will catch everything from the smallest sunfish . . .

to 150-pound tarpon.

Almost everyone today has used or seen a spinning outfit, and to understand just what fly casting is, a comparison of it and spin casting may be helpful. Let's take a look at two fishermen, both casting from a boat for bass, both using a minnow imitation.

A typical spin fisherman's lure weighs about a quarter of an ounce. One common type of spinning lure is carved from balsa wood or cast from plastic and is shaped like a minnow. It has a silvery painted finish, and a cup-shaped lip in the front makes it wobble like a minnow when retrieved through the water. His tackle consists of a 6½-foot spin rod and an ultralight spin reel that contains 200 yards of level 6-pound test monofilament line. The lure is tied directly onto his line. Holding the rod at about the 10:00 position in front of him, he uses his wrist to bring the tip of the rod back to 12:30; then a snap of the wrist quickly brings it back to 10:00. At the same time, he straightens his index finger, which has been crooked around the line. The flex of the rod snaps the lure off into space, pulling the line smoothly off the reel. Air resistance and gravity slow the lure's trajectory about sixty feet away, and it hits the water with a gentle splat. The fisherman retrieves his line and fishes the lure by turning a crank on the side of the reel; a mechanical bail gathers the line back onto the spool, moving the lure through the water with a minnowlike wobble. When the lure reaches the boat, he reels in more line until the lure is hanging a few inches below the tip of the rod. He is ready to make another cast.

Now let's take a look at the fly-fisherman. His objective is the same, but both his lure and tackle that presents it are quite different. The lure consists of a hook dressed with tinsel and feathers. The tinsel is wound around the straight part of the hook, forming a shiny "body" that reflects light in imitation of a minnow's silvery scales. The "wing" of the fly consists of two chicken feathers. The feathers, which have black centers with white edges, are an impressionistic view of a minnow's black medial stripe. This fly is called a streamer fly, and it would take a couple dozen of them to equal the weight of the spin fisherman's balsa wood version.

As the fly has virtually no weight, it lacks the momentum necessary to peel line off the front of the spinning reel. Even if you take a fly in your hand and heave it as far as you can, it will barely reach effective fishing distance. You can always dap the fly off the end of your spinning rod, as our primitive ancestors did with their embryonic fishing tackle, but there are more efficient ways to present a fly.

Instead of a long, level piece of nylon, the fly-fisherman relies upon a weighted line to deliver his fly. The line may float or sink once it hits the water, but it has enough weight to deliver the fly over a hundred feet away (although the average cast is much less, more like thirty feet). The thick fly line is separated from the fly by a leader of tapered nylon monofilament, basically the same stuff the spin fisherman's entire line is made of. The leader provides a flexible, relatively invisible connection between the fly line and the fly. It makes the fly appear lifelike and unattached on the water, and its air resistance allows the fly to settle gently to the water's surface.

Let's observe a fly-fisherman in action. After tying the fly to his leader, he pulls ten feet of fly line out beyond the tip of his fly rod. Then he pulls thirty feet of fly line off the reel and holds it, coiled, in his left hand. With a quick back-and-forth flicking motion, using his right forearm and wrist, he moves the tip of the fly rod from straight out in front of him to just past the vertical. As the fly line moves through the air it describes a tight, elongated arc. The arc flattens, parallel to the water, both behind and in front of him. He does this three or four times, without letting the fly or line hit the water, releasing some of the coiled fly line in his left hand every time he finishes a forward stroke. When he finishes the fourth "false cast," as they are called, his fly, leader, and line settle gently to the water, forty feet away.

The streamer, a type of wet fly, sinks slowly beneath the surface, pulling the leader along. The fisherman begins to retrieve line, moving the fly through the water. Instead of using his reel to retrieve line, as the spin fisherman does, he hooks the fly line over the index finger of the hand that is holding the rod and pulls the fly line with his other hand. Each pull of the line makes the fly dart through the water like a minnow. And each length of line is carefully coiled in his left hand, ready to be worked out on the next cast. When the fly is about ten feet from the boat, our fisherman will begin another cast, repeating the process.

You can fly-fish from a canoe in a small pond...

5

. . .or right from shore.

At first glance it seems as if the fly-fisherman has to go through a lot of effort for a single cast. All the spin fisherman has to do to deliver the lure is flick the tip of his rod once, while the fly-fisherman has to move his rod a few times before his fly reaches an effective fishing distance. But fly-fishing has its advantages. For one, if the fly-fisherman suddenly sees a feeding fish, he can pick up that entire forty-foot length of line, change the direction of his cast in midair, and lay it down right in front of the fish. The spin fisherman must reel in all his line before he can even think about making a cast to another spot. And there are other advantages.

Although fly-fishing is probably the most enjoyable way to fish for trout, it is not always the most efficient method. In early spring, when the water is cold, the trout are not inclined to move for a drifting fly. A worm put right in front of their noses is much more appealing. One early spring afternoon, I was walking the bank of my favorite river, searching for surface-feeding trout. A worm fisherman was carefully and methodically working one of the runs, and I envied his ability to place his worm right on the bottom. Bait is effective just sitting there, but a fly must move or drift with the current to entice trout.

I sat on the bank, keeping my eyes peeled for those characteristic rings on the surface of the water that indicate trout feeding on emerging insects. At this time of year I could expect to see grayish-colored mayflies emerging at about 2:00 P.M. The trout often feed on these insects to the exclusion of other types of food.

Sure enough, about 1:45 I saw the sailboat wings of the mayflies glittering in the weak spring sunlight as they rode the currents, drying their wings. A dozen adult mayflies were soon airborne, flying slowly but steadily upstream. Then two dozen. Then three. By 2:00 the surface of the water was covered with struggling mayfly adults, and the trout finally took notice, as mayfly after mayfly disappeared into the concentric rings of surface-feeding trout. It was the kind of opportunity that fly-fisherman often yearn for but seldom see.

I waded out into the pool with a light gray dry fly, an imitation of the floating mayfly, tied to my leader. The normally elusive brown and brook trout of this river must have forgotten the lessons they learned last season. It seemed that every time I put my fly over a fish, it was taken. I was elated—so elated that I forgot about the worm fisherman sitting on the bank behind me until he started exclaiming: "Ooh! Oh my God! Oh!" Every time I hooked a fish, his awe became more apparent. Finally he gave in.

"What kind of bait are you using?"

"Dry flies," I said.

"Live ones?"

"No, artificials made out of fur and feathers."

"I've been fishing worms all morning, couldn't get a strike," he complained. "Usually worms work out pretty good."

"Guess they just want flies today," I replied. "It isn't always this easy."

He pelted me with more questions, while I played and released fish almost continuously. Finally the worm fisherman thanked me for my patience with his questions and began walking to his car, dejection showing in the slump of his shoulders. He turned to me once more.

"Is it hard to learn?"

Natural and deceiver: the Hendrickson mayfly and a dry-fly imitation.

2
Fly Rods
and Line Sizes

A fly rod is a tool for casting and repositioning line and playing fish. But since it seems to have a personality of its own, you might think of a fly rod as an extension of your own anatomy—a long, skinny finger.

The phrase "casting a fly" is not really an accurate description of what you do when you wave a fly rod back and forth. A fly rod casts a weighted fly line; the leader and fly go along for the ride. Casting energy is transferred from your forearm and wrist through the rod to the line, which provides the energy to drive the leader and fly up to ninety feet away. Thus, it's difficult to discuss fly rods without talking about fly lines. In fact, when we name a fly rod, we generally describe it by length and line size: 8½-foot for 6-weight line, or 9-foot for 9-weight line. The material the rod is constructed from and the weight of the rod are also important parameters, though less important than length and line size.

Too often, fly-fishermen will ask: "I have a 3⅞-ounce bamboo rod. What kind of fishing can I do with it?" Describing your fly rod by weight alone is like describing someone by saying he weighs 190 pounds. Giving a rod's length, line size, and material, however, is like describing his personality, his purpose in life, his faults and his strong points, as well as his physical properties.

A fly rod casts the line, repositions the line, and lets you play a fish without breaking the leader.

FLY-ROD TERMINOLOGY

Before we discuss fly-rod line sizes, lengths, and materials, let's identify the parts of a fly rod. Although one-piece fly rods exist, they are not terribly practical, because it's hard to fit an eight-foot rod inside the trunk of your car. The most common fly rods are two-piece, although three- and four-piece versions are also available and are quite practical. The thicker, lower section of a fly rod (the piece that includes the handle) is called the butt section. The skinny top section is the tip section, and the in-between sections on three- and four-piece rods have the imaginative designation "mid sections."

Starting at the extreme bottom of the fly rod, the metal cap is called the end plug. On some large saltwater and salmon rods this plug can be removed and replaced with a detachable butt extension or fighting butt. This attachment is used when the fly-fisherman expects to be playing large fish for a long time. He can brace it against his stomach or belt, taking a lot of the strain out of his arms—a most pleasant weariness that generally accompanies big-game fishing.

The end plug is attached to the reel seat, which is available in an almost endless variety of materials. Although the reel seat's sole pur-

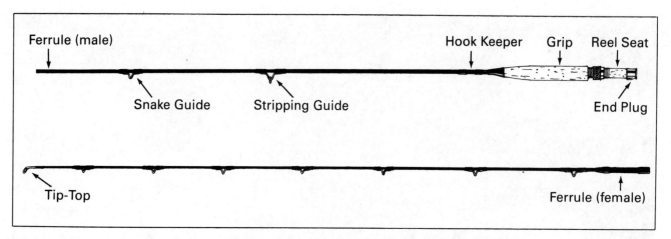

Ferrule (male)

Snake Guide   Stripping Guide

Hook Keeper   Grip   Reel Seat

End Plug

Tip-Top

Ferrule (female)

Parts of a fly rod.

pose is to hold the fly reel securely to the rod, fly-rod manufacturers and amateur rod builders often spend an inordinate amount of time discussing the relative merits of designs and materials. The reel seat usually consists of a metal frame, which actually holds the reel, and a filler. The frame is usually a strong, lightweight aluminum alloy. The filler, for practical and cosmetic reasons, may be made from cork, walnut, maple, zebra wood, or other exotic woods. Premium hardware is often made from jewelry-grade nickel-silver (heavier and more expensive, but exquisite in appearance). In large saltwater rods the entire reel seat is made from chrome-plated brass, which is necessary to hold heavy saltwater reels and to resist the corrosive action of salt water.

A sample of the reel seats offered by modern fly-rod manufacturers includes:

Ring type. Designed for small reels and light fly rods, the ring type consists of two thin metal bands that are forced over the feet of the fly reel. Although they are more secure than they appear, avoid reels that weigh over three ounces with this type of reel seat.

Screw-locking. This type consists of a fixed metal hood at the bottom of the seat, combined with a hood at the top, which can be screwed down over the reel-seat foot. Probably the most popular type of reel seat.

Reversed screw-locking. Exactly the same as the screw-locking, except that the fixed hood is at the other end of the seat, and is often buried inside the cork grip. The screw band screws *up* toward the grip—in fact, this type is often called "up-locking," as opposed to the "down-locking" reel seat above.

Most other reel seats are simply variations on the above three types, incorporating such features as fixed fighting butts or, in the case of the two-handed salmon rod, a second grip located below the reel seat. As long as your reel seat is of the correct size to accommodate your reel, you should select a type for aesthetic reasons.

The grip functions as the handle of your fly rod. On all quality fly rods it is constructed from cork that was filed on a lathe and sanded smooth. Grip style, which varies in diameter size and in shape, is a matter of personal taste. Grips commonly used, in order of increasing diameter, include superfine, cigar, half wells, and full wells. People

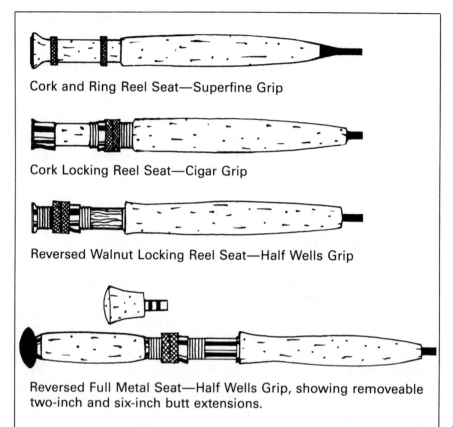

Cork and Ring Reel Seat—Superfine Grip

Cork Locking Reel Seat—Cigar Grip

Reversed Walnut Locking Reel Seat—Half Wells Grip

Reversed Full Metal Seat—Half Wells Grip, showing removeable two-inch and six-inch butt extensions.

Commonly used reel seats and grip styles.

with small hands generally prefer the smaller-diameter grips; those with big hands feel more comfortable with something like a full-wells grip.

Working your way up along the rod, you'll find a small metal ring or hook called the hook keeper. When you are not fishing, your fly is hooked here to keep it from catching in streamside brush (or your clothing!).

Next you'll encounter the first guide, called the stripping guide. The purpose of fly-rod guides is threefold: to hold the line to the rod during casting, to funnel the line along the length of the rod when shooting line (releasing extra line to obtain additional distance), and to distribute properly along the entire length of the rod, the stress of playing the fish. The stripping guide, being the first part of the rod the line encounters after leaving the reel, receives a lot of wear and tear. To reduce friction, the stripping guide is made from an abrasion-resistant material, usually hard chrome or ceramic. The rest of the guides, of which there should be at least as many as the rod is long in feet, are simple bent pieces of wire called snake guides. Guides are distributed along a rod according to a specific formula that is unique to each length of rod, and are attached to the rod with nylon thread, which is varnished three or four times for durability and protection from the elements. The last guide, which sits at the extreme top of the tip section, is called the tip-top.

Some fly rods feature ceramic stripping guides or single-foot ceramic guides along the entire length of the rod, instead of snake guides. But these are so heavy and air-resistant that they change the action of the rod. The idea is to lessen the friction between guides, enabling the caster to shoot more line.

Ferrules are the joints that connect the sections of multiple-piece rods. They are designed to hold the pieces of a rod together throughout a day of fishing, yet pull apart easily when you want to put your rod away. Ferrules on bamboo rods are made of nickel-silver metal, while those on graphite, fiberglass, and boron/graphite are "self-ferrules," which involve a tapered sleeve of the rod material itself, glued to the tip section, that fits snugly over the butt section.

LINE SIZES

To understand why line size is so important, you must realize that fly-fishing is immensely versatile. If everyone fished with flies that were ¼-inch to ¾-inch long, in streams fifteen to thirty feet wide, in a place where winds were always moderate to light, we'd need only one line size. But flies range in size from ⅛ inch to over six inches in length, and the corresponding differences in air resistance of these different-sized flies require lines of different weights. Generally, the heavier the fly line, the larger the fly you'll be able to cast, the fewer problems you'll have with wind, and the farther you can cast. The lighter your line, the more delicate and accurate your presentation will be with smaller flies.

A well-made fly rod is designed for a particular line size. The shape of the loop on your line cast is very important, and it is necessary to keep the fly line moving through the air in a special fashion. To cast properly, a fly rod must exhibit a happy medium between flexibility and stiffness. These characteristics are derived from a well-designed fly rod, good casting form, and the weight of the fly line pulling on the rod. A heavy fly line will exert more pull on a fly rod during casting; thus, a rod designed for throwing large flies into the wind will be stiffer than a rod designed to present tiny dry flies with a light fly line.

In order to cast a line, a fly rod must flex in a special fashion. This flex cannot come from the weight of either the fly or the leader; it must come from the weight of the line. "Fly-rod balance" is the key. If a line is too light for your rod, the rod will not flex enough, making you work extra hard in order to cast. If the line is too heavy, it will overload the rod and cause sloppy presentation.

Eventually, every fly-fisherman asks: "Can I get one fly rod that will do everything for me?" That depends upon what is meant by "everything." If you will be fishing for, say, trout and nothing else, the answer could be yes. However, if you want to fish for many different kinds of fish on rivers, lakes, ponds, and oceans, you will probably need a number of fly rods.

The all-purpose fly rod can be likened to an all-purpose golf club. It's possible to play eighteen holes of golf with a putter, but it's certainly not efficient (and not much fun).

Chart I shows the range of line weights used by fly-fishermen, the typical rod materials and lengths used, and the situations in which you would use these sizes. The number designation of each weight correspond to the weight in grains (437.5 grains = 1 ounce) of the first thirty feet of line. This system was adopted by the American Fishing Tackle Manufacturers Association in 1961, and is used throughout the world by all fly-line manufacturers. This weight may range from 100 grains for a 3-weight line to 380 grains for a 12-weight.

Why do we use weight at all? Why not diameter? Actually, before 1961 fly lines were classed by diameter, with letters of the alphabet referring to particular diameters. All lines were made of silk, so diameters were consistent with weight. With the advent of modern floating, sinking, and intermediate-weight lines, with their varying densities, this system had to be scrapped and was replaced with the modern system based on weight.

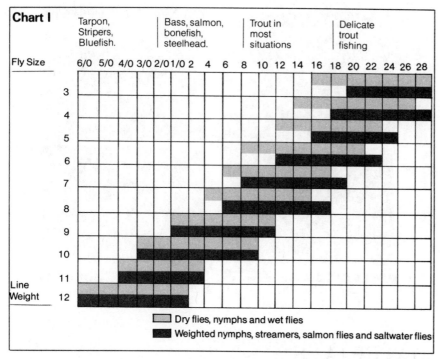

Fly rod/line size relationships.

Some fly rods, especially modern graphite and boron/graphite rods, will cast two or three line sizes with minor adjustments in casting technique. Whether a particular rod can do this depends on its design, and you will have to try different lines on a rod to find this out. As a rule of thumb, you can get away with one line size heavier if your casts will be consistently under thirty feet, and one line size lighter if they will be consistently longer than forty feet.

Again referring to Chart I, you can see that, for any type of fishing or fly size range, you have a choice of two or perhaps even three line sizes. This leeway allows you to choose your line size to fit prevailing weather and water conditions. For example, in stream trout fishing we generally use fly sizes 12 through 18. These would call for a 4-, 5-, or 6-weight line. If casts are frequently long and wind is a constant factor, the 6-

weight would be the best choice. If your streams lie in protected valleys and winds are light, or if the fish are skittish, the 4-weight might be a better choice. For a little bit of both, go with the 5-weight.

Rods that call for 11- or 12- weight lines are unlike any other kind of rod, because they are designed more for playing large fish than for casting. Usually called "tournament tarpon" rods, they allow the fly-fisherman to muscle large tarpon, sailfish, or sharks. You might be able to hook and play a 150-pound fish with a lighter fly rod without breaking the rod, but a lighter model will bend to such a degree that you'll never be able to put enough pressure on a huge fish to land it.

All fly rods made by reputable manufacturers are marked with the recommended line size. This recommendation is usually either engraved on the butt plate or inscribed on the butt section of the rod.

The important raw materials used in fly rod construction, and portions of the finished product: bamboo, fiberglass, graphite, and boron.

MATERIALS

In selecting a fly rod, the other two variables involved are material and length. The material that the rod is made of will to some degree determine the personality of the rod, or the casting tempo or "action" it exhibits. The material will definitely determine both the appearance and the price of your rod.

A bamboo fly rod, or "split bamboo" or "split cane" rod, is known even to non-fly-fishers as the hallmark of the affluent sportsman. Fly rods handcrafted from bamboo, with a heritage dating back over a hundred years, are sometimes thought to be fragile and easily broken. This belief has about as much basis in truth as does the proverbial story of the young boy with a bent pin outfishing the experienced sport. The finished bamboo fly rod is a solid, six-sided shaft. The glowing brown and amber bamboo is polished and varnished to produce a fishing rod that is unmatched in appearance. Most of the steps in making a bamboo rod are hand operations performed by craftsmen, and other than electric saws and milling machines, they use hand tools. It takes a month or more to produce each quality bamboo fly rod.

Briefly, raw bamboo is graded and sorted, strips are cut from the bamboo poles, and the strips are tapered on a milling machine to tolerances of a few thousandths of an inch. Six strips are glued together to form the solid rod, the outside of the rod is lightly sanded, and only then can the reel seat, grip, guides, and ferrules be mounted to the rod. A bamboo fly rod carries a pride of ownership that only the fly-fisherman and perhaps a custom woodworker can appreciate.

Before the advent of fly rods made from synthetic materials, starting with fiberglass in the mid-1940s and continuing with graphite and boron in the 1970s and '80s, bamboo was the only material of any significance, at least in the twentieth century. Manufacturers experimented with other types of wood and with tubular steel, but these produced inferior fly rods. Thus, bamboo was used for all types of fly rods, from the biggest, heaviest saltwater and salmon rods to the most delicate trout rods.

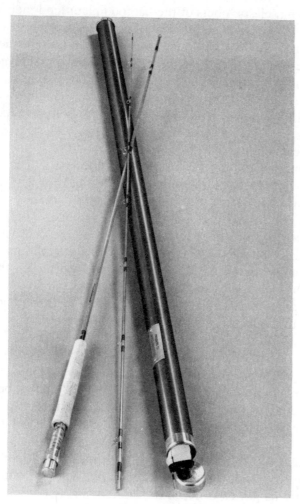

A bamboo fly rod: the highest expression of a rodmaker's craft.

15

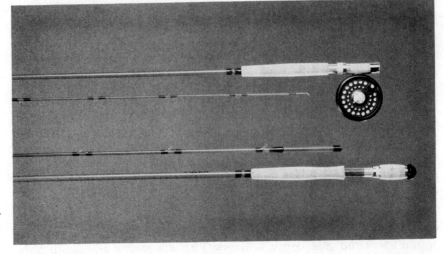

Fiberglass fly rods: a large salmon/saltwater rod at bottom and a standard trout model on top.

Bamboo rods are heavier for a particular class of rod than any of the synthetics, and in the 8- to 12-weight sizes they have been edged out of the market by the lighter and more powerful synthetics. Who wants to cast all day with a nine-ounce bamboo fly rod when a four-ounce graphite rod can do the job as well or better?

The strong, elastic fibers of the bamboo plant lend their personality to the bamboo rod, giving it a special casting sensation that is unique. These fly rods are neither better nor worse than those made from synthetic materials, but they are different. Bamboo fly rods feel more flexible when casting, lending themselves to a relaxed casting style. This is because bamboo fibers stretch more than, say, graphite to deliver the same amount of power. Some fly-fisherman, myself included, feel that bamboo is superior for delivering tiny, delicate flies to sophisticated trout in clear water.

A beginner should not shy away from a bamboo fly rod, but merely respect its limitations, namely weight and price. For fly-fishing in salt water, or wherever large flies must be cast long distances, bamboo is surely not as efficient as graphite or boron/graphite. This is not to say that bamboo is more fragile. A good bamboo rod can withstand the shock of being whacked against a tree limb or steady thrumming against a boat gunwale much better than synthetic rods, with their hollow construction. For trout fishing, pan fishing, or fishing with the smaller bass flies, at normal casting ranges (up to sixty feet) bamboo is as good as any synthetic fly rod, and many aficionados feel it is better.

Fiberglass was the first successful synthetic material used to make fly rods, and it is still with us today. Since the 1950s, fiberglass has been improved with new resin systems and fibers that are more consistent in their properties. Fiberglass fly rods are round and hollow, because they are formed by wrapping fiberglass around a stainless steel form, or mandrel, under pressure. The mandrel is removed, leaving the hollow fly rod.

Fiberglass is lighter than bamboo but it must bend more to deliver the same power; thus, when stressed on a long, powerful cast, a fiberglass rod will lose its power, or reach its elastic limit, under less stress than will a bamboo, graphite, or boron/graphite rod. However, this limit can be reached only within the abilities of a tournament caster, and is something that we ordinary mortals don't have to worry about. Fiberglass is also less sensitive to casting subtleties and less forgiving of casting mistakes.

Fiberglass rods have a big edge on all other types of modern fly rods in that a good one costs about half the price of a graphite or boron/graphite rod, and about one quarter the price of a bamboo rod. Fiberglass is an inexpensive raw material, and the fabrication techniques require much less labor. But the inexpensive nature of fiberglass has led to many poor-quality, mass-produced rods that are little more than spin rods with fly-rod guides. Buy your fiberglass fly rod from a reputable *fly-rod* salesman, not a sporting-goods clerk who feels more comfortable selling tennis rackets or bicycles.

Fiberglass rods are made for all types of fly-fishing, from trout to tarpon. They are also very rugged; thus, they lend themselves well to youngsters, who tend to be impatient with things like fly rods.

Graphite is a polyester fiber that has been subjected to intense heat and pressure. It was developed by the aerospace industry as a light, heat-resistant alternative to metals. As used in fly rods, graphite consists of thousands of tiny, hairlike filaments held together by epoxy resin. A flat piece of this material, cut to a taper, is rolled around a

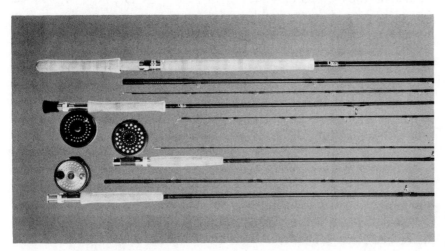

Graphite fly rods. From top to bottom: a two-handed salmon rod, a heavy tarpon rod with fixed butt extension, a trout or bass model, and a light saltwater or salmon model with a full-metal reel seat.

tapered mandrel and subjected to heat and pressure, after which the mandrel is removed. The resulting fly rod is extremely light, has tensile strength greater than steel, and, most important to us, makes a very fine fly rod.

That a graphite fly rod is lighter than a bamboo or fiberglass rod is not terribly significant when you are comparing trout-size models, as the difference in weight is a fraction of an ounce. When you compare the longer, thicker-walled saltwater, salmon, or bass rods, however, the weight differential is extremely significant. The fact that a nine-foot bamboo salmon rod weighs almost seven ounces and a fiberglass rod almost six, while a graphite rod weighs only three, doesn't sound significant—but

17

when you are wielding this rod through hundreds of casts a day, using only the muscles of your wrist and forearm, you appreciate the difference.

Graphite also has a special virtue: a comparatively high modulus (degree) of elasticity. This means that graphite has a high resistance to bending—or, quite simply, it's stiffer. Being stiffer without breaking is desirable up to a point, as it enables a rod to flex less to deliver the same length of line; this means that it will hold a longer length of line in the air, will have a quicker response rate between back and forward casts, and can be made thinner, cutting down on air resistance. All of these factors produce a higher line speed. More line speed produces more line momentum, so your fly line travels farther than if you expended the same effort with a bamboo or fiberglass fly rod.

In order to direct the fly line to the proper spot, your fly rod should bend when you direct it to and stay still when you want it to. The high modulus of elasticity also means that graphite rods have a quick recovery rate. When you finish your forward cast and the rod is pointing to where you want the line to go, the less your rod wiggles the more efficient and accurate your casting will be. Graphite fly rods are the most efficient casting rods known today.

Obviously, graphite's qualities lend themselves well to rods for big flies and heavy line sizes. How about delicate fishing and light line sizes? Because graphite is stiffer than bamboo or fiberglass, long (over eight-foot) rods for light fly lines (3-, 4-, and 5-weights) can be practical fishing tools, rods that would not be possible with either bamboo or fiberglass.

Graphite is also more forgiving of casting mistakes than any other material, and our years of experience in the Orvis Fly Fishing Schools have substantiated this belief. The hardest problem a beginning caster encounters is producing a high, flat back cast. Mistakes in timing that would be disastrous with a bamboo rod can produce a passable presentation with a graphite rod.

True all-boron fly rods are at present made by only one person, on a limited basis. They are solid, thin fly rods, reminiscent of delicate bamboo rods. They are presently being made only in the lighter line sizes.

Boron/graphite composite fly rods, as made by Orvis, are stiff and powerful. Adding boron to graphite gives the rods an even higher modulus of elasticity than graphite alone. They are special-purpose rods, designed for medium to heavy line sizes and long casts. They produce extremely high line speed and cast very well into the wind. As a result, boron/graphite fly rods are popular with fly-fishermen who fish large flies at long distances, over wide waters where problem winds are often encountered.

ACTION

Fly-fishermen often say, "That rod has good action," or "The action of this rod is poor." Great—all that tells us is that this fellow likes the way one rod feels in his hands, with his own particular casting style, and doesn't like the other. "Action" merely describes the way a fly rod flexes under stress.

In the golden age of bamboo rods, action was supposed to dictate what kind of flies could be used with a particular rod. "Fast action" was stiffer, and this type of rod flexed almost entirely in the top 25 percent of the rod. Flicking excess water from a dry fly was its purpose. "Slow-action" rods flexed all the way into the grip during casting, and were designed *not* to flick the water off a wet fly. "Fast action" became synonymous with dry-fly action, an "slow action" was equal to wet-fly action. "Medium action," obviously, was somewhere in between. The "slow" and "fast" came from the fact that it takes a lot more time to develop the power needed for a cast when the rod bends all the way into its lower sections than it does for a rod to flex just at the tip.

The fact that modern graphite, boron, and fiberglass rods behave so differently from bamboo rods has made comparisons of actions obsolete. For rods of comparable length and line size, fiberglass is usually the slowest, bamboo is next, graphite faster, and boron or boron/graphite the fastest. This comparison is based only on the stiffness of the materials involved. Theoretically, by thickening the walls on a fiberglass rod you could make it faster than graphite, but it would be extremely thick and heavy.

Most modern fly rods are built to a progressive taper or "progressive action," which means that as the rod is loaded with more line, it flexes lower and lower. Variations in action occur between manufacturers and between different models made by the same manufacturer. There are really no set rules for building fly-rod action.

LENGTH

Standard lengths for trout and bass fly rods run from seven and a half to eight and a half feet. These particular lengths in line sizes 5, 6, 7, and 8 (the most common line sizes used today) achieve a balance between lightness, manageability, and casting efficiency. As rod length becomes shorter, casting efficiency decreases, because the mechanical advantage obtained (the whole reason for using a fly rod) decreases as the arc through which the tip of the rod moves decreases. A fly rod less than six feet long is a novelty and not particularly pleasant to cast. To a lesser degree, fly rods longer than these lengths also decrease in efficiency, mainly because of added weight and air resistance. With graphite, though, it is possible to make a practical fly rod for a 6-weight line as long as ten and a half feet. Graphite salmon rods are made as long as fifteen feet, but these are two-handed rods and are used almost exclusively on European salmon rivers. The long, powerful two-handed rods are capable of picking up eighty feet of line and redirecting it to another spot in the river in a single cast.

Short fly rods have their advocates, and a six-and-a-half-foot fly rod is

Tight quarters call for a short fly rod.

more manageable than an eight-footer in brushy country; it is lighter by almost a full ounce, and it has faster action than a longer rod for a corresponding line size. The shorter rod is faster because it is stiffer, as the same amount of line weight has to be held in the air by less material. Short fly rods make it easier to drive in a fly under overhanging brush, because of their faster line speed and greater maneuverability. Short fly rods are also deadly-efficient tools for fighting large fish. It is much easier to lead a fish into the net at close quarters with a short fly rod.

The practicality of longer fly rods is due to graphite fiber. For example, a nine-foot fly rod for a 4-weight line in bamboo or fiberglass would be heavy and as limp as cooked spaghetti, yet such graphite rods are commonplace today. Long (over eight and a half feet) fly rods for the heavier line sizes (9 to 12) have always been made, because a seven-foot rod for a 10-weight line would have to be so stiff that it would hardly bend at all. But graphite's light weight has almost entirely edged bamboo out of the area of heavy lines/long rods. Long fiberglass rods are also used, but almost entirely in the heavy line sizes.

Thus, a fly-fisherman with an eye toward big game fish in the open ocean or salmon on a raging Norwegian river almost *has* to choose a longer rod. What about the trout-and-bass fisherman? Should he consider a rod over eight and a half feet long, even if he never has to cast over forty feet?

The question of fly-rod length can become quite personal, and if a fly-fisherman "just likes" the idea of an ultralight, short fly rod or a long rod, more power to him. Long fly rods have their advantages under certain circumstances, and it's important to recognize the helping hand that a long fly rod can provide. Remembering that a fly rod is merely an extension of your hand and arm, it's obvious that a rod over eight and a half feet long will be a great help when the fishing situation calls for repositioning the fly line and/or fly on the water once the cast has been made. For example, imagine that you are standing in an area of fast water in the middle of a trout stream, and trout are rising in the slower water against the far bank. With a short rod, as soon as the fly line hits the water, the fast current at your feet will immediately begin to pull on it, whisking the fly out of the slower water. A long rod will extend your reach, enabling you to hold the fly line above the fast water. By repositioning line on the water, you can also control the speed at which a wet fly drifts through the current.

Bass fishermen who wade in the edges of small lakes and ponds prefer long fly rods for a number of reasons. One advantage of a long rod is that it will keep a fly line out of the vegetation along the shoreline, enabling you to control your fly or bug with greater precision. Whether you fish in lakes or in streams, a long rod, with its greater vertical reach, will keep your back cast out of low trees and shrubs. When you're casting from a sitting position in a boat, a long fly rod will also keep your fly line from slapping the water.

Long fly rods also offer certain casting advantages. They are a great help when the situation calls for a long cast, holding more line in the air, helping you to overcome gravity on your back cast. By enabling you to pick up more line off the water, a long fly rod can also place your fly back on the water with a single cast. A six-foot fly rod just cannot develop enough momentum to pick up sixty feet of line with a single casting stroke.

Fly rods longer than seven and a half feet also offer smoother, longer roll casts. (This is getting ahead of ourselves a bit—roll cast is essentially a cast that has no back cast. The roll cast is a lifesaver when you find yourself backed up against a wall of streamside brush and trees.)

FLY-ROD SELECTION

I'll stick my neck out and recommend that your first fly rod be between eight and nine feet long, and be made from graphite. This seems to be the most efficient length for easy fly casting, and graphite is more forgiving of casting mistakes than any other material. If you fish small streams, lean toward an eight-footer; if you fish big rivers, lakes, or salt water, an eight-and-a-half- or nine-foot rod will be easier for long casts or when the wind is blowing.

Because these lengths are the most popular among fly-rodders, they come in the complete range of line sizes. If all your fly-fishing will be done for trout in clear water or for panfish, pick a rod that calls for a 4- to 5-weight line. For all-around trout fishing, choose a 6-weight rod, by far the most common line size used by trout fishermen. For both trout and bass, get a 7-weight outfit. For just bass, salmon, and smaller, inshore saltwater species, get an 8-weight. Only if you are fly-fishing just for the larger saltwater species or salmon or steelhead should you go as heavy as a 9-weight outfit, as these rods are heavier and more tiring than trout or bass rods of the same length.

Take time before you choose. Ask a knowledgeable friend or a trusted fly-fishing dealer. Good fly-fishing schools can provide solid advice. Always try the rod with a matching line before you buy.

3
Lines and Reels

FLY-LINE OPTIONS

You are now the proud owner of a new fly-rod outfit, including rod, reel, and a weight-forward floating line of the proper size for your rod. Is this line the only one you'll need? Can you fish wet flies with a floating line? What's the difference between a double taper and a weight-forward taper?

Modern fly lines come in an array of tapers and densities. A battery of different fly lines, mounted on extra spools that fit your fly reel, can help you increase the distance of your casts and keep your fly just under the surface, twenty feet below the surface, or anywhere in between.

Take a look at the line packages in a fly shop. You'll see them marked with a code that might read "DT5F" or "WF6S" or "ST8F/S." You already know the meaning of the number—it's the line size. The first two letters designate the taper, or how the line varies in thickness throughout its length. The last letter or letters tell you the line type—whether the line floats, sinks quickly, sinks slowly, or only partly sinks.

Taper

Standard fly lines are between eighty and ninety feet in length. The weight distribution along this length is tapered, except in level (L)

DT—Double Taper

WF—Weight Forward

ST—Shooting Taper

L—Level

S—Sinking

F—Floating

F/S—Sinking Tip

I—Intermediate

Fly Line Tapers and Line Types

lines, which are practically worthless in terms of their casting and presentation qualities. Many of us made the mistake of trying to learn how to fly-fish with a level line. After all, a tapered line costs two to three times as much. Why spend all that money on something you may give up after a season?

Giving up after a season is exactly what you may do if you start with a level line. Tapered lines are designed to take advantage of a gradual decrease in weight that transmits energy smoothly to the leader and fly, resulting in that feather-light delivery we associate with no other method of fishing. An accomplished caster can appreciate the niceties of increased accuracy and delicacy, but even a first-time fly-caster can see how much easier it is to cast with a tapered line.

All fly lines start thin at the end to which the leader is attached, to minimize the disturbance when your cast touches the water. The line gradually thickens into what is called the belly, which is at least thirty feet long. This is the portion of your line that you hold in the air when casting. Weight-forward (WF) lines taper down quickly after thirty feet of head to a thin running line that takes up the rest of the length. Double-taper (DT) lines form a mirror image if you cut them in half; the belly does not thin and extends through to a taper on the opposite end. Shooting-taper or shooting-head (ST) lines replace the running line with fine-diameter floating fly line or monofilament. The actual fly-line part of a shooting head is only thirty feet long. A loop is spliced into the back end of the line and into the running line, making a quick change from a floating to a sinking line without your having to replace the reel spool.

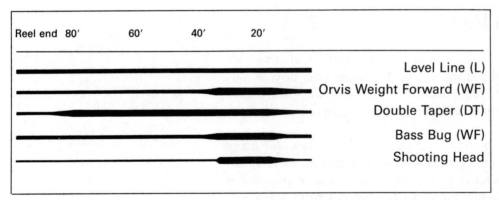

Reel end 80'   60'   40'   20'

Level Line (L)

Orvis Weight Forward (WF)

Double Taper (DT)

Bass Bug (WF)

Shooting Head

Fly line tapers.

Weight-forward lines are best for the beginning caster, because they cast and shoot easier than a double taper. They were originally designed for distance casting, because concentrating the weight up front enables the caster to shoot longer lengths of line with less effort. Modern weight-forward lines have a gentle front taper and are every bit as delicate as the traditional double-taper line.

Besides the standard weight-forward, you may also see lines listed as bass-bug or saltwater tapers. These are lines with a steep front taper, designed especially for casting large flies into the wind. These lines are not versatile, because they lack delicacy, so many bass and saltwater fly-fishermen stick with standard weight-forward lines.

Double-taper lines offer the advantage of economy, because if one end of the line becomes damaged or worn out it can be reversed. The myth that double-taper lines are more delicate than weight-forwards does not hold true today because of the gentle tapers incorporated into modern weight-forward lines. Double-taper lines do roll cast long lines well, because the heavier middle portion helps to develop the roll, rather than the hinging effect that occurs when you try to roll cast a weight-forward line with more than thirty feet of line on the water. The purported ability of double-taper lines to false cast long lengths of line is dubious at best; a fifty-foot false cast can be controlled only by a most skillful fly-caster. Using a weight-forward line's shooting properties is a much more efficient way to get distance. For small-stream work, though, the double taper is a most efficient and economical fly line, with its roll-casting advantages and reversibility.

Shooting tapers were originally designed for tournament casting; they were never intended to be used in practical fishing situations. Replacing the running line of a weight-forward line with a running line greatly reduced in diameter reduced both friction between rod guides and air resistance. A group of ingenious West Coast steelhead fishermen discovered that by using shooting-taper lines, not only could they reach the far bank of unwadable rivers, they could also cheat strong winds and get their flies deeper in fast-moving rivers. The same qualities that lessen air resistance also help fast-sinking shooting heads cut through heavy river currents.

Shooting-taper lines are now used in all types of fly-fishing where extra-long casts and strong winds are the rule. They are limited in their application, though, because they lack delicacy. Many fly-fishermen also find it difficult to handle shooting tapers, since those coils of thin

25

running line tangle much more easily than the thicker fly line. Fishermen who employ shooting heads may strip coils of line in a shooting basket that straps onto their waist when wading, or use an improvised plastic garbage can when fishing from a boat. These devices let them shoot great lengths of line with less chance of tangling.

Line Type

Most fly fishermen use a floating line (F) as their basic line. Floating fly lines incorporate tiny glass microballoons in the coating that forms the taper of the line. Although they need to be cleaned periodically, they need no grease or line dressing to float them, as did the old silk lines. Some floating fly lines actually have a hydrophobic coating that repels water.

Floating lines are the workhorses of fly-fishing; they are not limited to use only with floating flies. Wet flies sink of their own accord, because they are tied on heavy wire hooks; they can also be weighted with lead wire wrapped around the shank of the hook before the fly is tied. Leaders can be weighted with tiny split shot or lead strips. Thus, floating fly lines can be used to fish wet flies several feet below the surface; in small streams and shallow ponds a floating line is all you'll need. Sinking lines do not offer the same versatility, as they cannot be used with floating flies.

Floating lines are the easiest of all lines to cast and handle, for a number of reasons: they pick up off the water easily, they're easiest to manipulate on the water, and they're the most air-resistant of all lines. Greater air resistance means that it will be much less of a chore to keep the line high on your back cast. Sinking lines, with their greater density (less air resistance), need an experienced sense of timing to cast, otherwise your back cast will fall below the rod tip, with a resulting loss of power. Needless to say, your first attempts at fly casting and fly-fishing should be made with a floating line.

We'd all like to fish with floating lines 100 percent of the time; they're pleasant to use. Sooner or later, though, you'll need some sort of sinking line. Sitting in a boat with only a floating line, knowing that the smallmouth bass are on a shoal ten feet below you, makes you feel helpless; so is being on a deep, rushing steelhead river when you just can't get your fly down to the fish. Sinking lines sink throughout their length. They come in various types, such as sinking, fast-sinking, and extra-fast-sinking. The sink rate is usually listed on the package. It can vary from one and a half inches per second to almost ten inches per second. The deeper or faster the water you want to fish, the greater the sink rate you should choose. For real bottom-scratching, sinking shooting heads sink quicker than standard sinking lines, because the thin running line presents less resistance to the water.

Full-sinking lines are inconvenient in some respects. The fact that they sink means you have to retrieve most of your line before you make another cast. (Picture trying to pick up fifty feet of sunken line and throw it back over your shoulder with a single casting stroke.) For the

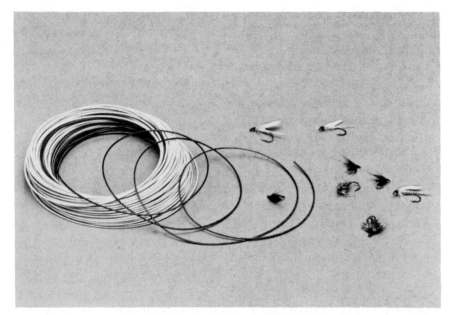

*Sinking tip lines have ten to twenty feet of
sinking line (dark color); the remaining line is
a standard floating line (light color).* Orvis

same reason, line mending, or repositioning the line when it is on the
water, is almost impossible with sinking lines. Sinking-tip (F/S) lines
are a practical compromise. They offer a ten- to twenty-foot tip of sinking line, with the remainder of the line standard floating line. Although
they don't reach the depths that full-sinking lines do, sinking-tip lines
get deep enough to be practical on small to medium streams and all but
the deepest parts of ponds and lakes. The floating portion lets you
mend line easily, and picking up line for another cast is less of a struggle.

Another alternative to full-sinking lines are intermediate-weight lines.
Just slightly denser than water, intermediate-weight lines sink very slowly,
and are quite useful in shallow, weedy lakes where even a sink-tip line
would drag your fly into the weeds on every cast. Intermediate-weight

Fly line types and their relative sink rates.

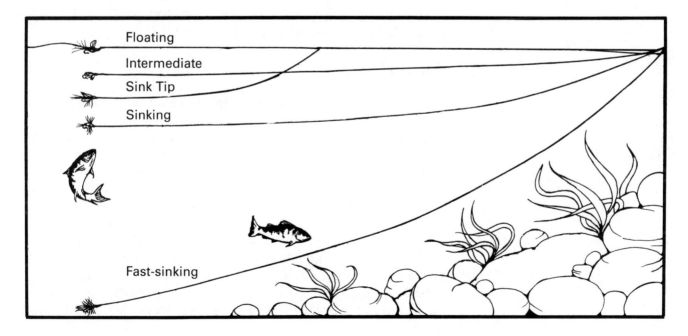

lines are also very thin and can be cast into the wind more easily than corresponding floating lines of the same weight. Because they ride just under the surface, intermediate-weight lines can be fished on a choppy lake surface without being affected by wave action. The casting characteristics of these lines are so pleasant that many fishermen prefer them to floating lines. In fact, an intermediate line will float when periodically greased with line dressing.

Fly-Line Color

Fly-line color is a minor consideration but one that is worth a few thoughts. It is generally agreed that sinking lines should be dark, as subdued colors are less noticeable to the fish and blend with the background colors of a stream or lake. A fish is surrounded by drifting debris all his life, and unless a subsurface object makes a threatening move, it's usually ignored.

The color of a floating line is probably immaterial from the fish's vantage point. I subscribe to the theory that all floating fly lines are equally visible against a backlighted sky, but I've seen some theories that run contrary to this. There is an argument that light-colored lines are more visible to the trout when they are in the air. The perfect fly line would be completely transparent, but even leaders, which are close to being transparent, cast shadows on the bottom.

There are good reasons for using floating lines that are bright, even garish, in color. Fluorescent lines in shades of yellow, orange, and red are more visible to you than other colors in early-morning and late-evening light. Under these conditions you'll seldom be able to see your fly, but if you can see the end of your fly line you'll at least have a clue. Keeping an eye on your fly line when it's in the air also helps correct casting problems. Most casting difficulties originate when the line is behind you, and bright colors show up vividly against streamside foliage. Incidentally, this quality makes them photograph extremely well in color, and in black-and-white when a yellow filter is used.

Backing

Backing is a thin, inexpensive, supple Dacron line that is knotted or spliced to the "back" end of your fly line. Because fly lines are only eighty to ninety feet long and many game fish can run for a hundred yards before slowing, backing lets you keep control of a frisky fish when you run out of fly line. A tarpon fisherman, for instance, will make sure that his fly reel holds not only a 12-weight fly line but also at least two hundred yards of backing. Small-stream trout fishermen also use backing (usually only fifty yards or so), not so much for insurance as to fill up the narrow diameter of a small single-action reel. Fly line that is tied directly to a reel spool tends to retain tight coils when stripped from the reel, coils that might interfere with casting and shooting line.

Braided Dacron is the best material for backing; regular monofilament line retains coils that may foul on rod guides. Freshwater fly-fishermen generally use 20-pound test Dacron for backing. For saltwater, 30-pound is best, not for its strength but because the larger diameter has much less chance of binding on the underlying layers when reeled under the heavy pressure of a big fish.

FLY REELS

A fly reel's purpose is to store line, provide smooth, uninterrupted tension (drag) when a fish makes a long run, and counterbalance the weight of your fly rod when casting. In general, as the size and tenacity of the fish you catch increase, so does the importance of your reel.

Fly reels are simple devices, and even the most complicated has fewer moving parts than a spinning reel. Fly reels consist of a foot that secures the reel to the rod, a handle, an outside frame, a spool that turns around a pillar attached to the frame, and some sort of drag system that puts tension on the revolving spool. Somewhere on the outside of the reel you'll find two levers or knobs: one is the spool release, which enables you to change spools; the other is the drag adjustment, which regulates the tension on the spool.

A single-action fly reel that uses the rachet-and-pawl drag system. The frame, with reel seat, pillar, and drag system, is on the right; the spool containing the line is on the left.

Drag Systems

Fly-reel drag systems have two purposes: they prevent spool overrun, with its resulting line tangles, when you strip line from your reel during casting, and they tire running fish by exerting tension against line running in the opposite direction. Fly-fishermen who catch fish that weigh less than a pound, such as small trout or bluegill, may never use the drag of their reel when fighting a fish, merely stripping the fish in by

29

hand. Their reels are simply line-storage devices. In the tight, brushy confines of small streams, fly reels keep excess line away from clutching branches and abrasive streamside gravel.

On the other hand, a bonefish, tarpon, salmon, or even a large trout can strip a hundred yards of line from a reel in seconds; in this case the reel can become the most important part of your tackle. The tension put on a running fish must be smooth, because a drag that stutters can cause an uneven buildup of pressure on your leader. The mechanical, adjustable tension that a drag system provides is smoother and more consistent than anything you could ever achieve by pinching the outgoing line between your fingers.

Mechanical drag systems may be either rachet-and-pawl, which clicks audibly when the spool is revolving, disk drags, which are silent, or a combination of the two. Many reels also feature a spool rim that is exposed on the outside of the reel, allowing the fisherman to exert additional drag by placing his palm up against the bottom of the reel.

Rachet-and-pawl drag systems are the simplest and most common. A rachet on the inside of the spool engages a pawl or a pair of pawls mounted on the reel frame. A leaf spring is connected to a knob on the outside of the spool, and variable tension can be applied to the drag pawl by turning the drag adjustment knob. The pawls are shaped so that the tension on the spool is always light when you're reeling in line. The tension on the spool when the line is running out can be made

Palming the exposed rim of a reel for additional drag. Orvis

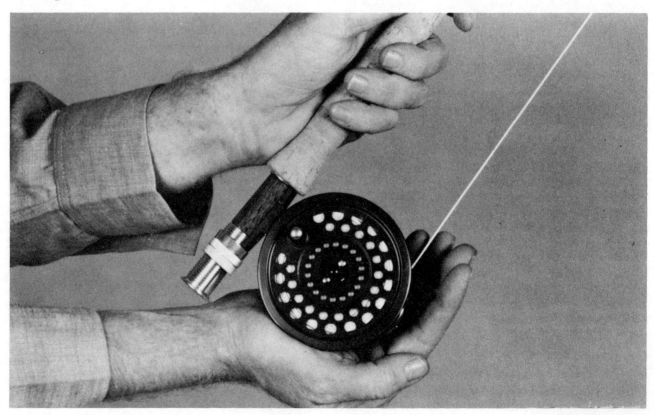

lesser or greater, depending upon the strength of your leader and how much pressure you dare put on the fish.

Disk drag systems incorporate cork or Teflon pads that exert pressure directly on the reel spool. One type utilizes a disk that rests on the rim of the spool, with tension provided by a leaf spring. Another type, similar to drum brakes on a car, features a pad on the inside of the spool face. Tension on this type is provided by a coil spring inside the spool pillar, adjusted by a nut on the outside of the pillar. Disk drags are most often used when fish will be heavy or strong and where leaders will be correspondingly heavy. Disk drags can exert a great amount of smooth pressure against a reel spool without seizing up.

Retrieve Systems

Fly reels offer three types of retrieve systems: single-action, multiplying, and automatic. Because the reel is not used to retrieve line after every cast, this aspect of the reel is not as important to the fly-fisherman as it is to the spin or bait caster.

The single-action reel, by far the most popular variety, gets the vote of most fly-fishermen because it is light and simple to maintain and has only a few moving parts to wear out or break down. One complete turn of the handle completes one turn of the spool.

Multiplying fly reels add a multiplying gear, which retrieves line faster than a 1:1 ratio. In other words, one turn of the handle produces anywhere from one and a half to two turns of the reel spool. The faster line retrieve comes in handy if you're fishing for such fish as Atlantic salmon, which sometimes run toward the fisherman at terrific speeds. Another time you might want to get excess line out of harm's way and onto the reel is when fishing from a boat with gear strewn all over. When a fish makes its initial run you want those loose coils of line packed neatly into your reel, not wound around canoe paddles, cameras, or tackle boxes.

Automatic fly reels incorporate a large coiled spring that surrounds the inside of the reel spool. The spring becomes progressively tighter as each length of line is pulled from the reel. By pressing a release lever, the fisherman can retrieve great lengths of line in just a few seconds. I must confess a prejudice against automatic fly reels that dates back to my first attempt at field maintenance. Upon prying the spool apart, I found myself surrounded by a twitching mass of steel spring that it was impossible to squeeze back into its original position. Automatic reels are also substantially heavier than single-action reels of the same capacity, and their drag systems tend to be quite heavy-handed, making them unsuitable for use with light leaders. Extra spools are also difficult to obtain and tricky to exchange, making changing from a floating to a sinking line time-consuming or impossible.

Saltwater Reels

Saltwater fly reels are often merely upscaled versions of single-action

31

A heavy-duty saltwater reel that has corrosion resistant parts, a disc drag, a rachet-and-pawl drag, and an exposed rim for palming.

trout reels. They may incorporate disk drags or rachet-and-pawl drags; regardless of the drag system used, it must be capable of applying heavy pressure without seizing up. A 150-pound tarpon can put an incredible amount of strain and heat buildup on a fly reel. The reel frame itself must also be substantial, so saltwater fly reels are quite heavy—between six and ten ounces, as opposed to three to six ounces for freshwater fly reels.

These reels may be either direct drive or antireverse. In direct-drive reels, the reel handle turns as the line is running out, which sometimes makes a mess of careless knuckles. Antireverse reels have a locking mechanism that prevents the handle from turning, yet allows the spool to rotate under drag tension when the line is running out.

All other considerations aside, a saltwater fly reel must be constructed from corrosion-resistant materials, usually anodized aluminum for the frame (to save on weight) and stainless steel or chromed or cadmium-plated for internal parts. Salt water is extremely corrosive and can cause electrolysis between unlike metals.

Choosing a Fly Reel

The most important consideration when purchasing a fly reel is its capacity. All good fly reels are rated for capacity; you can find this information on the box, in the instruction sheets, or in catalog copy if you're buying through the mail. Typical capacity information will read something like this: "To WF8F with 150 yds. backing." Because lighter line sizes are smaller in diameter, you know that a WF7F line is also OK on this reel with at least 150 yards of backing, probably 175 yards. Sinking lines are finer in diameter than floaters, so you can probably fit a WF9S line on the same reel with the same amount of backing. Double-taper lines fill up a spool more than weight-forwards, so our same reel with a DT8F line will most likely hold only 100 yards of backing.

Except for the smallest and simplest single-action reels, fly reels are available in right- and left-hand retrieve versions. The difference is merely in which direction the drag tension is applied. In single-action reels with rachet-and-pawl systems, switching from right- to left-hand retrieve is accomplished by merely removing a pawl from its post and flipping it over. Some single-action reels offer a double-pawl system, which means one pawl can be engaged for right-hand retrieve while the other merely acts as a spare and does not engage the rachet. The second pawl may also be flipped to achieve a stronger drag.

Some reels have metal line guards at the bottom, which are usually attached by one or two screws. When you switch from right- to left-hand retrieve, also switch the line guard, by loosening the screws and reversing the direction the line guard is facing.

Disk drags are usually a bit more difficult to switch over. Some require a completely different set of parts and cannot be changed over without returning the reel to the manufacturer. Before ordering a fly reel with one of the more complicated drag systems you should decide whether you want to crank right- or left-handed.

If you're right-handed and spin or bait cast as well as fly-fish, you'll probably want to crank left-handed, as nothing is more frustrating than to reach for the handle of your reel in the excitement of playing a fish and find it on the opposite side of the reel. Many right-handers, however, are oriented so strongly in that direction that they find it uncomfortable to reel with their left hand. This necessitates switching the rod from right to left hand when reeling in line or playing a fish, but it becomes almost second nature and really presents no problem at all. Regardless of whether you are right- or left-handed, decide which way is more comfortable for you and purchase or convert your fly reels accordingly.

Some fly-fishermen say that the reel should balance the weight of the rod beyond the grip; when the reel is mounted on the rod the whole arrangement should balance perfectly when the middle of the grip is placed in the index finger. Others contend that the fly reel should be as light as possible. A third faction feel comfortable with a reel that is heavier than custom dictates, especially if they pursue long-running fish and need extra capacity for added backing. Rest assured that if you own a fly rod that calls for a 6-weight line, a single-action reel that will hold a WF6F line plus 150 yards of backing will be perfectly comfortable. At both extremes of fly-fishing tackle you may have to be a little careful in choosing a fly reel—those little cork-and-ring reel seats used on tiny 3-weight rods may only fit over the thin feet of the lighter fly reels, and the substantial feet on the heaviest saltwater reels may require a full-metal reel seat.

4
Leaders and Knots

The leader is not only as important as the rod, reel, and line, but at times more important than the correct fly pattern. The leader is a device for deception as well as presentation. It deceives by being transparent, and even more by its flexibility. With the proper leader, your fly should appear unattached. It should move freely with every shift of the current or sink unhindered.

All modern leaders are made from nylon. Nylon, or monofilament, is strong for its diameter, flexible, and stretches somewhat without breaking. The fact that nylon is transparent may also be helpful in fooling fish, although I'm convinced that fish can always see the leader. Its transparency may make the connection to the fly just a little less blatant.

Before nylon was first used for leaders, in the late 1940s, leaders were made from drawn silkworm gut. Level pieces of gut were joined with knots to form tapered leaders, which cast and straightened very well. However, gut is brittle unless soaked in water for a few hours, and it mildews and rots if not carefully dried and put away. Gut cannot be drawn with any kind of quality control in diameters less than .009-inch. Today we use nylon in diameters as fine as .003-inch and a nylon leader is two or three times as strong as a gut leader of the same diameter.

Gut did have one advantage over nylon: it was straight. Because lead-

34

ers are so long, they must be stored coiled, and nylon retains a "memory" that must be removed. You can remove almost all the kinks and curls from nylon leaders by carefully stretching sections between your hands or drawing them through a piece of gum rubber or leather. The heat generated by this process, along with the slow, steady pull, realigns the molecules in the nylon and eliminates most of the memory.

Pulling a leader through a special leader straightener to remove kinks in the nylon.

Leaders designed to present flies properly follow tapers developed by theory and by trial and error, just as fly rods and fly lines are tapered. In fact, the whole system is one continuous taper, from the butt section of the rod to the hair-thin end of the leader. All three work together to transmit and dampen the tremendous speed and energy developed in your casting arm, to place the line, leader, and fly on the water so gently they barely ripple the surface.

Leaders can be tapered by two methods, knotted and knotless. I prefer compound-tapered knotted leaders, which consist of as many as ten pieces of monofilament of different diameters in specific lengths, joined by knots.

A knotless leader is a single, continuous piece of nylon that gradually decreases in diameter. The diameter of a knotless leader must decrease at a constant rate, due to the manufacturing process that extrudes the leader.

Knotted leaders do not decrease in diameter at a constant rate. They straighten better when built according to a compound taper, which consists of about 60 percent heavy butt section, a 20 percent section of a number of pieces that step down the taper quickly, and 20 percent level tippet. The heavy butt section connects to the fly line and assures a smooth transmission of casting energy; the step-down sections continue this process into the tippet.

Knotless leaders do offer advantages in weedy waters. If you're trying to slip a weedless bass bug across the lily pads, a knotted leader can catch on vegetation. The knots may also pick up small clumps of algae, which can make casting difficult. Still, whenever possible you should stick to knotted leaders with their superior casting properties. Knotless leaders appear to be simpler, but I'd be willing to bet that poor-quality leaders have discouraged as many would-be fly-fishermen as have poorly matched fly-rod/fly-line outfits.

The easiest way to understand a leader is to construct one. Anyone who can tie a shoelace and use a tape measure can make his own leaders. Here are the specifications for a standard 9-foot, 4X trout leader, one that is used under average midseason water conditions with fly sizes 12 through 16.

LENGTH (INCHES)	DIAMETER (INCHES)
Butt section	
36	.021
16	.019
12	.017
Midsections	
6	.015
6	.013
6	.011
6	.009
4X tippet	
20	.007

Start by taking a level piece of monofilament leader material that measures .021 inch in diameter and is a little bit longer than thirty-six inches. Tie a loop in one end with a surgeon's loop or perfection knot. This loop will be attached to the fly line. Next take a piece of .019-inch nylon that is just a little longer than sixteen inches and tie it to the .021-inch section with a surgeon's knot or barrel knot. Tie the twelve-inch section of .017-inch nylon to the .019-inch in the same manner, and continue the process to the tippet.

Notice that ordinary square knots were not used. Nylon is slippery stuff, and knots that hold in rope will slip right out when tied with nylon. You also may have observed that there is never more than .002-inch difference in diameter between connecting leader sections. The greater the difference in adjacent strands, the weaker the connecting knots, especially if you use the barrel knot.

The barrel, or blood, knot is the traditional knot you'll see used most often in leaders that are available commercially. It's a smooth, neat knot, but it requires some practice to tie properly. It's a good idea to practice this knot and all other fly-fishing knots with heavy string or rope before you try your hand with thin, slippery leader material.

Barrel Knot

The barrel knot will not slip if properly tied. If, when you inspect your finished knot, both tag ends stick out the same side, the knot is not properly tied and may break. When tied correctly, the tag ends should emerge from the knot at a 180-degree angle to each other.

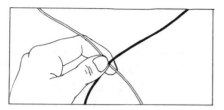

Barrel knot: Cross both pieces of material in an "X," leaving plenty of overlap.

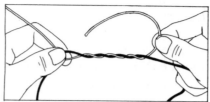

Wind one end around the standing part of the other piece three or four times.

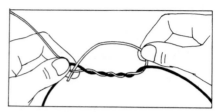

Pass this end back through the loop formed by the intersection of the two pieces.

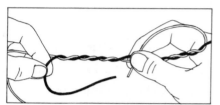

Pinching the first half of the knot to keep the end from slipping back through, wind the free end around the standing piece in the opposite direction three or four times.

Pass this end through the same loop as the first end. The ends must enter the loop from opposite directions.

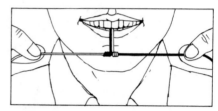

Hold both ends together while pulling on the standing parts to tighten. The easiest way to keep them from slipping through is to hold them in your teeth. Don't put any pressure on the short ends when tightening.

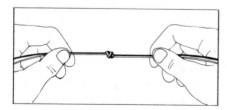

Trim the tag ends as closely as possible.

Surgeon's Knot

The surgeon's knot is slightly stronger than the barrel knot and is easier to tie. It is not quite as neat in the larger diameters; most fishermen use it for tippets and for the finer sections of tapered leaders. If you have to join pieces of leader material that differ more than .003 inch in diameter, the surgeon's knot is stronger than the barrel knot.

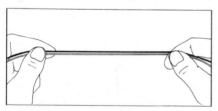

Tippet replacement: Clip off old tippet, lay new tippet parallel beside the end of your leader so the two strands overlap for about four inches.

Form an overhand knot in this doubled section by forming a loop, bringing the tippet and the end of the leader around and through the loop (treat these two as if they were a single strand). Do not tighten the overhand knot yet.

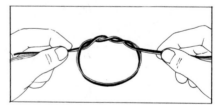

Make the double overhand by bringing the same double strand around and through the loop once more.

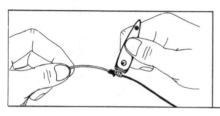

Tighten by holding all four ends tightly and pulling.

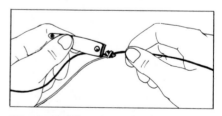

Trim the tag ends as close to the knot as you can without cutting into the knot.

Loops

Loops can be tied in the butt section of your leader with one of two knots, either the perfection knot or the surgeon's loop. They have equal strength; the perfection knot is a little neater and the surgeon's loop is easier to tie.

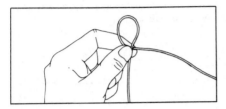

The perfection loop: form a single loop by bringing the end around behind the standing part of your leader. The end should be on the right hand side.

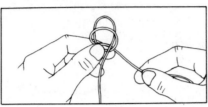

Form a second loop by bringing the end to the left and in front of the first loop and around the back of the first loop. The second loop should be smaller than the first.

Take the end and pass it between the two loops, folding it from right to left.

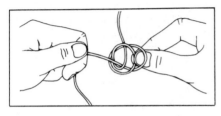

Holding the end in place, reach through the first loop from behind and pull the second loop

through. Tighten by pulling on the second loop and the standing part of the leader. Do not pull on the tag end. While tightening slowly, make sure the end stays at right angles to the loop and the standing part of the leader.

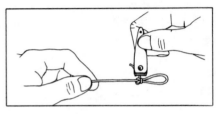

Trim the tag end as close to the knot as possible.

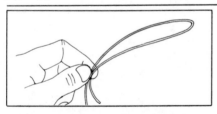

Surgeon's loop: form a loop in the end of your leader. The end should be held parallel to the standing part.

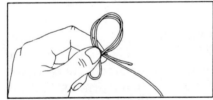

Form a second, larger loop in the doubled portion of your leader. You should now have a doubled loop and a single loop.

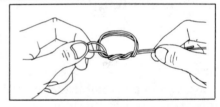

Wrap the single loop around and through the doubled loop twice.

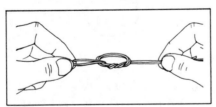

Tighten by pulling on the single loop with one hand and the standing part of the leader and the end together in the other hand.

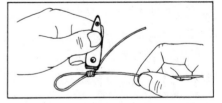

Trim the tag end as close as possible.

The two most popular knots for tying flies to the tippet are the clinch and the double turle knot. The clinch is easier to tie, it is stronger, and you generally don't use up as much leader material when you tie on a new fly. Although the double turle knot is harder to tie, some fishermen prefer it because the leader comes straight out of the hook eye. The clinch knot can sometimes cock the fly off to one side.

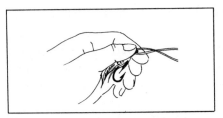

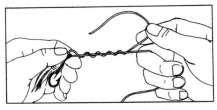

Clinch knot: pass the tippet end through the eye of the fly, either from above or below the eye. Pull three or four inches of leader material through the eye.

Wind the end of the leader around the standing part of the leader five times, keeping the loop immediately adjacent to the hook eye open. Tight, even turns are important. To do this, hold the fly with the thumb and index finger of your left hand, cradling the standing part of the leader with the last three fingers of your right hand. Wind by holding the end of the leader with the thumb and index finger of your right hand, wind away from you, catch the material on the far side with the middle finger of your left hand, and return it to the right hand (it's easier than it sounds). As you are winding, keep the loop next to the hook eye open by pinching it with the same two fingers that are holding the fly.

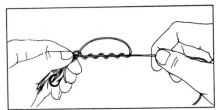

After five turns around the standing part of the leader, bring the end back around and pass it through the loop immediately in front of the hook eye. Catch the end with the two fingers that are holding the fly.

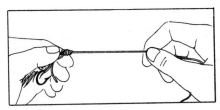

Tighten the knot by pulling the standing part of the leader and the fly in opposite directions. Do not pull on the tag end of the leader —merely hold it alongside the fly so it does not slip back through the loop. (Pulling the tag end of the leader will tighten the knot improperly, resulting in a much weaker knot.) Trim the tag end closely—the knot will not slip if tied properly.

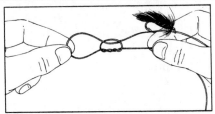

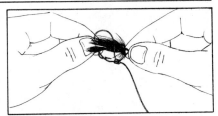

Turle knot: pass the leader through the top of the hook eye. Slide the fly down the leader and out of the way.

Tie a double slip knot in the leader and draw it tight, forming a loop.

Bring the loop formed in the leader over the top of the fly.

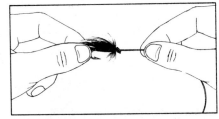

Tighten by pulling on the standing part of the leader while holding the fly. Make sure that the tag end stays forward of the loop as you tighten. Trim the tag end close.

Another reason for preferring the clinch knot is that you can remove the knot simply by grasping the knot just ahead of the hook eye and pulling away from the fly. The double turle knot must be clipped off when you replace flies.

The improved clinch knot, in which the tag end is passed back through the large loop, is needed only when the diameter of the hook eye is much greater than the diameter of your tippet.

TIPPETS

The tippet is the most important tool for deception in a fly-fisherman's bag of tricks. At least when trout fishing, a .001-inch difference in the diameter of your tippet can make a marked difference in your success. Diameter increases the relative flexibility or stiffness of you final connection to the fly, and thus the fly's credibility as an unattached morsel of food.

Leaders are described by their length and tippet size. Though tippets may be identified by their diameter in inches, in the finer sizes a more common system is to assign "X" numbers to specific diameters.

The system, which is universal regardless of the manufacturer of the the leader material, is as follows:

TIPPET SIZE	DIAMETER	BALANCES WITH FLY SIZES	APPROXIMATE POUND TEST
0X	.011″	2, 1/0	6.5
1X	.010″	4-6-8	5.5
2X	.009″	6-8-10	4.5
3X	.008″	10-12-14	3.8
4X	.007″	12-14-16	3.1
5X	.006″	14-16-18	2.4
6X	.005″	16-18-20-22	1.4
7X	.004″	18-20-22-24	1.1
8X	.003″	22-24-26-28	.75

When fishing for bass, salmon, steelhead, and the saltwater species, you'll want a heavier tippet, since the flies will be larger, casts will be longer, and you are not concerned with a delicate presentation. The tippet sizes used are larger, too large for the X system. The following designations are used:

	DIAMETER	POUND TEST	FLY SIZES
Ex. Light	.011″	6.5	8, 10, 12
Light	.013″	8.6	4, 6, 8
Medium	.015″	11.6	1/0, 2, 4
Heavy	.017″	15.1	3/0, 2/0, 1/0
Ex. Heavy	.019″	19.2	5/0, 4/0, 3/0

Thus, a nine-foot leader with a tippet of .007-inch will be called a "nine-foot 4X leader." In the heavy saltwater, bass-bug, or salmon leaders the tippets are often larger than 0X. We would call a nine-foot leader with a .015-inch tippet a "nine-foot .015 leader" or a "nine-foot medium salmon leader" or even a "nine-foot 11-pound leader." The 11 pounds refers to the minimum breaking strength or pound-test of that .015-inch section.

The diameter of your leader tippet must exhibit a happy medium between stiffness for proper presentation and flexibility for deception. Flies vary greatly in terms of size and air resistance, so you must be adaptable in your choice of leaders.

For example, if I'm going to fish for trout with a #14 dry fly I'll usually choose a leader with a 4X tippet. From experience I know that a 2X tippet is too stiff and will make the fly behave unnaturally as it drifts in the currents. If I use a 6X tippet, I find that the last half of the leader won't straighten, because the 6X material is too fine to overcome the air resistance of a size 14 fly. If I can't straighten my leader, the fly won't go where it's supposed to—and if the tippet falls in a big heap around the fly, it's tough to fool the fish.

If you look at the tippet size/fly size chart, you'll see that I could use a 3X or 5X tippet. If the water is very clear or if conflicting currents are pulling on the leader and making the fly drift unnaturally, I'll use 5X. If the water is dirty or fast and the fish are easier to fool, I might use 3X instead, with its greater breaking strength.

Leaders also come in varying lengths, which may vary from as short as three feet to as long as fifteen feet. Very short (three- to six-foot) leaders are used with sinking or sink-tip lines. The specific gravity of nylon is so close to that of water that leaders tend to float, especially if contaminated with line dressing or grease from your hands. A long leader with a sinking line tends to buoy the fly toward the surface, defeating the purpose of using a sinking line. Sinking lines are seldom used under clear, shallow water conditions where the fish are spooky, so having the heavy line in close proximity to the fly is not a problem.

The slap of a fly line seldom scares voracious fish like largemouth bass, northern pike, or bluefish, and short leaders, from three to seven and a half feet, are used for these species. When fishing for bluefish with big poppers, in fact, I've used a level piece of 60-pound mono-filament. Bluefish aren't afraid of much, and I could conceivably tie the popper right to the fly line. The only problem is that the teeth of a bluefish can cut through fly line in a single chop, whereas nylon is more resistant to abrasion by sharp teeth.

Certain fish are what is called "leader-shy," but "line-shy" is actually more appropriate. Trout in fresh water as well as salt, bonefish, permit, and sometimes striped bass fall into this category. If a heavy fly line lands too near them, they may cease feeding or actually bolt for cover. Whenever this kind of nervous fish is found in calm, clear water, it's best to use a leader longer than seven and a half feet.

Because a leader is thinner and more air-resistant than fly line, a longer leader gives you added delicacy. Nine- or ten-foot leaders are considered standard for trout and bonefish under most conditions. At times, when the water is very shallow and clear, or on a calm lake surface, you may find even a ten-foot leader frightening the fish. Longer leaders, twelve- to fifteen-footers, may be used under these demanding conditions.

Unless it is windy, a properly made twelve-foot leader will straighten as well as a seven-and-a-half-footer, as long as the casts you make are over twenty feet. In small, narrow trout streams, though, the short casts you make seldom develop enough line speed to straighten a nine-foot leader. Luckily, trout in small streams usually aren't as leader-shy, and you can get away with a seven-and-a-half-foot leader.

Your leader can be modified during a day's fishing; in fact, you should be prepared to change your tippet quite frequently. Suppose you start fishing with a nine-foot 4X leader. The tippet on this leader, as it comes to you in the package, will be about twenty inches long. Every time you change flies, you'll have to tie a new one on with a clinch or double turle knot, losing a small piece of tippet in the process.

As the tippet shortens with each fly change, the delicacy of your presentation decreases, especially when it gets down to fifteen or six-teen inches. You need that twenty inches of air-resistant tippet to slow down your fly at the end of the cast. If you're properly prepared, you'll have spools of tippet material in your fishing vest; merely pull off a piece that's just over twenty inches long (you'll lose some tying it to your leader). Clip off the remaining 4X tippet and tie on a new one.

Windy conditions and certain casting problems can put what are called wind knots in your tippet. Wind knots are simple overhand knots. They should be removed immediately, as they can weaken the breaking strength of your tippet as much as 50 percent. Check your leader frequently while fishing; if you see a knot where it isn't supposed to be, remove the tippet and tie on a fresh one. It's almost impossible to untie these tiny overhand knots, and even if you can pick them apart I wouldn't trust that tippet. Once the damage to the tippet is done, it is irreparable.

Sometimes if it's very windy you'll find wind knots in the heavier sections of your leader. Since the tippet is the weakest link in the system, I wouldn't bother trying to remove them anywhere else.

You can also see another advantage of knotted leaders over knotless ones. After each fly change with a knotless leader, or each time you break off your fly in a fish, your tippet becomes heavier. Knotless leaders have a gradual taper, so after a half dozen fly changes it may be 3X or even 2X. Of course, you can tie new tippets on knotless leaders, but you never know exactly when you should unless you carry a micrometer.

It's easy to change tippet sizes with a knotted leader. Suppose you need to fish a smaller fly, say a size 20 with that nine-foot 4X leader. The 4X tippet is too heavy for a size 20 fly. Take your nine-foot 4X leader, which looks like this:

LENGTH (INCHES)	DIAMETER (INCHES)
36	.021
16	.019
12	.017
6	.015
6	.013
6	.011
6	.009
20	.007

Cut your tippet back to six inches and make it an extra intermediate section. Add a twenty-inch tippet of 6X. Your leader now looks like this:

LENGTH (INCHES)	DIAMETER (INCHES)
36	.021
16	.019
12	.017
6	.015
6	.013
6	.011
6	.009
6	.007
20	.005

Yes, you now have a nine-and-a-half-foot 6X leader and the taper varies slightly from a store-bought one. However, as long as that 60-20-20 butt-mid-tippet formula remains relatively intact, you can add or subtract a few midsections without affecting the leader's casting dynamics.

Don't forget not to jump more than .002 inch between diameters. In the same light, you can change that nine-foot 4X leader to an eight-and-a-half-foot 2X by cutting back to the .011-inch section and adding twenty inches of .009 inch.

I often fish for weeks with the same basic leader, adding or subtracting sections as needed. It's much easier than changing the entire leader every time I need to change tippet sizes.

There are two little metal devices sold that can be attached to your leader. They were designed to cater to our reluctance to tie knots. One is a little metal clip that goes onto the tippet end of your leader, enabling you to change flies quickly. Avoid it. It ruins your fly's action and can even sink a dry fly.

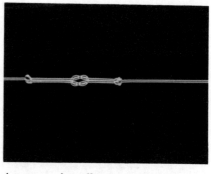

A permanent loop of heavy monofilament epoxy-spliced or nail-knotted to your fly line allows quick, easy leader changes. Orvis

The other contraption is a metal ring with a barbed pin on one end. The barbed end goes into the core of your fly line; you tie the butt of your leader to the loop. These things tend to rust, and may also ruin your fly line.

A convenient way to attach a leader to your fly line is to nail knot a six-inch section of heavy leader material to your fly line. Tie a perfection knot or surgeon's loop on the other end of the section. When you want to change leaders, just make a loop-loop connection with the loop on the butt section of your leader. That six-inch looped section is a permanent part of your fly line, and saves you the trouble of tying knots or having to clip a piece of your leader or fly line every time you change leaders. After a season or two, the fly line coating may crack next to the nail knot, which causes a hinging effect when you cast. If this happens, cut off the end of your fly line and nail knot a new loop to the line.

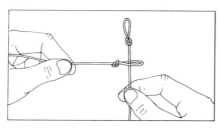
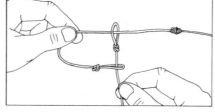
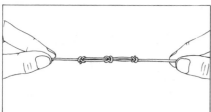

Above left: The loop-to-loop connection. Pass the permanent loop through the leader loop. Above right: Pass the end of the leader through the permanent loop. Left: Tighten by pulling the loops away from each other. You can disconnect the loops by pushing them toward each other and reversing the joining process.

Nail or Tube Knot

The nail knot can be used to permanently attach a six-inch secton of heavy monofilament to your fly line, with a perfection loop on the other end. This makes it easy to change leaders, with a loop-to-loop connection. You can also attach the butt section of your leader directly to the fly line with this knot.

43

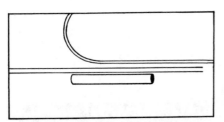

Nail knot: For this knot take a one-inch plastic or metal tube, fly line, and a piece of .023", .021", or .019" monofilament. Lay the three parallel together.

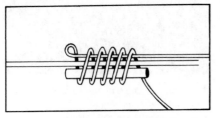

Pinch the tube, monofilament, and line together with one hand. Grasp the end of the monofilament opposite the end of the fly line and wind it toward the line's tip. Wind it over itself, the tube, and the line at the same time. Have at least six inches of monofilament to work with, and make your turns tight and lying neatly next to each other. Five turns are plenty.

Tests have shown that the butt section of leaders used with 3- and 4-weight lines should be about .019 inch, with 5- through 9-weights .021 inch, and for the real heavyweight 10-, 11-, and 12-lines .023 inch. The permanent loop that you attach to your fly line should be of the same diameter material as the butt section of your leaders.

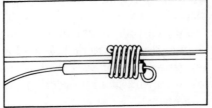

Pass the end you've been working with through the tube so that the end passes back under the turns you've just made. Pull the ends of the monofilament in opposite directions, tightening them on top of the tube.

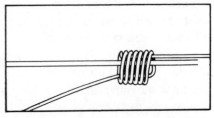

Carefully slip the tube out while you continue to tighten.

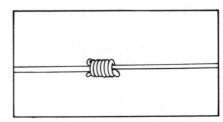

Clip fly line extending outside the knot and clip the tag end of the monofilament. Tighten the knot further by holding the fly line with one end and pulling on the monofilament with a pair of pliers.

Albright Knot

The Albright knot is a good knot for attaching backing to fly line. It can also be used anyplace you need to join sections of monofilament that vary greatly in diameter.

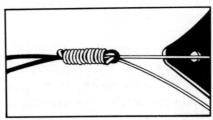

Albright knot: Form an open-ended loop in the fly line (or larger diameter strand of monofilament). Pass the backing (or smaller diameter strand) through the loop and take one turn around itself and the neck of the loop.

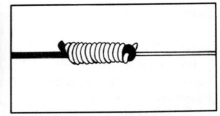

Wind ten to twelve turns toward the loop. Pass the backing back through the loop.

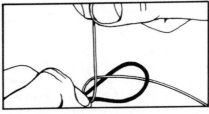

Tighten by pulling on the standing part of the fly line with your hand and on the backing with a pair of pliers.

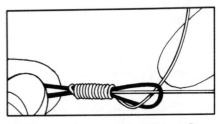

Trim the tag ends of fly line and backing neatly.

Backing should be attached to the other end of your fly line. You should have a spool of backing of the length specified for your reel model with the particular line size you're using. Tie one end of the backing to the reel spool and wind it on with fairly tight turns, level-winding it from side to side so it goes on evenly. When all but a few feet are on the reel, tie the backing to the fly line with a smooth, secure knot. I like the albright knot, but a nail knot with seven or eight turns instead of the usual five is also fine. Now wind on your fly line, using the same technique to distribute the line across the spool. The fly line should be wound loosely, because when you're fishing you seldom take the time to wind it tight. The line should come no closer to the rim of the spool than about a quarter inch, or you'll have trouble changing spools and the line will bind up against the frame of the reel.

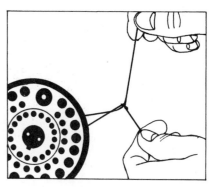

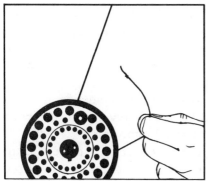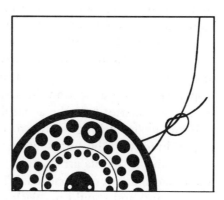

Tying backing to your fly reel.

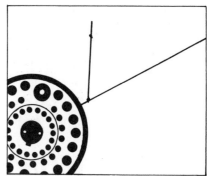

A supposedly clever trick is to wind the fly line onto the reel first, attach the backing and wind it on, then take the whole thing off and wind it back on in reverse order. The idea is to see exactly how much backing you need, cutting it at the proper point. The problem is you then end up with about a hundred yards of backing and thirty yards of fly line in a big heap that you have to untangle and wind back on the reel. I prefer to trust the reel manufacturer's specifications, throw caution to the wind, and wind everything on in the proper order. If I find the spool is filled too much, I'll just strip off the fly line, cut off some of the backing, and tie a new albright.

Take care that the knot you use to attach the backing is as smooth as possible and all tag ends are trimmed closely. You may not need your backing very often, but if that trophy of a lifetime runs away with your fly line you don't want your backing connection to catch on one of the guides on your fly rod.

An epoxy-splice process is offered for front loops and the backing-to-fly-line connection. These splices have to be done with brand-new fly lines, so they should be ordered when you purchase your fly line and backing. These splices are the smoothest possible connections to your fly line and eliminate the need to tie both nail knots and albright knots.

For saltwater species that are suspicious and look their food over critically, such as bonefish, permit, and striped bass, you'll want to use a standard saltwater leader with the 60 percent butt section/20 percent

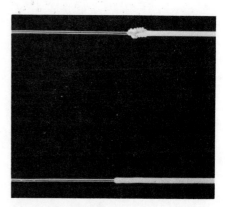

Top: leader butt nail-knotted to fly line. Bottom: leader butt epoxy-spliced to fly line. Orvis

midsections/20 percent tippet formula. Fish like bluefish, barracuda, or mackerel are voracious feeders with sharp teeth and are oblivious of what is attached to your fly. A simplified leader formula with a shock tippet is advised. Shock tippets, as I see them, are more to protect your leader from abrasion against sharp teeth, scales, or gill covers than they are to soften the shock of a sudden strike.

Saltwater shock leaders are usually constructed like this: two feet of 25- to 40-pound monofilament, eighteen inches of tippet, and about twelve inches of heavy 40- to 100-pound monofilament. The tippet is there to make things more sporting. To qualify for International Game Fish Association records it must be at least fifteen inches long; the shock tippet must be no more than twelve inches long.

The butt section of a saltwater leader can be connected to the tippet by tying surgeon's loops in both pieces. Connect them with the same loop-loop connection you use to attach your leader to a permanent fly-line loop. The shock tippet can be easily attached to the tippet with an albright knot. By permanently attaching a butt section to your fly line and tying a surgeon's loop on the other end, you can tie up extra tippet–shock tippet sections in advance. If you wish to change tippets, it's an easy matter to make a simple loop-to-loop connection.

If you're not fishing for the record books, simply attach the shock tippet directly to the butt section with an albright knot.

Wire shock tippets are sometimes used for species with very sharp teeth, like bluefish or barracuda. The wire should be multistrand plastic coated wire, and should be black or brown rather than silver, because fish will strike a shiny silver leader. The wire should be attached to the rest of your leader with an albright knot. Because wire is stiff and will affect the action of your fly, use no more than six inches.

Attach the fly to the wire by threading the fly on the leader and then tying a surgeon's or perfection loop in the end, so that the fly is inside the loop and able to swing free. A three-turn clinch knot can also be used, but will not allow the fly to move in the water as well.

Most fly-fishermen pay less attention to their leaders than they should. A change in leader length or tippet size will sometimes be more important than a change in fly patterns.

5
Fly Casting

The basics of fly casting are easy. You can learn to cast well enough to catch fish with just a few hours of practice. As with any skill that requires eye-hand coordination, like tennis or golf, there will be times where almost no skill is required; other times you'll have to call upon every minute of practice you've ever spent.

It is easier to learn to spin cast than to fly cast, but fly casting is less mechanical and requires more manipulation by the fisherman. This greater control and sensitivity is fly-fishing's greatest appeal.

The first step toward learning to fly cast is to relax and think about what you're doing. Don't relate fly casting to spin casting. Don't think about throwing a fly as you would cast a spinning lure. Never lose sight of the fact that you cast a *weighted line* that propels the fly and leader.

I'd be foolish if I told you that you can learn fly-fishing as well with this book or any book as you can with a teacher standing at your side. If your budget and time allow, go to a fly-fishing school. Organized fly-fishing schools are reasonably priced, and the instructors are experienced in picking out exactly what you're doing wrong. Second best is a patient fly-fishing friend, preferably not a relative or spouse.

There's nothing wrong with learning to fly cast from a book, it just takes longer. If you do expect to learn from this book, proceed slowly and patiently. Watch other fly casters in action. Above all, don't try to fish while you're practicing—at least for a couple of sessions.

GETTING READY

Find a quiet, unobstructed place to practice. The ideal place would be a pond that contains no fish, but a lawn will do, at least for the basic forward cast. Find a place away from prying eyes. I know that my laboriously slow progress in fly casting was the result of neighbors snickering over a young boy with a book lying open on the lawn next to him, flailing away with a long, skinny fishing pole.

For practice you'll need a properly balanced rod, reel, and line combination, plus a leader. Leave the flies at home. Flies weigh almost nothing, so they add nothing to the cast. Besides, they're distracting, and until you've practiced a bit they tend to embed themselves in pants, shirts, and ears.

Take the rod out of its case and seat the ferrules by pushing them together until they're hand-tight. You can prevent damage to your rod by holding the rod close to the ferrules when you do this. Line up the

*Push the ferrules together with your hands
placed close to both ferrules.*

guides by eye. When taking a rod apart, it's best to hold the rod out in front of you with one hand above and the other below the ferrule. Shrug one shoulder back, making sure that you get a straight pull. Bending the rod while unseating a ferrule is the easiest way to damage a rod, and is a common reason for careless rod breakage. Fiberglass, graphite, and boron rods should be twisted slightly, but metal ferrules on bamboo rods should always be kept completely straight when you unseat them.

Attach the reel securely to the rod, making sure that the handle is on the correct side and that the line guard, if there is one, is facing forward.

The proper way to take a rod apart, ensuring a straight pull.

Pull off about ten feet of fly line from the reel. While resting the butt of the rod against the ground, string up the rod by doubling the fly line over just near its junction with the leader. Doubling the fly line is easier than trying to pull the fine leader through the guides, as you invariably lose your grip on the leader just as you reach the last guide.

Set the rod down again and pull out about twenty feet of line beyond the tip of the rod. Ready to cast? Check behind you for obstructions. Now, get the line out in front of you any way you can. Thrash around a little bit; get the feel of the rod and forget about technique for a moment. You're ready to start when that twenty feet of line is straight out in front of you, the rod and line are both at a 90-degree angle to your body, the rod is pointing straight out in front of you at waist level, and your feet are planted comfortably with toes pointing straight out in front of you.

The easy way to string up a rod.

HOLDING THE ROD

How are you gripping the rod? There are two basic grips, the thumb-on-top and index-finger-on-top. If you don't have one or the other on top of the grip, you won't be able to point the rod precisely and may sacrifice some accuracy. Most people find using the thumb more comfortable and less tiring, but use whichever style feels more natural to you.

The thumb-on-top grip.

The index-finger-on-top grip.

There is a third, little-used grip called the free-hand or V grip. This grip puts the V between your thumb and forefinger on top of the rod grip. It is supposed to be more comfortable and efficient on long casts, but I've never seen anyone other than tournament casters use it consistently. You might want to switch to the V grip occasionally, to relieve cramping in your casting hand.

If you're right-handed you should cast a fly rod with your right hand; left-handers should cast with their left hands. If you are totally ambidextrous I would recommend that you learn to cast with one hand and stick with it. Trying to learn to cast with both hands usually results in a mediocre ambidextrous caster rather than an accomplished one-handed caster.

Your other hand, which I'll refer to as the line hand, actually does more work when you're fishing. The line hand controls your line, and as a result is always doing something. The casting hand operates only when you're casting or mending line or playing fish.

When you first begin practicing, you should think about your casting hand and not about the other. Grasp the line between the reel and the stripping guide with your line hand and, as you cast, allow the line hand to follow the rod as it comes up into the back cast. As you finish the back cast and are ready to begin the forward cast, your line hand should be level with your breast.

The starting position, showing the line hand pinching the line tightly.

THE FORWARD CAST

Using your forearm, lift the tip of the rod straight up to the point just past the vertical. If you were looking at yourself from the side, the rod should start at the 9:00 position and stop at the 1:00 position. Turn your head and see where the fly line goes. With proper technique, the line should form a loop as you're moving the rod and then straighten beyond the tip of the rod, forming a line that is parallel to the ground.

This is called the back cast, and when you finish it the line should be

Forward cast: starting position.

Lift the rod and accelerate quickly from here...

. . .to here.

Wait for the back cast to straighten.

*Begin the forward cast, applying power
from here...*

...to here.

The loop will carry the line forward.

Follow through with the rod to the starting position, allowing the rod to drift down as the line settles.

bending your rod as it straightens behind you. The line will shortly fall to the ground, because you haven't learned the forward cast, but during actual casting the fly line should never drop below the tip of the rod on the back cast. The rod must flex in order to transmit casting energy properly to the line, and if you bring your rod back too far the rod will not flex enough.

You should be able to feel the rod bending as you cast. Some fly casters liken a fly rod to a spring: the energy that is built up by the fly line bending the rod is released, slinging the line out in front of you. Nonsense, others say, the fly rod must bend because it allows the tip to travel in a straight line, obtaining a greater mechanical advantage between your casting hand and the energy it imparts to the fly line.

As you practice the forward cast, which is by far the most important cast, keep in mind that while the line travels back and forth while you cast, fly casting is really an up-and-down motion of your forearm and rod, working together as a single unit. This motion keeps the fly line pulling at an almost perpendicular angle to the rod, which puts the fly rod to its best mechanical advantage.

With thirty or forty feet of line on the water in front of you, lifting all of that line out of the water, into the air, and back behind you is a lot to ask of a simple movement of your forearm. This is where the mechanical advantage of the fly rod becomes apparent. Don't shortchange yourself by starting a cast with the fly rod held too high. You can't move much fly line by starting a cast at 10:30 and stopping at 1:00.

Too much slack line on the water presents a similar problem on a back cast. Your fly rod will work properly only when the fly line is bending it throughout the execution of a forward cast. Otherwise, you might as well be casting with a broomstick. If you start a back cast with slack line on the water, the rod won't bend enough until all the slack is lifted off the water, which doesn't give you much room to lift the rest of the line into the air.

To get the most out of your fly rod on a forward cast, always lower the rod tip and eliminate any slack by stripping in some line before starting the cast.

Get the line back out in front of you and make another back cast. This time, though, turn your head and watch for the instant that the line is perfectly straight behind the tip of the rod. With a hammering motion that uses both forearm and wrist, quickly bring the rod tip back to its starting position in front of you. Don't try to throw the line; merely direct it out in front of you with the tip of the rod.

Back in the days of long, limber bamboo fly rods, students were taught to cast with a book under their elbow, using a flick of the wrist to move the rod. Any greater effort on their part would have overpowered the limp "spaghetti rods" popular in those days. With today's progressive-taper rods, casting with the elbow tucked tightly into your side is not only impractical, it's plain uncomfortable.

On the forward cast, your elbow should start by hanging comfortably at your side, at about waist level. During the back cast it should come up to the level of your shoulder, returning to that relaxed position at

Good rod position at the end of the back cast. Your wrist should not bend back any farther than this.

your side on the forward cast. Your elbow movement should always be more of an up-and-down motion than back-and-forth.

Your first cast probably did not look like poetry in motion. Relax and don't let it bother you. Most likely you tried to use your wrist too much. Try to take your mind off the grip of the rod and out toward the tip. Thinking about where you're holding the rod makes you use your wrist as the pivot point of the cast. Instead, make your forearm pivot around your elbow. If the wrist is not locked into position at the end of the back cast, it may dip the rod tip too far back, throwing the line below the point where it is effectively pulling on the rod.

If you have trouble with your wrist breaking on the back cast, try this: before starting the cast, while the rod is pointing straight out in front of you, notice the angle between the rod and your forearm. Make a couple of back casts, never taking your eyes off your wrist. Forget

57

about the line for a moment. On the back cast, that angle between your forearm and wrist should remain constant. Now look at your back cast. Is it flat and parallel to the ground?

If your rod tip is coming to a dead stop at 1:00 every time and the back cast drops too low, you may not be putting enough emphasis into the back cast. If you try to throw the fly line up in the air over your head rather than over your shoulder, it may be easier to keep the back cast where it belongs.

The back cast should be a gradually increasing acceleration, starting at 9:00 and ending at a dead stop at 1:00. Watch the fly line on the water. As you begin to raise your rod tip, the fly line will begin moving toward you; then it will suddenly leave the water. At this point, increase your acceleration to a maximum. This is called the power stroke. It's a difficult concept to visualize until you've done it correctly once or twice.

Once the back cast is mastered, you have more than half the task accomplished. It's easy to make a good cast with a good back cast, but nearly impossible to make a good cast with a poor back cast.

The timing of the forward cast is important. If you begin to come forward before the back cast has straightened, you'll probably hear a sharp crack—and the line will fall in a big puddle in front of you. You cannot develop enough power on the forward cast until the line is straight behind the tip of the rod, pulling on the rod. If you wait too long, gravity will take over, causing the fly line to fall below the tip of the rod. Again, you're not getting maximum power out of your fly rod.

You should always begin the forward cast at the instant the fly line straightens behind you. It's perfectly all right to turn your head and look; even the best casters turn and check their back casts occasionally. After some practice this timing will be almost intuitive and you won't have to look. Different lengths of line require different timing. With a short cast the pause is very short, but with a long cast it takes longer to straighten all that line behind you.

The forward cast is almost like pounding a nail into a wall that is about one foot in front of you. When pounding nails, most of the power comes from the forearm, with the wrist adding that final crispness to the stroke. Just as you wouldn't throw your arm forward too far when pounding that nail, try not to throw your arm forward on the cast. Your upper arm can move a little on the forward cast, but you shouldn't end up with it any farther forward than your shoulder. The forearm should end up exactly where it started—at waist level pointing straight out over the water. If you're wading in deep water, over your waist, the forearm will end up higher than waist level, but it should end up parallel to the water.

Problems sometimes occur on the forward cast because power is not directed properly. There is a power stroke on the forward cast, and it should be applied between 1:00 and about 10:30. As the rod reaches 10:30 the line should be almost straight in front of you; from 10:30 to 9:00 the rod drifts down, following the line as it settles on the water. Too much power too late will make the line splash on the water instead of straightening just above the water and settling gently to the surface.

Misdirecting the forward cast can also cause the line to splash or puddle. Don't forget that the tip of the rod directs the line. Keep your eyes on it. If you aim the tip of the rod *on* the water, you will *put* the line on the water. You're actually trying to straighten the line two to three feet above the water, letting the air resistance of the line and leader take over at the end to produce a delicate delivery. There are two ways of looking at this, and you should use whichever idea works best for you: either aim two feet high or else make sure that the tip of the rod never ends up pointing below the horizontal when you complete the forward cast.

Now we're ready for some fine points. You may have hit your shoulder or the back of your head with the leader as the rod came forward. Make sure that, for now, the tip of your rod moves in a straight vertical plane as you cast. In other words, as you lift the rod on the forward cast you slice upward through a vertical plane; make sure that you slice back through this same plane on the forward cast.

You may also have hit the rod itself with the leader or line. If you had a fly on the leader it would probably be hooking on the leader or line as you came forward. This is called a trailing loop, and usually happens because you are pushing and pulling, rather than raising and lowering your forearm. If you push forward, the rod tip, leader, and line all move forward in the same plane and something has to tangle. Dropping your arm on the forward cast gets that rod tip out of the way as the line, leader, and fly pass over your head.

SHOOTING LINE

It's time to lengthen your cast. This technique, called shooting line, is done by pulling some line off the reel, holding it with your line hand, and releasing it on the forward cast. The momentum of the line traveling forward on the forward cast will pull this line through the guides.

Strip about ten feet from your reel. Hold this line tightly so that the slack is below your line hand. The line between this hand and your stripping guide should be tight. The slack line can be coiled in this hand, but for now just let it hang to the ground. Start a back cast, making sure that the line is held tightly between your thumb and forefinger. Don't release any line while the line is behind you. As your rod comes forward, at about 10:30, release the line you're holding. It should slip through the guides and add another ten feet to the cast.

It will take some practice to determine exactly when you should release the shooting line. Most problems come from releasing the line too early, which directs the shooting line straight up in the air rather than out in front of you. After you release the line, funnel the line through the stripping guide by forming an "O" with your thumb and forefinger. This directs the line to the stripping guide, lessens friction, and prevents tangles. With practice you should be able to shoot at least twenty feet of line comfortably.

LINE CONTROL

Line control is an essential part of casting. After your cast hits the water the line will be hanging in that O you've made with your fingers. Grab the line again with your thumb and forefinger. Never let go of the fly line—some fish strike as soon as the fly hits the water, and if you don't have control of the line, you'll miss your chance.

You can retrieve line by transferring the line from your line hand to between the forefinger and third finger or between the third and fourth fingers of your casting hand. Pull the line through these fingers by grasping it behind your casting hand. As the line is gathered, it can either be coiled in your line hand or just dropped to the ground or water surface next to you. The speed at which you retrieve line is also the speed that your fly will move through the water. When fishing, try to give action to your fly by using this retrieve rather than moving the rod tip. Moving the rod tip around produces slack line, and it's difficult to set the hook or pick up for another cast with a pile of slack on the water.

Stripping line. The left hand has just brought the line over and hooked it over the index finger of the right hand.

Pull down to retrieve line, then reach up for another coil.

You can hold as many coils as you need in your line hand.

A helpful drill is to make a cast, shoot some line, transfer the line to your rod hand, strip in some line, then cast and shoot the line again. When transferring the line from your right to left hand becomes second nature, you're well on your way to mastering line control.

An alternate way to retrieve line is to use the hand-twist retrieve. For this retrieve you don't need to transfer the line to your casting hand. Begin the hand-twist retrieve with the line in the palm of your noncasting hand, palm up. Pinch the line between your thumb and forefinger, at the same time turning your hand upside down. Reach forward with your other three fingers and catch the line on the edge of your little finger. Turn your hand so that the palm is facing up again. You should now have a single small coil of line in your hand. Palm this coil while reaching forward again with your thumb and forefinger, grasping a new section of line. Repeat the process. You'll soon have a handful of small coils that will pay out and shoot through the guides without tangling.

The hand-twist retrieve is useful when you want your fly to move through the water at a slow, steady pace. It's not as versatile as the strip retrieve, because you can't retrieve line quickly, nor can you impart an erratic action to your fly.

Accuracy in fly casting is obtained merely by pointing your thumb or forefinger, whichever is on top of the grip, at the spot where you want your fly to be delivered. Don't forget to aim a couple of feet high. If you

The hand-twist retrieve: Turn your palm up-side down . . .

. . . and catch the line on the outside of your little finger.

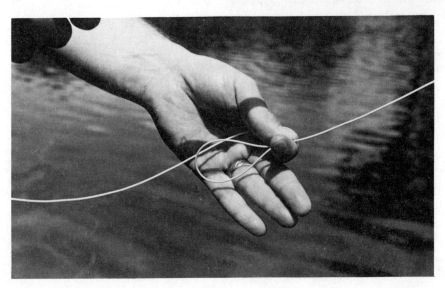

Turn the palm back up and palm the coil you have obtained.

point down at a spot, your fly, leader, and line will slam into the water, rather than straightening above the water and settling gently to the surface. A change of direction in fly casting is accomplished by picking up the line with an ordinary straight-up movement of the rod, then pivoting your body and coming forward with the rod at a different angle. A change of direction of more than 45 degrees, however, is best accomplished with a false cast in between.

FALSE CASTING

False casting is merely making a cast or series of casts without letting the line touch the water. Suppose you're standing at the edge of a lake with the line straight out in front of you. You spot a fish cruising along the shoreline to your left, 90 degrees from where your line is sitting. If you pick up the line and try to place it near the fish with a single change-of-direction cast, your presentation will be poor, because the rod can't flex enough when you come forward at an angle that's radically different from your pickup angle. A false cast in between will allow you to alter the direction of your forward cast a little at a time.

To practice the false cast, make your back cast in the standard way and come forward as you would normally—but don't follow through on the forward cast. Stop the rod tip at about 10:30, wait for the line to straighten out in front of you at about shoulder level, then start another back cast. Repeat the process three or four times, then on the last false cast let the rod follow the line to the water as it straightens.

It will take a bit of practice to false cast without having the line slap the water in front of you. Most problems occur when you stop the rod tip too low or when you don't allow the fly line to straighten both in front and behind you. And don't forget that it's still an up-and-down motion with the rod. Pushing and pulling the rod on your false cast will only cause your line, leader, and fly to slam into the rod. It's OK to use mostly wrist on the false cast, so long as your motions are crisp, short, and up-and-down.

False casting performs other useful tasks. It allows you to work out line gradually, shooting a little line on each forward cast without letting the line touch the water. Distance can be obtained this way quicker than putting the line on the surface three or four times, and the water is disturbed less. It also allows accuracy without trial-and-error casts that disturb the water. By watching the line on a false cast, you can estimate where the fly is going to fall and make corrections by changing direction or shooting a little extra line. Finally, dry flies absorb water on the surface, and a few short, quick false casts shake this water off efficiently.

I emphasize short and quick because there is a temptation to make half a dozen false casts or to false cast forty or fifty feet of fly line. False casting requires fairly tricky timing, and the longer you try to hold your fly line in the air, the more you compound the problem. There is never any need for more than four false casts. False casting with long lengths of line should also be avoided. Again, the more line you try to hold in the air, the easier it's going to be to lose your timing. If you have to cast sixty feet, false cast with forty and shoot the remaining twenty when you follow through on the last one.

VARIATIONS ON THE FORWARD CAST

The forward cast and false casting can be done in planes other than the straight up-and-down. You can cast with the rod 90 degrees off to the side, 45 degrees to the side, or at any angle so long as it's not lower than 90 degrees from the vertical. Below 90 degrees you'll slam the line into the ground or water behind you on the back cast. You can also turn the forward-cast angle so that you throw the back cast over your opposite shoulder. You'll hear these called such things as "cross-body casts," "side casts," and so on, but that terminology bothers me because they aren't different casts, just basic variations on the forward cast.

Casting with the rod at a 45° angle from the vertical.

These casts can be used to get you out of tight spots. For instance, suppose you're right-handed and there's a tree behind your right shoulder. By angling the back cast over your left shoulder, which is clear of obstructions, you can get the fly on the water without ending up in the tree.

Casting off to your right side gives you a horizontal cast. With a cast that is parallel to the water's surface you can fire your fly in under overhanging trees on the bank of a river or lake. Everything else —shooting line and false casting—is exactly the same, except that it's turned on a different plane. When you false cast with a side cast your 9:00 to 1:00 is parallel to the water instead of perpendicular to it.

Casting to the side or across the front of your body also lets you cast curves into your line, controlled curves. For instance, suppose you're

Casting with the rod at 90° from the vertical.

Using a sidearmed cast to drive a fly under overhanging trees.

right-handed and have a rock directly in front of you. There is a trout feeding on the far side of the rock. Make a side cast off to the right side of the rock, false casting a few times. On the last cast, stop your rod at about 10:30, just as if you were going to make another false cast, but let the line fall to the water. Don't follow through with the rod. The line will snap back against the rod, forming a curve that hooks to the right. Hopefully, the fly and leader will fall in front of the rock, with the line off to the right side. You can make the curve even more pronounced by pulling back slightly on the rod after you've come forward.

A curve to the left for right-handers can be made in a similar manner by casting across your left shoulder, again stopping the rod high.

Don't become enthralled with curve casts. They're tricky, and even with a lot of practice they can be inconsistent. You could have reached that trout in front of the rock merely by moving a few feet to the right and presenting a regular overhead forward cast to him—with much greater chance that your fly would land in the proper spot.

65

Using a cross-body cast to keep the fly out of the brush off to the right of the fisherman's body.

DISTANCE CASTING

There may be times when you need to cast a fairly long line, over fifty feet. Remember: the longer the line you cast, the more difficult it is to be accurate and precise. It's always better to make a short, easy, accurate cast than a difficult, long, sloppy one.

The first step toward adding distance to your cast is to raise your arm up a little. Start at the normal starting position, but instead of bringing your elbow up to your shoulder, raise it above shoulder level when you make your back cast. This does two things: it keeps your rod tip higher, allowing you more ground clearance behind you, and it gives you a longer, more powerful casting.

Just raising your arm should give you the added power to make most long casts. On very long casts you can also let your rod tip drift back to almost 2:30, just make sure that you give the back cast enough power to prevent it from falling below the tip of the rod. Increasing the distance the rod tip travels is another way of obtaining a longer, more powerful casting stroke.

THE DOUBLE HAUL

A variation of the forward cast known as the double haul is the final step in increasing line speed and thus adding length to your casts. The faster a fly line moves, the more momentum it has. Greater momentum allows you to shoot longer lengths of line. The double haul is used for long casts, over sixty feet, and/or a lot of wind, because greater line speed will overcome either obstacle.

The double haul can be done efficiently only with weight-forward or shooting-taper lines. Both of these lines utilize thirty feet of head or thicker line; the remainder of the line is thin-diameter running line. It's easy to see this junction in a shooting-taper line, since the head and fly line are different types of materials, and sometimes different colors. With weight-forward lines this junction is not immediately apparent, because the head and running line are continuous, the demarcation being where the head tapers down quickly, about thirty feet from the tip of the line. It's important to find this point with either type of line. You'll use the head to load the rod, while the running line will be pulled through the guides by the forward momentum of the head.

Start the double haul with about thirty feet of line on the water in front of you. Lower your rod tip to about two feet above the water and eliminate any slack by stripping in some line or else making a single forward cast. Begin the forward cast as if you were going to pick up a lot of line, bringing your arm up as you cast, letting your elbow come up above shoulder level. Your line hand should be holding the line tightly, quite close to the stripping guide. Watch the fly line—as soon as the line leaves the water, haul on the fly line by bringing your line hand down forcefully toward your waist. As the rod tip reaches 1:00, let your line hand drift back to the stripping guide. The line that you hauled will become part of the back cast. Let the rod tip drift back to 2:30 as the line straightens behind you.

That's a single haul, and may come in handy all by itself if you have a wind at your back and are having trouble straightening the back cast.

To complete the double haul, begin to come forward, simultaneously hauling by bringing your line hand back to your waist. When the line hand reaches your waist, the rod tip should be at about 10:30. Your casting arm and the rod tip should be one straight line pointing above the horizon. Now, release the line with your line hand. Since you didn't have any slack in reserve, the line will snap against the rod with quite a bit of power and fall to the water.

Now practice the double haul with twenty feet of slack line held below your stripping hand, piled neatly on the ground. The powerful line speed you've developed by hauling, combined with the high trajectory of the rod tip, will allow you to shoot great lengths of line.

The high rod tip is essential because, unlike any other type of forward cast, you are actually throwing or propelling line through the air. If the rod tip ends up too low, everything will pile up into the water.

With a shooting-head line, it's possible to shoot sixty to eighty feet of running line on a single cast. Running line has less friction and air resistance than the back end of a weight-forward line, so it travels farther. When using a shooting head, make sure that the last couple of inches of fly line are just inside the guides. Otherwise, you'll form a hinge at the junction of the fly line and the running line and lose a lot of casting power. Fly-fishermen using shooting-head lines often hold the coils of

The double haul: starting position.

Haul with the line hand while making the back cast.

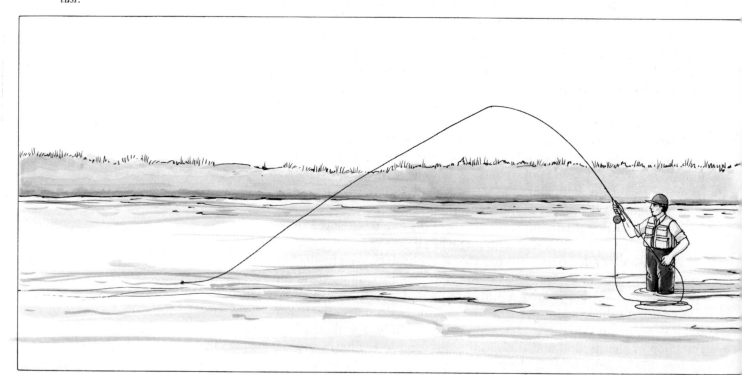

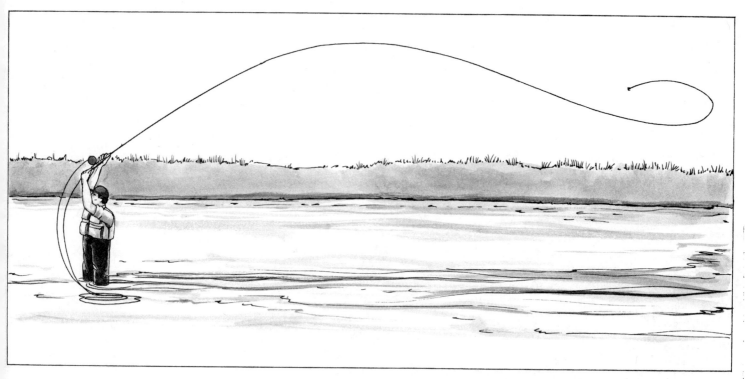

Let the line hand drift back to the stripping
guide, lengthening the back cast.

Haul at the start of the forward cast.

Release the line immediately after hauling.

Keep the rod high as the line shoots.

running line in their teeth or coiled in a stripping basket attached to the chest. In a boat, shooting line can be held in a plastic bucket at your feet.

For optimum performance, you should get the kinks out of shooting-head running line. Point your rod tip at your fishing partner and have him pull on the end of the running line as he walks away from you. If no one is around to help, you can hook your front loop over a branch or nail and accomplish the same thing.

The double-haul and shooting-head lines are both designed for one purpose—distance. Neither will straighten a delicate twelve-foot leader. They should be used only when it is necessary to cast consistently over sixty feet—most often in big steelhead and salmon rivers, lakes, and in saltwater fishing.

DEALING WITH WIND

The double haul, with its tremendous line speed, is a great advantage in the wind, but in most cases a simple modification of the forward cast will suffice. It's mostly a matter of common sense. For example, if you have the wind blowing toward you, it's going to be easy to form the back cast, harder to straighten the line in front of you. Put a little less effort into the back cast, be a little more casual about it, but hammer the rod down quickly on the forward cast. When casting into the wind, don't try to *push* the line *into* the wind—slice down *through* the wind. As long as you keep your rod tip from pointing below the horizontal, you can come forward as hard and as fast as the wind dictates without slamming your line into the water.

With the wind coming from behind you, use a forceful back cast and an easy forward cast.

Wind coming from either side presents a different set of problems. If you're a right-handed caster and you have a crosswind blowing from left to right, merely lead your target a foot or two to the left to compensate for the wind. With a wind blowing from right to left, you have two options: either change your position or use a cross-body cast. If you stand there and try to use a standard forward cast, you're asking for a fly in the back of the neck.

THE ROLL CAST

The roll cast is a useful technique in tight spots and quite easy to learn, but I see it as a last resort in most situations. The reason: the roll cast is not as accurate or as delicate as a properly executed forward cast. Also, it is harder to shoot a lot of line with it—it can take four or five roll casts to get out forty feet of line.

The roll cast offers two advantages: the line never goes behind you

71

and it can be accomplished with slack line on the water, which would ruin a forward cast. The roll cast can be used when you have an impenetrable wall of trees or brush behind you. If you've made a bad cast and have piles of slack line on the water, a quick roll cast can straighten those coils in preparation for a proper forward cast. In fact, it's frequently used to get the line in the water quickly when you approach a new spot.

Because the roll cast does not have a back cast, it must be started slowly in order to keep the line from going behind you. To start, very slowly raise the rod tip to the vertical. As you do, bring the rod off to the side just enough to keep the line on the far side of the rod. The line will move toward you, and will form a curve of line between the rod tip and the water. Keep moving the rod tip up and back until part of this curve is behind the rod, forming a semicircle with the rod as the radius. Stop. Wait until everything stops moving. Now, with a forceful motion, using your wrist and forearm as you would on a forward cast, snap the rod tip straight down in front of you. The line should roll neatly onto the water in front of you.

The longer your fly rod, the longer the roll cast you'll be able to perform, because the rod tip will travel a longer distance, imparting more force to the line. Still, with any kind of rod, roll casting over fifty feet in length is a tricky and inconsistent business.

You can change the direction with a roll cast so long as the line is directed away from the side of the rod that the loop is formed on. In

The roll cast: starting position. Raise the rod slowly to this point.

Keep moving back slowly until there is a semicircle of line along the outside of the rod.

Snap the rod tip quickly to this point.

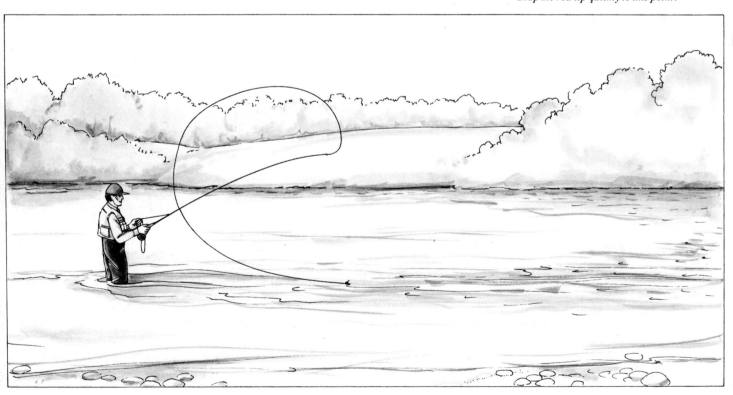

The rolling loop formed will carry the line out...

...and deliver the fly to its target.

other words, a right-handed caster can make a change of direction only to the left of where his rod tip is pointing. If he tries to roll cast to the right, the line as it rolls will come up under the rod, and the fly will probably catch on the rod.

A roll-cast pickup can be used to lift the line off the water in preparation for a false cast. It is done by making a roll cast but not allowing the line to touch the water in front of you; thus, the rod tip should be directed a little higher than normal. When the line straightens in the air in front of you, make a single false cast and follow through as you would on a normal forward cast. With sinking lines, the roll-cast pickup serves to bring the line to the surface instead of back toward your face, since it's difficult to lift a sunken line straight off the water. For a deeply sunken line it may take two roll-cast pickups—one to bring the line to the surface, the other to lift the line into the air.

The roll cast can be performed as a cross-body cast, across your opposite shoulder, but it's an uncomfortable and difficult motion for most people. For right-handers, it is done by slowly bringing the rod tip up and across the front of your body, over the left shoulder. Keep the fly line off to the left of the rod, or the line will roll up into your face when you cast.

SLACK-LINE CASTS AND LINE MENDING

Fishing in moving water, there are times you'll want to manipulate the line with the rod just before or just after the line hits the water. When imitating an insect floating on the surface of the water or drifting in the current, your fly line must move at the same speed as the fly. A river or stream is composed of many different current speeds from bank to bank or from top to bottom; if your fly line is lying in a current that is faster or slower than that in which the fly has been placed, some manipulation is necessary.

The most typical example is when you find yourself in the middle of a fast river with a fish feeding in the slow water next to the bank, directly across from you. If you cast your fly to the fish, the faster water between you and the fish will pull on the fly line, forming a belly in the line and whisking the fly from the slower water near the bank. Not only will the fly be pulled away from the fish before he can see it—if you're using a dry fly a little wake will form behind it, making it look like a miniature motorboat. Most insects don't skid across the surface of a stream. This unnatural movement, called ''drag,'' is very apparent, even frightening, to a feeding fish.

In instances like this, drag can be avoided by purposely throwing slack into your line. The faster current has to pull all the slack out of the line before it can begin to pull on the leader and fly. Throw slack either by overshooting your target, overpowering the cast, and stopping the rod higher than normal (about 10:30), or by wiggling the rod from side to side as you follow through on the forward cast.

You have other options in your bag of tricks for avoiding drag. One is to throw a curve cast with the arc of the curve upstream of the fly's position. The faster current will have to invert this curve before it will pull on the fly.

Mending line means throwing a curve into your fly line after the line hits the water. In the circumstance described above, you would cast to the fish directly across from you; then, with the rod held low in front of you with a stiff arm, flip the rod by rolling your wrist in the upstream direction. The result is an upstream curve that the current will have to invert before it will pull on your fly. It's best to release some slack line as you make the mend, otherwise you'll move the fly when you reposition the line.

Mending line. Dotted line indicates the line's position before the upstream mend is made.

The so-called reach cast is merely an aerial mend. Just before the line hits the water on a forward cast, you move your rod upstream of where it would have ended up on a standard forward cast. This offers the advantage of not moving the fly, since you are making the mend just before everything hits the water.

A mend or a series of mends is often used to sink a wet fly deeper and to keep it moving at approximately the same speed as the current. A line that is bellying downstream will pull a fly faster than the current and also draw it toward the surface. Every time the line bellies downstream, make an upstream mend. On a long cast across the stream you may have to mend line three or four times to get a natural drift. This technique is especially useful with sink-tip lines, because the floating portion of the line is easy to mend. It is almost impossible to mend sinking lines once they are in the water.

Although the most common mend is made in an upstream direction, you may occasionally have to mend the line downstream. A typical situation would be where you are standing in fast water and casting into a slower current. If you don't mend line downstream, the line nearest you will hang upstream of the fly, making the fly drag against the current. In this instance, just reverse the process and flip your wrist in the downstream direction.

Every place you ever fly-fish will present a different set of challenges. For precise placement of a fly you should use the standard forward cast whenever possible, but with the many variations of the forward cast, the roll cast, and line mending you have an impressive set of skills with which to meet many different fishing conditions.

6
Flies

Flies can imitate almost anything a fish will eat. Trout flies are tied to resemble the various insects that trout eat, as well as minnows, leeches, and crustaceans. Bass flies imitate frogs, mice, and minnows. Saltwater flies mimic the color and shape of saltwater baitfish, crabs, and squid. The best flies are constructed by winding fur, feathers, tinsel, and hair on a hook. Lightweight synthetic materials like nylon, latex, polypropylene, and some plastics are used as replacements for, and sometimes improvements upon, natural materials.

Flies called attractors stimulate nonfeeding fish. Some trout and bass flies look like nothing that occurs in nature and can be considered attractors; no one really knows why fish strike them. Perhaps fish see them in a different light than we do, and actually take them for items of food. It is said that attractor flies arouse curiosity or anger or boredom in fish, but this theory is probably more anthropomorphical than biological in origin.

I believe that fish don't see flies as we do. There can never be a perfect fly, because a perfect fly would not contain a hook. All flies have that great big, obvious point sticking out of them. Every time a fish inhales one of your flies, it's by mistake.

With our flies we are trying to create the impression of "something alive," not an exact duplicate of live bait. Exact molded-rubber or plastic imitations of fish and insects have been around for years but are soon discarded after a fly-fisherman tries them, because these stiff, hard facsimiles don't give an impression of life in the water.

HOOKS

Hooks for tying flies come in a variety of styles and sizes suitable for constructing flies that imitate everything from a tiny insect to a large baitfish. Most quality fly-tying hooks are made in Norway, England, and the United States. All the important manufacturers follow a universal sizing scale, so when an Icelandic salmon-fishing guide says to try a size 8 fly, you can reach for the correct size in your fly box.

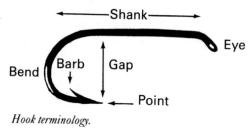

Hook terminology.

Hook Terminology

Eye. The eye of a hook is a closed loop or ring of wire at the front end. It enables you to tie flies to your leader. The most common type is a turned-down eye, which means that the eye is bent down from the shank of the hook. Turned-up-eye hooks have the eye bent upward from the shank, and the ring-eyed hooks have a straight eye that is parallel to the shank. Certain types of eyes are supposed to offer better hooking advantages in various situations, but I've never seen any of these theories proven conclusively. Most standard trout flies use turned-down-eye hooks, most salmon flies are tied on turned-up-eye hooks, and most saltwater flies feature ring-eye hooks, but the habit seems to follow tradition more than anything else. As a fly-tier, I'm offended by a classic dry fly on a ring-eyed hook, but I'm sure if it's properly tied it will catch as many fish as one tied on a turned-down-eye hook.

Shank. The shank is the long, straight part of the hook that is used for the base, to which fly-tying materials are attached.

Bend. The bend occurs between the shank and barb of the hook. Bends come in several varieties, such as sprout, limerick, and model perfect, but the subtleties in bend shapes are more for aesthetic than utilitarian purposes.

Point. The point penetrates a fish's jaw so that the bend can hold. Hook points should be sharp but not too long, because long, thin points can easily be broken. The hook point on a fly should be sharp enough to scratch your thumbnail if drawn across it lightly. Examine hook points before you begin fishing and periodically while fishing, especially if you've missed a fish or dropped your back cast. If the point has been lightly nicked, touch it up by drawing it against a sharpening stone or special hook hone. If it is badly broken, the fly should be thrown away and replaced.

Barb. The barb helps to keep the bend in place once the point has penetrated. Because a fly has little weight that a fish can throw or work against, many fly-fishermen use barbless hooks or carefully mash down the barb with a small pair of pliers or forceps. Barbless hooks make it much easier to release fish unharmed, and may even offer hooking advantages because there is less resistance to penetration.

Hook Size and Style

Hook size. Hook size, and thus fly size, is measured by an arbitrary scale based on distance between the point and the shank, also called the gape. Hook sizes that are used for flies range from less than one eighth inch in length for the smallest to three inches for the largest.

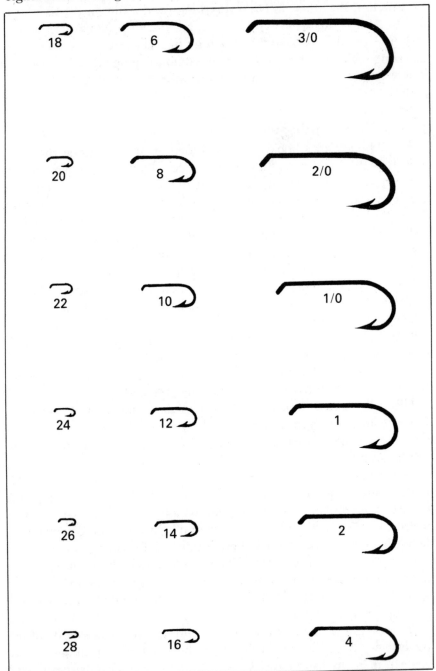

Hook sizes. All are standard length.

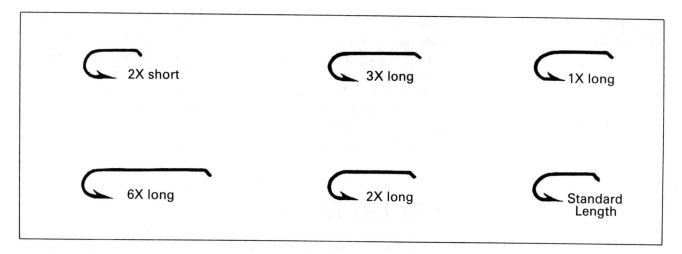

The actual size of a fly can be much larger; in some saltwater flies the materials used will extend up to six inches beyond the bend of the hook. In the smaller trout-sized hooks we use even numbers 2 through 28; the larger the number, the smaller the fly. Hooks larger than size 2 use a numbering system that increases as the size increases, using a slash/zero after the number to distinguish them. Thus, the hook size scale, in increasing order of size, would be 28, 26, 24, 22, 20, 18, 16, 14, 12, 10, 8, 6, 4, 2, 1/0, 2/0, 3/0, 4/0, 5/0. Hook sizes larger than 5/0 are too heavy to be cast with fly-fishing gear, and hooks smaller than size 28 have a gape that is so small it's impossible to hook a fish.

Shank length. For a given hook size, the standard shank length is about twice the gape of the hook. Some hook styles, however, have shank length longer or shorter than normal. This gives you a longer or shorter fly with the same hook size. An X system is used to designate these hooks—for example, a sixe 6 2X long hook has a shank length equivalent to a standard hook that is one size larger than a size 4 hook, because even though odd-size hooks aren't made they are still counted in the X scale. A size 22 1X short hook has a shank length equivalent to a size 21 hook.

Hooks that are 1X to 3X long are generally used for nymphs, or imitations of immature aquatic insects. The 3X to 8X styles are used for long, skinny baitfish imitations called streamers. Short-shank hooks are less commonly used, but a short shank can be an advantage in the tiny, #20 and smaller hooks, when you want to imitate a small insect but want the hooking advantage offered by a larger gape. Spiders, special dry flies designed to be skated across the surface of the water, are sometimes tied on 2X short hooks. Hooks shorter than 3X short give poor leverage when playing a fish and are seldom used.

Wire diameter. The size of the wire used to construct hooks is proportional to hook size. Thus, a size 2 hook is made from heavier wire than a size 4. Standard-wire hooks are generally considered wet-fly hooks; dry flies should be tied with hooks of finer wire, or they won't float properly. As with shank length, we use an X system, and a 2X fine hook is made from wire that is two sizes finer than the standard hook in that size. Most dry flies are tied with 1X and 2X fine-wire

Different shank lengths of the same-size hook.

hooks; 3X fine hooks are available, but they break or bend quite easily. Salmon, saltwater, and steelhead hooks are 1X and 2X stout, or 1- and 2-hook sizes heavier, because these species can put a lot of pressure on a diminutive hook.

Hook finish. Most flies are tied on bronzed or japanned (blackened) hooks, which are coated to keep them from rusting. Saltwater flies are always tied on stainless-steel or nickel or cadmium-plated hooks because of the corrosive properties of salt water.

FLY PATTERNS

Flies are tied according to specific patterns, some of them hundreds of years old, others dreamed up by fly-tiers the night before they go fishing. All will catch fish at one time or another, but the ones you see in the fishing catalogs year after year have withstood the test of time, because a trout will eat the same insect tomorrow that trout were eating a hundred years ago. Some patterns are limited in their use; for example, a size 28 black midge will catch trout when they are feeding on tiny midges, but a 20-pound pike or 185-pound tarpon won't even notice this speck on the water. Other flies have broad application. Under the right conditions, a plain black-and-white streamer fly will catch any fish in fresh or salt water that feeds on baitfish—and that includes most of them.

Fly patterns range from sublimely simple to ridiculously complicated. Some steelhead flies are merely clumps of fluorescent yarn that imitate salmon eggs, while the Baron, a classic Atlantic salmon fly, calls for thirty different kinds of tinsel, floss, and feathers.

Parts of a Fly

Head. The head of a fly is right behind the eye of the hook, and usually consists of the thread that has been used to tie the fly. Properly made heads are small and neat, and have been finished with a special knot called a whip finish, then laquered or varnished for durability.

Body. The body of a fly is the part that occupies most of the hook shank. Fly bodies can be made from almost any imaginable material, but the most common are fur, tinsel, nylon or silk floss, wool, plastic, cotton chenille, and spun and clipped deer body hair.

Rib. The rib is a spiral decoration that is sometimes wound around the body. It may imitate the segments of an insect's body or, if made from tinsel, add flash to the body.

Wings. Wings imitate the wing of an insect or the back of a minnow. Wings are usually made from feathers or hair.

Hackle. The hackle imitates the legs of an insect or crustacean, and in most dry flies is the part of the fly that provides flotation, by trapping the fly in the surface film. The hackle is almost always made from a neck or body feather of a bird.

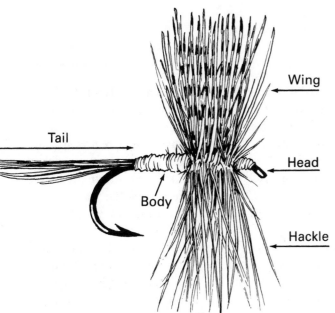

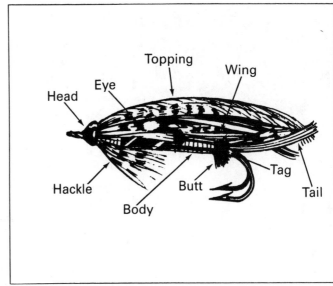

Parts of a dry fly (left), and a wet fly (right).

Throat. Sparse hackle or hair often replaces the hackle proper on streamer or wet salmon flies.

Tail. The tail extends beyond the bend of the hook, and is usually composed of a small bunch of hackle fibers. On dry flies the tail helps support the fly in the surface film, on some flies it is merely a decoration that adds a bit of color, and on many wet flies and nymphs it imitates the tails of an insect larva.

Tag, tip, or butt. Some flies have a short piece of tinsel or floss that is actually a part of the body but is a different color or material from the rest of the body. The tag is located just in front of or just behind the point where the tail originates. The tag is usually just a decoration, but it may imitate the egg sacs of some insects.

Eyes, cheeks, horns, topping. These are adornments that are commonly found on fancy, complicated streamer or salmon fly patterns. They add nice touches of color to a fly, but their utilitarian value is questionable.

IMITATING INSECTS

Most fly-fishing is based on imitating the creatures that fish feed on. The size, shape, color, and behavior of this food is what we strive to imitate. The plausibility of the first three criteria depends on the fly pattern you use, the last one on the way in which you present your fly.

Most flies used to catch trout and some that are used for bass and panfish are imitations of immature or adult insects. Aquatic insects, the primary source of food for trout, live as larvae underwater. They hatch into winged adults at specific times of year, according to species. When these hatches occur, the insects are extremely vulnerable, so the fish feed with reckless abandon and are quite easy to catch—if you have the right fly pattern.

83

An adult mayfly.

Mayflies

Mayflies are the genesis of fly-fishing. The majority of the flies we use for trout are designed to imitate some stage in a mayfly's life. Thus, understanding the life cycle of this order of insects is bound to make you a more successful trout fisherman.

Mayflies are the most common insect in most trout streams and the most important source of food for trout and other stream fishes. They are also common in ponds or lakes, but are usually not the main source of food in still waters. Mayflies, like trout, are intolerant of warm or polluted water. The distribution of mayflies throughout the world closely parallels the range of trout, both native and introduced.

Eggs are deposited by adult mayflies by various methods. In streams, the adults usually drop the eggs into the water and the eggs sink and fall into crevices on the stream bottom. Many pond insects and some stream dwellers crawl underwater on vegetation and deposit their eggs. The eggs soon hatch into tiny larvae or nymphs, which feed on algae and dead plant matter, maturing and growing as the season progresses. Some nymphs burrow into silt on the stream bottom, many varieties cling to the bottoms of rocks, and a few are free-swimming and move like tiny minnows, propelling themselves by expelling water through their abdomens.

Almost exactly one year after they hatched from eggs, the nymphs are ready to hatch. Some species of mayfly may hatch at the same time of day for a few days; others may hatch sporadically throughout the day for almost a month. Just before hatching, the nymphs become restless. Some drift in the current; others clamber around on the stream bottom and migrate toward the shallows. Then, according to environmental cues that include water temperature and sunlight, the nymphs begin drifting in the current, rising to the surface by gases that form inside their exoskeletons.

When a mayfly reaches the surface, the exoskeleton splits and a winged form, called a subimago or dun, crawls out onto the surface film. The adult may fly away immediately, or it may sit on the surface of the water for a minute or so to expand and dry its wings.

Mayfly nymphs are drab in color, camouflaged against the stream or pond bottom, as are most animals that are preyed on by other animals. Most are olive, brown, tan, or cream in color. The swimming varieties of mayfly are long and skinny, and the species that cling to the bottoms of rocks are flat and wide. Some clamber along bottom debris; in shape this type is halfway between the streamlined swimmers and the flattened clingers. A fourth type burrows in the mud on stream and lake bottoms and has very prominent gills.

All mayfly nymphs have gills along the abdomen. Some have prominent, feathery appendages; in other species the gills are tiny hair-like filaments that aren't visible without a magnifying glass. Tails are always two or three in number. The legs of mayfly nymphs are often tucked under their bodies when they swim or drift; thus, some artificial nymphs don't even attempt to imitate the legs, or may simulate them

This mayfly nymph was discovered by turning over a rock on the stream bottom.

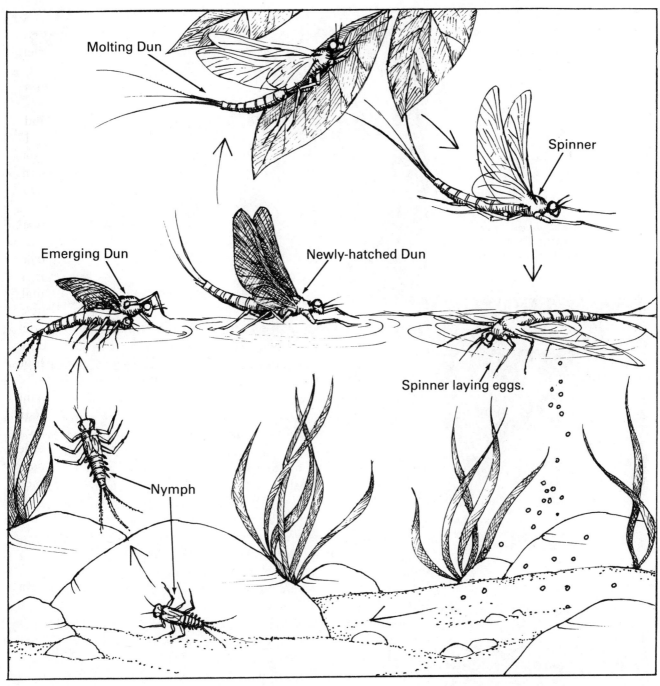

Molting Dun

Spinner

Emerging Dun

Newly-hatched Dun

Spinner laying eggs.

Nymph

The mayfly's life cycle.

with a few fibers of fur that are picked out from the thorax. The wing pads or cases of mayfly nymphs extend across the top of the thorax. Just before hatching, the wing pads become darker and more prominent.

Newly hatched mayfly duns have a distinct sailboat-like appearance on the water, and are quite easy to identify. The wings are translucent gray, yellow, or cream, and some species have brown or black mottling. Bodies range in color from almost white to olive, pink, brown, cream, yellow, and black. Mayflies always have two or three slender tails and six delicate legs. Dry-fly imitations usually have more than three hackle

85

Examination of the stream bottom turned up these four different types of mayfly nymphs in a very small area. Note the gills along the abdomen.

A mayfly spinner. Note the clear wings (with the exception of the dark speckles on the front of the wings, which is typical of this particular species) and long tails.

A mayfly spinner laying spent on the surface of the water.

fibers for tails and more than six fibers for legs, but nature has the edge in flotation and we need more materials to keep our hooks on the surface. Harry Darbee, the famous Catskill fly-tier, is often quoted as saying, "If the trout could count, we'd all be in trouble."

The adults, if they survive predation by fish and birds, will then fly to streamside brush and molt a final time, changing into the imago form, known as the spinner stage. The spinners will mate, lay eggs, and die over their parent body of water. Some mayflies mate immediately after hatching, molting in midair, their entire adult stage lasting less than an hour. Most mayflies return to mate the following day. The life of an adult mayfly is so brief that it doesn't even feed in the adult stage. In fact, their mouth parts are nonfunctional.

After mayfly duns have molted and hatched into spinners they retain the basic mayfly profile, but colors may change. The wings are transparent, bodies are thinner, and tails are usually longer. Bright yellow or orange egg sacs are often visible on the abdomens of the females. It is by their behavior, though, that spinners are instantly distinguished from duns. While the duns are slow, clumsy fliers and can be easily captured with a swipe of your hat, spinners are quick fliers and quite agile. Before the mating flights begin, you'll see squadrons of them moving upstream, flying quickly at treetop level with obvious purpose. When mating, they will hover over the water, periodically dipping up and down. These swarms of glistening insects can be so thick that you can barely see the opposite shore.

All of the mayfly stages—nymph, dun, and spinner—are part of a trout's diet when they are available. Because most mayflies do not swim in the current or on the water's surface, but merely drift with it, they are most vulnerable to trout during their hatching stage. Although trout will root nymphs out from under rocks and vegetation, it's a lot of work, and they prefer the easy capture of a nymph drifting in the current or a dun or spinner floating on the surface.

Once mayfly nymphs reach maturity, they vary little in size through emergence and mating. Thus, a size 12 nymph will hatch into a size 12 dun, which will molt into a size 12 spinner. Mayflies range in size from a size 6 hook down to a size 28, with most species you'll encounter being sizes 12 through 20.

Colors, however, may vary drastically between life stages. *Ephemerella subvaria*, the species of mayfly fishermen call the Hendrickson, has a nymph stage that is brown-olive in overall coloration. The dun has a creamy pink body with medium gray wings. The spinner has clear wings and a dark reddish brown body, and the female carries a ball of bright yellow eggs on the end of her abdomen.

Mayfly hatches are predictable not only with regard to the time of year that they'll hatch, but also to the time of day. For example, I know that at 2:00 in the afternoon during the second and third weeks of May on my favorite trout stream I'll see red-bodied mayflies with gray wings, about size 14, and that they'll hatch for two hours and then stop. I can fish a Hendrickson dry fly, which matches the dun, and catch trout, if I'm lucky, for this two-hour period. I can also catch trout on a Hendrickson nymph an hour prior to the hatch. If it's a warm, clear evening, I'll be able to catch trout on a spinner imitation in the evening, when the flies hatched yesterday return to lay their eggs.

The Hendricksons will be preceded by, followed by, and overlap with hatches of other aquatic insects. This predictable pattern has been written about and researched in the many trout fishermen's entomologies that are available to the serious trout fisherman. The seasonal sequence of hatches will vary with differences in geography and altitude, but in a given section of the country at a given time you can expect the same hatches year after year.

Many trout streams are so rich in insect life that there is almost always a hatch in progress during the day (few insects hatch after dark), and you may see four or five species hatching at once. Trout can be very selective in their feeding habits, choosing one insect and feeding on it all day long, to the exclusion of all others. That's when the fun begins! By watching the trout or by trial-and-error fly changes you'll find the fly that is closest to what they're feeding on. Then you're in the ball park.

Mayfly species vary with each region, but a fly-fisherman who has a well-stocked fly box can catch trout anywhere in the world. The Blue-Wing Olive dry fly in sizes 14 through 26 will imitate over a dozen species of mayfly in the eastern United States alone, and this fly will also imitate olive-colored mayflies that hatch in Argentina and Chile, New Zealand, England, and the western United States. There are over five hundred species of mayfly in the United States, and to try to achieve a one-to-one correspondence between our imitations and the naturals would be both futile and unnecessary.

Caddisflies

Caddisflies rival mayflies as important food for trout. They also have a larval stage that trout feed on, and some caddis larvae live alongside mayfly nymphs under rocks. Other caddis larvae spin nets that trap food for them. The great majority of caddis larvae, however, build cases from pieces of gravel, sticks, or vegetation. Each species has its own preference as to the type and size of debris it uses for its case, and species of caddis can be identified by the shape of their case or even what size stick or leaf particle they use. The cases serve as protection and as ballast to keep caddis larvae from being swept away in the current. Trout aren't always fooled by caddis camouflage, and if you examine the stomach contents of the fish you've killed you may find bits of sticks or

Caddisfly life cycle.

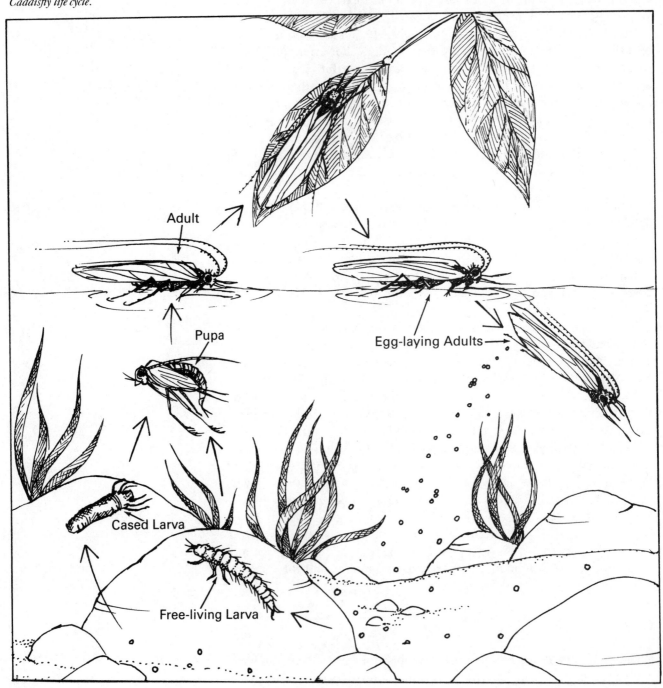

Adult

Pupa

Egg-laying Adults

Cased Larva

Free-living Larva

gravel. You can bet that your trout have been feeding on caddis larvae, or else they've been making a lot of mistakes in their food selection. Trout do make mistakes and pick up a stick or a stone once in a while. If they didn't make mistakes, we'd never catch them!

Unlike mayflies, caddisflies have a stage between the larva and the adult, known as the pupa stage. About a week before they hatch, the larvae become inert and change their shape, inside a cocoon that they build around themselves. When the hatch occurs, the pupae cut their way out of the cocoon and rise to the surface. Some species drift great distances; others pop right to the surface. The adult caddisfly emerges from the pupal skin, looking very much like a tiny, drab moth.

Adult caddisflies differ greatly in appearance from mayflies. Their wings are not held upright like tiny sails, but are folded tentlike, parallel to the body of the insect. Caddisflies have long antennae, but lack the slender, delicate tails that characterize mayflies.

A stick-caddis larva. Note the head and legs protruding from the right side of the case.

Four kinds of stone-caddis larvae cases and a free-living caddis larva.

A caddis pupa, caught at the surface of the water, just before hatching into an adult.

Caddisflies range in size from a size 8 hook down to a size 22, with most falling in the 14-through-18 range. Caddisfly hatches exhibit the same seasonal predictability as mayfly hatches, and often hatch at the same times. Cased caddisfly larvae are almost always white with black heads, while the free-living varieties may be tan, green, or orange. The adults are invariably drab, with tans, browns, and grays predominating, although a few species have bright green abdomens.

Caddisfly behavior can be quite different from mayfly behavior. Some species hop, skid, and flutter on the surface of the water. Many leave the water immediately, not even stopping to stretch their wings, as most mayflies do. Some ride the surface of the water sedately for four or five feet, providing easy meals for the trout and great sport for the dry-fly fisherman. Caddis adults live for up to a month before they mate and die; thus, they do feed in the adult stage, sipping water and nectar from streamside brush. They often form huge mating swarms at dusk, with battalions of flies moving upstream, bouncing on the water to drop their eggs, and stimulating the trout to feed on the surface.

An adult caddisfly inspects my fly box. Note the tent-shaped wings that are held parallel to the body.

Stoneflies

Stoneflies are another aquatic insect group that is quite important in a trout's diet. Stonefly nymphs look much like mayfly nymphs, although most species are larger than the average mayfly nymph, and have gills under the thorax rather than along the abdomen. Stoneflies have no pupal stage, and the nymphs hatch directly into adults. Most stoneflies do not hatch in the surface film, like caddisflies and mayflies, but crawl onto rocks or logs and then hatch into adults above the water's surface. Thus, although the nymphs are available as trout food, the recently hatched adults don't constitute an important source of trout food unless windy weather blows them back into the stream. Some large stonefly nymphs live for two to three years before they hatch, so they are always available to the fish.

Where mayflies and caddisflies are found in all areas of trout streams and ponds, from fast riffles to weedy bays, stoneflies are invariably found in fast, rocky, highly oxygenated water. The flattened shape of the nymphs reveals their habitat preference, as they are found clinging to the undersides of rocks. Stonefly nymphs are usually dark brown with amber mottling or black, and the adults look exactly like the nymphs, except for the flat wings, which are folded over the body when the insect is at rest.

Stonefly adults, like caddisflies, live for several weeks, subsisting on liquid food, and may fall into the stream on windy days, since they seldom stray far from the riffle where they hatched. Stonefly mating swarms also make these juicy morsels fair game for hungry trout, as the flies fall spent to the water after mating and egg-laying duties are discharged.

Stoneflies grow larger than mayflies. In fact, the famous Salmonfly of western rivers is the largest trout-stream insect and provides a tremendous source of food. Some fly-fishermen plan their vacations years ahead of time to coincide with the emergence of this fly on the Madison River in late June, because even the largest trout will feed on the surface at

A stonefly adult is quite similar in appearance to the nymph, except for the wings that lay flat along the body.

Two common species of stonefly nymphs.

this time. Salmonflies may be almost three inches long, imitated by size 2-through-6 hooks, but most stoneflies are in the 8-through-12 range. The smallest stoneflies are about a size 18.

Midges

Midges follow a life cycle similar to that of caddisflies: they have a larval, pupal, and adult stage. All three stages are important to trout, the pupal stage being the most important because it drifts in the current. Midge larvae, which look like tiny red, pink, or brown worms, burrow in the silt of lake bottoms or in the slower areas of trout streams. The pupae have a slender abdomen and a bulbous thorax, and the adults have two tiny veined wings and look much like mosquitoes, to which they're closely related.

As might be suggested by their name, most species of midges are quite tiny, sizes 18 to 28, although some are as large as size 14. Despite their tiny size, midges are important trout food because they hatch all year long, and may be the only source of easy food in a trout stream in the middle of winter.

Dragonflies and Damselflies

The familiar "darning needles," these brightly colored mosquito predators are much more important in ponds and lakes than they are in streams. The larvae favor slow water, and thus are found only in the still pools of trout streams. The nymphs are quite large (size 4 to 12) and are favorite foods of lake-dwelling trout, bass, and panfish. The adults are usually incidental sources of food for fish, because the nymphs crawl out onto vegetation to hatch.

Terrestrial Insects

When the spring and early summer hatches of mayflies, caddisflies, and stoneflies dwindle, trout turn to land-bred insects for much of their food. A large trout's explosive rise to a juicy grasshopper is an event to make even the veteran trout fisherman tremble. Ants, beetles, leafhoppers, inchworms, crickets, and many other kinds of land-bred insects find their way into the stomach of trout. Terrestrial insects are much more important to trout, bass, and panfish in areas where vegetation overhangs the shore, and on windy days when these insects get blown into the water the fish will be on the lookout for them.

CRUSTACEANS

In fresh water, scuds, sow bugs, and crayfish are important sources of food for fly-rod quarry. These animals never hatch into winged adults as insects do, so they are available to the fish year round. Scuds and sow

Midge pupa.

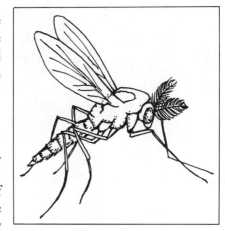

Midge adult.

Damselfly larvae are an important food for trout, bass, and panfish in ponds and lakes.

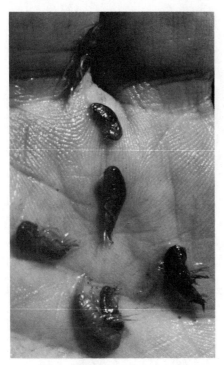

A handful of scuds from a weedy spring creek.

bugs occur in lakes and streams with large expanses of underwater weeds. Scuds look like tiny shrimp, olive or gray in color, while sow bugs look exactly like their gray "pill bug" relatives that live on land. Scuds and sow bugs range from size 10 to 18.

Crayfish, on the other hand, may reach six inches in length. They look like miniature lobsters, and apparently game fish feel the same way about them as humans feel about their larger relatives. Crayfish are found in lakes and streams with clear water and rocky bottoms. They are the number one food of smallmouth bass where they occur, and are also preferred by large trout.

OTHER INVERTEBRATES

Many other aquatic invertebrates find their way into the stomach of fish and can be imitated with flies, including leeches, crabs, shrimp, hellgrammites, aquatic beetles, and even snails.

An understanding of the life cycle of these insects is not essential for success, but it is valuable to know how they behave in the water. In most cases imitations designed for other kinds of animals will work for them. Large black stonefly nymphs, for example, make excellent hellgrammite imitations, and a brown marabou streamer will serve very well when the fish are taking leeches.

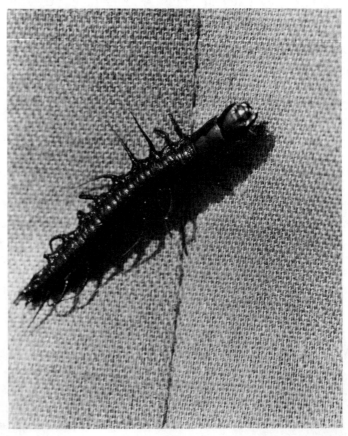

Hellgrammites, large, vicious larvae of the dobsonfly, are relished by large trout and smallmouth bass.

92

FORAGE FISH

Forage fish are small fish that provide food for larger fish. Most freshwater and saltwater game fish will eat smaller fish: thus, long, skinny imitations of baitfish are essential in anyone's fly box. The most popular forage fish in saltwater are menhaden, anchovy, herring, and mullet, all of which are silvery with white bellies and black, blue, or green backs. Freshwater baitfish include the young of most species of game fish, darters, sculpin, and members of the minnow family.

SINKING AND FLOATING FLIES

What's the difference between a dry fly and a wet fly? That is one of the first questions an inquisitive student of fly-fishing will ask. Quite simply, a dry fly is designed to float and a wet fly is designed to sink. How?

For a wet fly, the problem is an easy one. All flies are tied on hooks, and hooks are made of metal, which is quite easy to sink. Fly-tiers help wet flies sink by tying them on heavy wire hooks and using materials that absorb water quickly. Soft, webby feathers, tinsel, floss, and most bird feathers absorb water quickly and are essential materials in wet-fly construction. If you want your wet flies to sink very quickly, you can even buy weighted versions; by winding turns of lead wire on the shank of the hook before he ties the fly, a fly-tier can make a fly sink quickly.

Most dry flies won't float on their own, or won't float for long without a couple of quick false casts to dry them. Some, made from buoyant cork or plastic or hollow animal body hair, are actually lighter than water, but the delicate insects that most dry flies imitate just cannot be made with these bulky materials. Most dry flies aren't lighter than water, but are pinioned in the surface film, supported by delicate hackle and tails.

A typical dry fly (top) and a wet fly (bottom).

Dry flies are tied on hooks made of light wire, and the reduction in weight helps to keep them floating. Most dry flies have stiff, bushy hackle that is wound 360 degrees around the hook. This hackle not only disperses the weight of the fly over a wider area of surface film, it also increases the air resistance of the fly so it lands lightly. Stiff, shiny rooster hackle floats a fly better than dull, webby hackle, and it is used for both dry-fly hackles and tails. Stiff, hollow deer, elk, or moose hair is also used for tails on dry flies.

Wherever possible we try to use water-repellent materials for dry flies. For bodies, fur or synthetics like polypropylene are better than absorbent wool or floss. Finally, before using dry flies you should spray or dip them into some type of dry-fly flotant. These preparations are either silicone paste or silicone with a solvent, and enhance the water-repellent properties of a dry fly.

You can tell most dry flies from wet flies at a glance. Dry flies look light and bushy because of the amount of hackle used; wet-fly hackle is usually sparse and slopes back toward the point of the hook. It's not always so easy, though, because some dry flies are tied without hackle. Their floating properties depend entirely on light wire hooks, stiff tails, bodies tied from water-repellent materials, and a good silicone flotant.

POPPERS AND HAIR BUGS

Unlike true dry flies, poppers and hair bugs are really lighter than water. They fall in that gray area between flies and fly-rod lures, because they come very close in appearance to the plugs that spin and bait casters use, but they're much lighter.

Poppers are hard-bodied cork or plastic bodies that have been cemented to the hook. They are usually painted bright colors, sometimes to imitate frogs and sometimes just in appealing combinations of hues. They may be adorned with hackle, hair, or rubber legs. Poppers may have concave faces, in which case they make loud "burps" and "pops" when retrieved, or they can be made with a bullet-shaped head. The bullet-shaped head produces a less noisy, more subtle disturbance in the water. Both kinds have their place, according to the moods of the fish. Poppers may imitate frogs, mice, or wounded minnows, or they may just be noisy attractors. They are popular with bass, panfish, and pike, and with saltwater fly-fishermen, who often need to present a large, meaty, noisy fly to interest the fish.

Hair bugs are similar to poppers, being large, noisy, and usually dressed with rubber or hair legs. They are made by spinning hollow deer, caribou, elk, or antelope hair to a hook, often in bands of different colors, and clipping the hair to whatever shape is desired. Hair bugs are porous, so they don't float indefinitely as poppers do, but they are soft and are rejected less quickly once they are grabbed by a fish. Incredibly realistic mice and frog imitations can be made from spun and clipped hair—I once scared a waitress into hysterics with a hair mouse at a Trout Unlimited banquet. Because hair bugs are not as durable as poppers, they are not used for toothy saltwater fish and pike, but are very popular for bass, panfish, and large trout.

Various floating flies. Top: a standard dry fly and a cork popping bug. Middle: a saltwater skipping bug, a type of popper. Bottom: a deer-hair bass bug and a salmon dry fly.

DRY FLIES

Dry flies that imitate insects are the most diverse group of flies you'll see offered through a catalog or at a fly shop. There is a good reason for this: trout are selective feeders, which means that they often pick out one type of insect, find out that it's good to eat, and ignore insects that don't have its shape, size, and color. It is usually the insect that is most abundant on the water, regardless of size. Thus, a trout may feed on size 18 mayflies, ignoring larger juicy mayflies that are on the water at the same time. This selectivity may last for an hour or so, or it may last for weeks, depending on the relative abundance of the insect and how long it hatches. The dry-fly fisherman must be prepared to switch flies to accommodate the whims of surface-feeding trout. He's always looking for a dry fly that will work all the time, and thus each year fly-tiers come out with new lines of flies, much like the annual unveiling of Detroit's latest offerings.

Of course, merely changing the body color of a fly creates a new pattern, and the list of dry-fly types is almost endless. They can, however, be lumped in groups, depending on the construction of the fly or what it's supposed to imitate.

Traditional dry flies. Traditional dry flies are the most versatile of all the types of dry flies. Their construction has changed little in the past fifty years. They rely on stiff tails and hackle for flotation. Traditional dry flies were originally tied to imitate adult mayflies, and their wings are tied upright, at a 90-degree angle to the body, to simulate the distinctive upright wing of a mayfly sitting on the water. Some traditional flies leave the wings off and rely on hackle to give the impression of both the legs and the sparkle of an adult mayfly's wings.

Variants. Variants are traditional dry flies but with longer tails and hackle than on traditional dry flies. Whereas traditional dries have tails and hackle that are one and a half to two hook sizes in length, variants have hackle and tails that are equivalent to a dry fly that is one hook size larger. The long hackle and tail increase both the air resistance and flotation of variants. Because they land softly and float very well, they are an excellent choice for the beginning fly caster. Because variants float high on the water, some fishermen believe that the fish take them for insects that are fluttering above the water. Variants are usually tied without wings.

Spiders or skaters. Spiders are dry flies with very long, stiff, bushy hackle and tiny hooks. They are usually tied on a size 14 or 16 hook with hackle the diameter of a silver dollar, and most often without bodies or tails. Spiders are fished with manipulation by the fisherman, "skated" across the water. They are an interesting option when no other fly will work, but often result in short strikes or fish refusing the fly at the last minute. Some fishermen use spiders to locate large fish, returning later with more conventional flies.

Bivisibles. Bivisibles are flies that consist entirely of hackle. The hook shank is wound with hackle, usually brown or gray, with a few turns of cream or white hackle at the head. The light-colored hackle at the head makes bivisibles easy to see on the water, thus the name. Bivisibles are great floaters and, like variants, are probably taken for fluttering insects by fish.

Hair-winged flies. Hair-winged flies are robust, bushy dry flies that use durable hair for wings and tails. They float extremely well and are most often used in fast, broken water. These flies are extremely valuable for "fishing the water," which is fishing a dry fly in a likely place when no fish are visibly feeding.

Hair-bodied flies. Hair-bodied flies are dry flies made from spun and clipped hollow deer or antelope hair. They are tied with lots of bushy hackle and usually with hair wings and tails. Hair-bodied flies, because

A traditional dry fly—the March Brown.

A variant—the Grey Fox Variant.

A Brown Spider.

95

The Brown Bivisible.

Hair-winged dry fly—the Ausable Wulff.

The Irresistable is the most famous of the hair-bodied dry flies.

The Blue Dun Parachute.

A delicate Spent-Winged Pheasant Tail.

of the air trapped in the body, are the one type of dry fly that is actually lighter than water, and will float in the roughest of water. Excellent for fishing the water, they are a little too bulky and robust for imitating delicate mayflies during a hatch, but their large, juicy profile will often catch the attention of fish in foamy water that would hide a sparsely-tied traditional dry fly.

Parachutes. Parachutes feature a single upright wing with hackle wound around its base, parallel to the hook shank rather than perpendicular to it. Parachutes land lightly and float well. Some fishermen believe they look more realistic to the fish than flies with standard hackle.

Spent wings. Spent wings are imitations of mayflies or caddisflies that have fallen spent to the surface of the water after mating. Their wings, rather than being upright as in a freshly hatched fly, lie outstretched in the surface film. They are sometimes tied without hackle or with hackle that is clipped on the top and bottom so they float low in the surface film, just like the naturals.

Downwings. Unlike mayflies, caddisflies and stoneflies float with their wings parallel to their bodies, instead of upright and perpendicular to them. Downwings are tied with wings of feather or hair that are tied down along the body of the fly.

Terrestrials. These are imitations of ants, beetles, grasshoppers, crickets, and leafhoppers, land-bred insects that accidentally fall into the water. Terrestrial imitations aren't always easy to identify as dry flies, because they lack the bushy appearance of flies that are designed to imitate aquatic insects. Land-bred insects don't have the delicate buoyancy of aquatic insects. They plop into the water and float low in the surface film, so the imitations need little or no hackle; you want them to land in a clumsy manner and to float low in the water.

No-hackles, thorax flies, and comparaduns. The need for an exact adult mayfly imitation under very clear, flat water conditions when trout can look over your fly closely has spawned these recent innovations in dry-fly construction. The theory is that trout "key into" the silhouette of a mayfly's wings and body, and hackle obscures this silhouette. These

A down-winged caddis imitation.

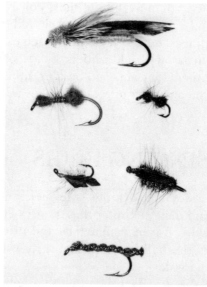

Terrestrials: a grasshopper, two ants, a leafhopper, a beetle, and an inchworm imitation.

Dry flies for fussy trout: a no-hackle fly, a parachute, a comparadun, and a thorax fly.

A tiny midge dry fly.

flies utilize little or no hackle, relying on stiff tails, water-repellent fur or polypropylene bodies, a good flotant, and light wire hooks for flotation. They are extremely effective for picky surface-feeding trout but do not float well in broken water—but trout are seldom as selective in fast water, because they can't see your fly as well as on a smooth, unbroken surface.

Midges. The term "midge" generally refers to any dry fly size 20 or smaller, but this is technically incorrect, because there are many tiny mayfly, caddisfly, and terrestrial species that are imitated by small dry flies. Midges tied to imitate the order of the aquatic insects called midges

97

are extremely simple flies, consisting of a few turns of sparse hackle and a thin fur body. They should float right in the surface film, as most midges are taken as they emerge. Midges tied to imitate tiny mayflies add a few hackle fibers for tails, but they usually don't have wings, either. Tiny ants and beetles, miniature versions of terrestrials, are also tied and are quite effective on midsummer days.

SINKING FLIES

The March Brown is a typical winged wet fly.

A soft-hackled wet fly, tied without wings.

Wet flies, nymphs, streamers, most salmon flies, most steelhead flies, and most saltwater flies are designed to sink. They are generally tied with absorbent materials and present a thinner profile than dry flies, as the bulkier or fuzzier a fly is, the more resistance it will offer to the water.

Wet flies. Wet flies are the original flies; all other sinking and floating flies are recent innovations compared to the wet fly. Nymphs were developed in the twentieth century to be more exact imitations of aquatic insects, streamers to be representative of baitfish, and dry flies couldn't be developed until hook technology developed a fine wire hook that could be floated when dressed with the proper materials.

What does the traditional wet fly imitate? Emerging aquatic insects possibly, at times small minnows, and perhaps at times wet flies just trigger something unexplainable in a fish that says "food." Fishing with a wet fly is probably the least scientific way to fly-fish, but at times it's extremely productive, especially when trout are taking insects at the moment they reach the surface and unfold their wings.

The difference between a wet fly and a nymph is merely that a wet fly has wings that lie sloping back over the whole body, like an emerging mayfly, and nymphs have a small wing case that is folded over half of the body, like a mayfly that is not yet ready to hatch. Some very simple nymphs and wet flies don't have wings or wing cases, just a fur body and few turns of soft hackle at the head.

Nymphs. Nymphs come in all shapes and sizes, and may imitate animals other than immature insects. Besides mayfly, stonefly, and caddisfly nymphs, artificial nymphs may imitate crustaceans such as scuds, sow bugs, or crayfish, or even leeches. A nymph is generally considered to be any sinking fly that is a fairly specific imitation of an aquatic animal other than a minnow. Thus, for every species of insect or crustacean that fly-fishermen feel is important as fish food, there is a nymph pattern.

Take heart! You don't need thousands of different fly patterns to catch fish on nymphs. A general representation of the shape, size, and color of whatever the fish are feeding on is all you'll need in most cases. The Hare's Ear nymph, for example, the most popular nymph pattern in North America, is probably taken by trout at various times for a mayfly nymph, stonefly nymph, caddis larva, caddis pupa, dragonfly nymph, scud, and even a small crayfish.

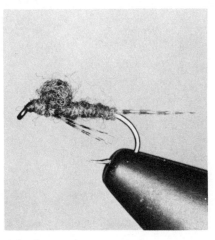

Nymph patterns, left to right from top to bottom: a scud imitation, stonefly nymph, caddisfly larva, hare's ear nymph, mayfly nymph, and midge pupa imitation.

Nymphs have the potential to be the most useful flies a trout fisherman has in his box, because there are nymphs available in a trout stream or pond twelve months a year. Dry flies are useless to the fisherman unless there are insects hatching to interest the trout in surface food, and even during a hatch when the fish are feeding on the surface they also take nymphs below the surface.

Emergers and floating nymphs are nymphs that are tied on dry-fly hooks, to drift just under the surface or in the surface film. During a hatch, aquatic insects will drift just under the surface, trying to break through the film and shed their nymphal skins at the same time. Trout often hold just under the surface, refusing both high, floating dry flies and sunken nymphs, accepting only those flies that are barely submerged. Emergers and floating nymphs have the body color and shape of the nymph that is emerging and short, embryonic wings made of feathers or small balls of fur or polypropylene.

A floating nymph.

Streamers and bucktails. Streamers and bucktails are long, skinny flies that are tied to be baitfish imitations or perhaps just "lures," as the English call them. Streamers were developed when it was found that long, skinny chicken hackles tied on a hook would catch fish that were feeding on smaller fish. It is generally thought that the modern streamer fly was first used around the turn of the century in Maine to imitate the smelt that landlocked salmon feed on, but research in fly-fishing literature has proven that English fly-fishermen were catching saltwater fish on feathered lures fifty years earlier.

Bucktails are streamers with hair instead of feather wings. The Black Ghost bucktail, one of my favorites, is exactly the same as the Black Ghost streamer except that the wing is made from white hair from a

The Dark Edson Tiger is a popular bucktail.

The famous Muddler Minnow.

deer's tail instead of white hackle feathers. Bucktail makes a more durable wing than hackles, but it doesn't have as much action in the water. I like to use bucktails in fast water, reserving the more lively hackled streamers for slow streams and lakes.

You can go one step further and use a marabou streamer, which has a wing made from soft, downy feathers from under the wing of a turkey. Marabou breathes and pulsates in the water, and often excites game fish.

The addition of a spun-and-clipped deer-hair head and collar to a streamer or bucktail produces an important variation called a Muddler or Sculpin. The original Muddler Minnow was tied this way to simulate the flat, blunt head and wide pectoral fins of a bottom-dwelling baitfish called a sculpin, which is a favorite food of large trout and bass. The Muddler, usually tied weighted or fished on a sinking line to keep it where sculpins dwell, has accounted for more large trout than any other fly in the past forty years. The deer-hair head appears to produce some kind of vibration in the water, and Muddlers are excellent flies even when the water is dirty and visibility limited. Muddlers or Sculpins can be tied with wings of hackle, hair, or marabou—the effectiveness of the fly doesn't seem to be affected so long as it incorporates that deer-hair head.

SALMON FLIES

Atlantic salmon are born in freshwater rivers, grow fat in the ocean or large lakes, and return to their natal rivers to spawn. They do not need to feed for nourishment on their spawning runs, but will occasionally take worms, aquatic insects, minnows—and flies. There are many theories as to why Atlantic salmon take flies. A logical explanation is that salmon have a vestigal, instinctive memory of feeding in rivers when they were young, and our flies trigger a reflex. An old salmon fisherman in Nova Scotia once told me, "Your fly's getting in the way, they don't like anything getting in the way when they're moving, so they swat it with their mouth." That would certainly explain why salmon take flies more readily when they're moving than when they're resting.

Regardless, Atlantic salmon do take flies. Where most trout won't move more than a few inches to feed, an Atlantic salmon may come from ten feet away to inhale a large wet fly. It doesn't make sense but it's a lot of fun.

Most Atlantic salmon fishing is done with large wet flies that are attractors in the purest sense of the word. The bodies of these flies may be richly embellished with brightly colored floss, hackle, and tinsel for visibility in fast rivers. Two basic kinds of wet flies are used: featherwings and hairwings. The featherwings are older, traditional European patterns and may incorporate from one to twenty different kinds of feathers. Hairwings are simpler, more durable flies, and many salmon fishermen feel that they are just as effective. Hair seems to have a more lifelike

Salmon wet flies. Top: a hairwing wet tied on a double hook and on a single hook. Middle: a tube fly. Bottom: a classic featherwing Atlantic salmon fly.

action in the water, so many fly-tiers duplicate the classic featherwing patterns with hair by substituting dyed hair for the less durable feathers.

Tube flies, used mainly on European salmon rivers and in Iceland, are thin plastic tubes (the size that hold ink in ball-point pens) dressed with bucktail. A tube is threaded onto your leader, then a hook (usually a double hook) is tied to the leader, and the tube is pushed over the eye of the hook. Tube flies are ridiculously simple, but they offer the advantage of a large fly without adding a lot of weight to make casting difficult.

When salmon rivers warm to over 60 degrees, dry flies can be effective, at least on North American rivers. For some reason, salmon seldom rise to dry flies on European rivers. Salmon dry flies are large, and because

Various dry flies used for salmon.

of the heavy hook needed are tied with lots of bushy hackle or deer-hair bodies. Most of them are merely oversized versions of fast-water trout dry flies. Certain salmon dry flies, such as the Salmon Muddler, Salmon Hornberg, and Buck Bug, are designed to be fished "damp,"—that is, in the surface film or just under the surface. These flies are skinned across the surface, and are often tried as a last resort when the salmon are sulking.

During low-water conditions salmon seem to be frightened by large flies. Low-water flies are sparsely tied wet flies that occupy half to three quarters of the hook shank. The advantage is that a relatively small fly can be presented on a hook large enough to hold a big salmon. Sparsely tied nymphs, similar to trout nymphs, are also used during low-water conditions.

You'll see some salmon wet flies tied on double hooks. Double hooks offer no real hooking or holding advantage, but add weight and thus are used when you want to fish a salmon fly in deep or fast water. Weighted flies are illegal in most salmon rivers, because it's easy to illegally snag a salmon with a weighted fly (even double hooks are illegal on some rivers). Some salmon fishermen also believe that double hooks keep the fly riding upright in faster water. Salmon seem to prefer a fly that is presented broadside to them, and double hooks ensure this profile in tumbling currents.

Pacific salmon rise to flies less readily than Atlantic salmon, but take flies well, especially when they are fresh, or have just ascended a river. Most Pacific salmon are taken on large, brightly colored streamer flies or oversized steelhead flies.

STEELHEAD FLIES

Steelhead are large, migratory rainbow trout that feed in the ocean or large freshwater lakes. Like salmon, they migrate into rivers to spawn;

Steelhead flies. Top: a single egg fly, a hair-winged wet fly, and a wiggler nymph. Bottom: a bead-eyed Comet, a marabou wet fly, and a Two-Egg Sperm Fly.

unlike them, steelhead feed occasionally. Where Pacific salmon spawn in the same rivers as steelhead, the steelhead may follow the salmon and feed on their eggs, which are bright orange-red. Most steelhead are caught on large wet flies that incorporate some red or orange in their dressings. At times, darker, less colorful flies will also entice steelhead.

Dry-fly fishing for steelhead can be successful, especially in summer, when the rivers are low, warm, and clear. Most dry-fly fishing for steelhead is done with patterns that ride in the surface film, such as Muddler-type flies.

BASS FLIES

Largemouth and smallmouth bass were being caught on flies long before plastic worms, spinner baits, and plugs were developed. Early bass flies were large, gaudy wet flies, oversized versions of flies used for brook trout.

Most modern bass flies are either brightly colored attractors or imitations of such large forage as crayfish, minnows, or frogs. Poppers and hair bugs are used as surface lures, as well as some Muddler-type streamers that float just under the surface. Bass flies are often tied with monofilament weed guards or on keel hooks so that they can be slithered over logs and through weed beds without hanging up. When bass are in deep water, streamers or leech imitations fished near the bottom with sinking or sink-tip lines may save an otherwise fishless day.

Sinking bass flies: a Prismatic Muddler, Prismatic Shiner, Marabou Muddler, and a Wooly Bugger.

Just like trout, smallmouth bass will feed on aquatic insects. I always take along a box of trout dry flies and nymphs when smallmouth fishing, although smallmouths aren't as selective as trout, and a little popper twitched near their feeding stations may make them forget the insects.

103

PANFISH FLIES

Sunfish, perch, crappie, and other warm-water panfish can be caught with a wide variety of flies. Small versions of bass bugs and sponge-rubber bugs with rubber legs are very effective for bluegill and other sunfish, and standard trout flies, especially terrestrial dry-fly imitations, are useful at times. Many panfish feed on aquatic insects, crustaceans, and small baitfish, so standard trout nymphs and streamers can come in handy.

A properly presented fly is a most efficient way to catch panfish, because only a fly rod can deliver the tiny artificials that mimic the small foods these popular fish eat.

PIKE, PICKEREL, AND MUSKELLUNGE FLIES

These voracious predators feed on large minnows, frogs, and even ducklings and young muskrats. Flies used for these species should be large and flashy, and the most effective kinds are large bass flies and poppers or saltwater flies. To my knowledge, there are no standard patterns tied specifically for pike, pickerel, or muskellunge, but so long as your fly is big and moving quickly, a hungry pike or pickerel is an easy mark. Muskellunge are caught infrequently on flies—but muskies are rarely caught on any kind of bait or lure.

SALTWATER FLIES

Although saltwater fish have been taken on flies for over a hundred years, this field of fly-fishing is still wide open in terms of possibilities for new fly patterns. Most saltwater fish feed on baitfish, crustaceans like shrimp and crabs, or squid, so the selection of flies is quite simple.

Saltwater flies can be lumped into three categories: large, simple streamers, which may be attractors or baitfish imitations; poppers, for surface-feeding fish; and bonefish and permit flies, which are imitations of crab and shrimp and look much like large versions of trout nymphs. Saltwater flies can be instantly recognized because they are always tied on nickel-plated or stainless-steel hooks.

Saltwater streamers are tied with simple tinsel or epoxied-thread bodies and wings of bucktail, hackle feathers, or artificial (nylon) hair. The most popular colors are blue and white, green and white, or all white, because saltwater baitfish such as menhaden, herring, and mullet have white bellies and green or blue backs. Other saltwater streamers, used as attractors, are tied in combinations of red, yellow, and white. They should be tied with the most durable materials possible, since most saltwater fish have impressive dental work. The heads and bodies should be given at least two coats of epoxy cement.

Saltwater poppers come in the same color combinations as streamers. They are designed to make a lot of noise when retrieved, imitating either a baitfish skipping across the surface of the water or the sound of other fish feeding on the baitfish.

Bonefish and permit flies are tied for these bottom feeders, as well as other fish that pick crabs and shrimp off the bottom, like redfish. They are designed to sink quickly, so that they can be placed near the bottom in front of a feeding fish. Most patterns are tied upside down, to ride with the hook point facing up, and won't catch on the bottom when retrieved. The bucktail or nylon hairwings imitate the legs and tentacles of crustaceans streaming behind them as they scoot from one spot to the next.

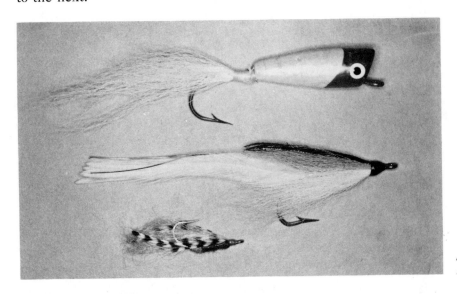

Saltwater flies: a floating skipping bug, a large Deceiver streamer, and a bonefish streamer.

SHAD FLIES

Shad, like salmon, live in salt water and spawn in freshwater rivers. When they're on the move, they will take brightly colored wet flies fished just off the bottom. Shad flies are usually just a floss or tinsel body with a hair tail, tied sparsely so that they sink quickly. After their spawning duties are completed, shad will feed on aquatic insects before they return to the ocean, and can even be taken with dry flies during heavy mayfly or caddisfly hatches.

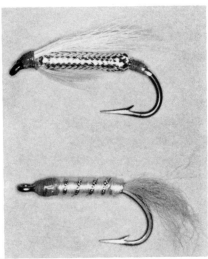

Don't be afraid to cross the boundaries between a fly that is meant for one kind of fish or another—and by all means try flies for fish not mentioned here. The walleye, a superb game and food fish, will take streamer flies and poppers. Bass will take saltwater flies, as will large trout and salmon. Steelhead will take salmon flies, and salmon will take steelhead flies. Versatility is an important part of our next topic—fly selection.

Two simple shad flies.

105

7
Fly Selection

The first rule of fly selection is that there are no rules. There is never a right or a wrong fly, only flies that work better under certain conditions than others.

One evening last spring I was fishing a favorite stretch of flat water on a local trout stream that is known for its selective brown trout. I was unusually successful with a dry fly that I had just developed, and throughout the evening I could see two of my friends above me and one below, all apparently doing as well as I, judging by the frequent bends in their rods. We gathered on the bank after dark.

"You guys must have discovered my secret pattern," I said as they viewed my new creation by flashlight.

"Wasn't even using a dry," said one. "This nymph did the trick for me."

"I was using a standard Sulphur," said the third.

The fourth fisherman was using a wet fly that resembled none of the other flies. So much for my secret pattern!

If you're going on a trip to unfamiliar waters, consult fly-fishing magazines and books, which often have lists of flies for particular areas. Call ahead to the tackle shop nearest your destination. They're usually eager to give you a list of fly patterns for the area, and may have one or two

Which one will work today?

local favorites that can't be obtained anywhere else.

Approach fly selection as a challenge rather than a chore. Finding the right fly through experimentation is one of the great satisfactions of fly-fishing. Remember—the worst thing that can happen is that you won't catch any fish.

There are two opposing philosophies on fly selection: the imitationist, who believes that with the correct fly you can solve all fishing problems, and the presentationist, who believes that any old fly will work so long as it's presented in the proper manner. The most prudent choice is to take the middle of the road.

You can also divide flies into arbitrary groups, attractors and imitators.

107

The latter are those flies that are designed to mimic a specific kind of fish food, like the deer-hair mouse used by bass fishermen. Attractors are not designed to imitate specific kinds of food, at least not to our eyes. Though attractors are usually brightly colored and outlandishly large, the fish may take them for something in nature, seeing them in a different light.

Take the Royal Coachman dry fly. With its green peacock herl and red rayon-floss body, plus white wings, it doesn't look like anything in nature. But wait until it gets wet. Peacock herl when wet turns a bronze-olive color, and red rayon floss turns dark brown. What we now have is a brownish fly with a narrow waist and two bulbs at each end. Something like an ant, maybe? The fish may think so.

My point is that fish don't put things in their mouth out of playfulness, anger, curiosity, or boredom. They don't have these emotions. They put things in their mouth so that they can obtain enough energy to spawn and pass their genes along to the next generation.

Fish take attractor flies out of reflex. If a fly is brightly colored it may stand out more, catching the fish's attention first. Brightly colored attractor flies are used a lot in sterile environments where a fish will attack anything that resembles food. Bright colors catch their attention quicker than muted tones that fade into the background.

Fish take their prey, and thus our flies, either by sitting and waiting for the current to bring food to them or by actively pursuing or ambushing their prey. The first feeding strategy occurs only in flowing waters and is characterized by trout, grayling, landlocked salmon, and smallmouth bass. Fish may also actively pursue their prey in streams, but they *must* ambush prey in still waters. Saltwater fish chasing a school of baitfish, a pike spearing a frog off the surface of a still pond, and a trout cruising for mayflies on the surface of the lake are common examples of ambushers. Of course, bass and trout in streams may also ambush their prey, but the energy expended in chasing the food and fighting the current must be balanced by the calories obtained. Fish, by some marvel of instinct, are quite good at judging this energy balance.

Fish that are actively pursuing prey are far less critical of your fly selection than those who are using the sit-and-wait strategy. The ambusher takes his food when he can get it, never knowing when his next meal might stumble by. The drift-feeding trout has an almost constant supply of food passing overhead, in what a fish-ecologist friend of mine calls "the buffet in the restaurant," his view of the current bringing food to trout in a stream. Trout don't always feed selectively from the buffet, but when they do you'd better pay attention not only to what insect they're taking but to what stage—nymph, dun, spinner, pupa, or emerger.

When trout are actively feeding they give us clues. The most obvious clue is called the rise, which occurs when the fish takes an insect off the surface of the water. The rise may be a violent splash, subtle concentric rings in the water with a few bubbles beside them, or merely the head, back, and tail of a fish gently porpoising above the surface. Each of these rises give us clues to what fly we should use.

A rise as the fisherman usually sees it.

The classic rise occurs when you see an unhurried dimple in the water that leaves a few bubbles behind. This occurs when a trout takes an insect that is resting on top of the water. It may be a mayfly dun, caddis adult, or stonefly, but the unhurried rise indicates that the insect is sitting sedately on the water and the trout knows he has an easy mark. In ponds and lakes the rise will form even, concentric circles; in a stream the current distorts the rise into a sharp wedge.

The splashy rise occurs either when the insect is actively fluttering across the surface of the water or when the trout is in fast current. Either way, the fish has to make a quick decision, and the splash gives away his haste. Be careful, though. When a splashy rise occurs without the accompanying bubbles on the surface of the water, your fish may have taken an insect just under the surface. The reason: when a trout takes an insect from the surface of the water he rises to the top, opens his mouth, and lets the current drop in the insect. When the fish closes his mouth he expels through his gills the air he took in along with the insect, hence the telltale bubbles. The splash without bubbles happens when a fish rises quickly to take an insect just below the surface. His momentum may carry his back or tail above the surface, but since he opened his mouth underwater there won't be any bubbles.

Splashy rises with bubbles often indicate a trout feeding on adult caddisflies, which skid across the surface of the water, large mayflies that hop and flutter on the water, or a big terrestrial insect like a grasshopper that is trying to oar its way back to land. Splashy rises without bubbles indicate an emerging caddisfly pupa or mayfly nymph.

A third, often misleading type of rise is the smutting or dimpling rise. Usually all you will see is a tiny dimple in the surface of the water, but occasionally you'll also see the back and dorsal fin of the fish behind the rise. This type of rise characterizes fish feeding on either tiny midges, mayflies, or terrestrials, and fish taking spent mayflies or caddisflies that are pinioned in the surface film. Either way, the food is lying

109

Bird's-eye view of a rise. Here the brown trout is visible as a shadowy form below the surface.

He finds his target, visible as a small white speck in front of his nose.

The tiny mayfly is taken.

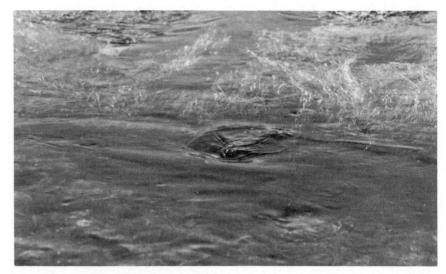

He turns his head down, making the rise form.

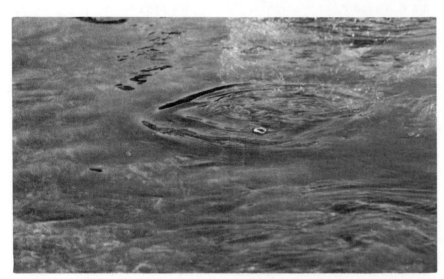

Note the bubble, an indication that the trout took a fly off the surface of the water.

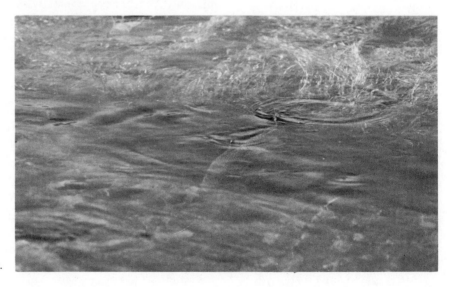

The trout returns to his observation position.

flush *in* the film, not on top of the water, like newly hatched mayflies or caddisflies. Emerging insects that are having trouble breaking through the surface tension of the water may also produce this kind of rise. The smutting rise may hide a trout of substantial size, as a big fish can just barely poke his snout above the surface and leave a tiny disturbance.

When fish are feeding below the surface of the water there are also clues, albeit less obvious ones. Unless the fish are feeding just under the surface, in which case they might leave a swirl with no bubbles, the water must be clear and relatively slow with an unbroken surface for you to see the clues.

Most subsurface feeding happens when a fish is resting his head on the stream bottom or hanging in the current. As a nymph drifts by, he'll merely tip his fins to move for the fly, open his mouth, and let the current wash it in—lazy and efficient, leaving no splashes, no flashes, no clues. If you can't spot the fish camouflaged against the bottom, as in broken or deep water, you'll never even know where he is, much less that he's feeding on something. Subsurface trout fishing involves a lot of guesswork.

You may have heard that flashes below the surface of the water reveal a trout taking nymphs. The flashes occur when a fish turns on his side to dislodge nymphs from the stream bottom, but unfortunately most of the time these flashes indicate suckers or whitefish, which feed this way much more often than trout. Trout prefer to intercept drifting nymphs in the current rather than grub around on the bottom, although they will sometimes root for caddisfly larvae or crayfish.

The other often-written-about-but-seldom-seen phenomenon is the tailing trout. If a trout is rooting in shallow water, standing on his head, his tail may wiggle or wave above the water. The only time I ever saw this was in a shallow, weedy stream where the trout were rooting for sow bugs and scuds in the vegetation.

Trout and other fish feeding on large forage like minnows and crayfish may also leave characteristic water disturbances. One type is a bulge in the current, accompanied by a quick flash as the fish turns to take a minnow. Another type, usually seen at dawn or dusk, is a torpedo-like wake streaking through the shallows, sometimes with tiny minnows jumping out of the water in front of the wake.

SIZE, SHAPE, AND COLOR

Whenever possible, you should try to determine what the fish are feeding on and pick the fly in your box that most closely resembles the natural food. That's fairly obvious, but which is most important—size, shape, or color?

Size in fly-fishing refers to the length of the fly. In most cases it is the most important characteristic for matching natural foods. Experienced saltwater fly rodders say that any color streamer will work when fish like blues or stripers are chasing bait, but if it's an inch or two larger or

The mayfly that was hatching had speckled wings and dark bands on the body, so the fisherman chose a fly with speckled wood duck wings and a quill body. The size is also very close.

smaller than the baitfish it will be ignored. There are days on salmon rivers when all the fish will be taken on different patterns but on the same size fly. Trout will often refuse a size 14 fly but eagerly accept an 18. If you can't match anything else to the natural, at least match the size.

Color and shape seem to vie for second place in fly selection. Migratory fish that feed little but take flies seem to have strong preferences for certain colors on certain days, as do trout, bass, and bottom-feeding saltwater fish like bonefish and permit. Bright colors may turn the fish on one day and off the next. Some days they seem to care less about color.

Fish that feed on prey that is below them, like bonefish rooting for shrimp, are very sensitive to colors, as are most fish when the sun is at an acute angle, since your flies are illuminated better when the sun is low in the sky. When the sun is high and flies are seen against a backlit sky, colors are difficult for fish to distinguish. Because surface flies are always seen from below, color is less important with dry flies and poppers than it is with sinking flies.

Shape or silhouette is especially important with surface flies. A bass that is accustomed to feeding on frogs may not be interested in a surface fly with a long, skinny silhouette. When trout are feeding on caddisflies they may take a standard dry fly with an upright wing, but a dry fly with a tent-shaped wing is bound to be more effective.

The shape and color of only a part of an animal may be enough to trigger a strike. The Brook Fin, an old wet fly used for brook trout in the north woods, incorporates a wing of red, white, and black—the color of a brook trout's pelvic fin. Why a brook trout will strike the fin of another is a matter for speculation (perhaps territoriality?), but they do seem to have an attraction to it.

Action, or the way a fly wiggles or pulsates in the water, is important at times, especially when fishing for bass. The wiggle of a marabou

This thorax fly matches the size, shape, and color of the Hendrickson mayfly.

streamer or the hackle of a Wooly Worm can excite a fish that shows no interest in other flies.

MATCHING THE HATCH

Choosing the correct fly at the height of an insect hatch, when the trout are selective, is the most complicated, exasperating, and, when you find the right fly, satisfying experience in fly-fishing. The challenge involves not only what species of insect the fish are feeding on, but also the stage—is it an emerging adult, a drifting nymph, or a spent egg-laying adult?

The classic case of dry-fly fishing is when you arrive at a stream or lake to find the trout rising and the water covered with hatching mayflies. You pluck a fly from the air or the surface of the water, lay it on the lid of your fly box, and choose the fly in your box that matches it in size, shape, and color. Then you proceed to catch lots of fish.

It's seldom that easy. Faults in your presentation may tip the fish off to the fact that your fly isn't real (we'll cover those problems in the next two chapters). You can have what is called a masking hatch, usually a larger fly that is more obvious to you hatching at the same time as a smaller, less obvious fly. But the trout may prefer the smaller fly, because it's more abundant or easier to capture.

Every trout-stream insect has a Latin or scientific name, and you may hear other fly-fishermen using these names. Latin names eliminate confusion about insect hatches between different areas of the country—an *Ephemerella subvaria* is called a Hendrickson in some parts of the country and a Whirling Blue Dun in others. It isn't necessary to know Latin names to catch fish. It isn't even necessary to know the names of the flies in your box until it's time to reorder. As long as you can match the natural to its imitation you'll be a successful fly-fisherman.

The secret is observation. Before you start flailing the water with your favorite dry fly, watch the fish that are rising. Find one that's rising steadily and keep your eyes glued to the spot. Did he take the big cream mayfly or the little gray one? Perhaps he keeps rising but the flies that float over his head remain untouched. Remember the bubbles? If there are none, he's probably taking the emerging nymphs just under the surface.

Using a fly with a down-wing silhouette is important when the fish are feeding on adult caddisflies.

Here is what usually happens during a hatch: from a couple of days to an hour before the flies hatch, the nymphs or pupae become restless and drift in the current or scamper around on the aquatic vegetation in a lake. Trout pick off these nymphs, but we have no clues unless there has been a hatch for the past few days or your fishing diary or a book on trout-stream insects tells you a hatch is due on this date.

Because the trout are preoccupied with underwater food, they'll probably ignore floating flies, so you'll want to try a wet fly or nymph. Turn over a few rocks on the stream bottom. The flies that are due to emerge will be more abundant on rocks at the stream's edge, and their wing cases will be almost black. Choose a nymph from your fly box that matches them as closely as possible.

At the beginning of the hatch you'll see a few flies in the air and a few on the water. Rises will probably be scattered and erratic. What you're most likely seeing is fish feeding just under the surface; occasionally they'll misjudge and break the surface or cause a swirl. This is the time for a wet fly fished just under the surface, an emerger pattern, or a floating nymph.

Trout feeding just under the surface can be exasperating. You see a fish rise, toss your dry fly to him, he splashes at it, the water bulges under it—and you strike and come away empty. This is called a refusal. It may occur because your fly is the wrong size, but often occurs because the fish doesn't want a fly that is floating that high. He puts on the brakes at the last second but his momentum causes him to break the surface. You might think that he missed your fly or you didn't strike quickly enough. Don't believe it. An adult trout seldom misses his target, and when he wants a dry fly it's tough to take it away from him.

Another clue to subsurface feeding is a splashy rise from which erupts an adult fly that flies away. The fish has chased a nymph off the bottom but hasn't been quick enough. This is a very common sight during caddisfly emergence. If you see little mothlike flies popping out of rise forms, put away your dry flies and fish a caddis pupa just below the surface.

During hatches of many mayflies and caddisflies, the trout take the emerging flies throughout the hatch and bother little with the adult flies resting on the water's surface. You may catch a few on dry flies, especially if your fly isn't floating too well, but you would have been more successful using an emerger or wet-fly pattern. In most hatches, however, there will come a time when there will be enough flies on the surface to tempt the trout to take the adult insects—and our high-floating dry flies. Rises will be deliberate, rhythmic, and you'll see bubbles.

Splashy rises indicate fish taking insects that are fluttering on the water; as I've said before, this usually indicates a caddis hatch. A downwing dry fly of the correct size and color should work. Rises to adult mayflies are usually more sedate unless the mayflies are very large or the wind is blowing them across the surface like tiny sailboats.

It's usually not good enough to gauge the size and color of a hatching fly by observing it in the air or on the water. Flies look larger in the air, and color in a moving insect can be deceiving. Catch a sample to be sure that your match is correct.

At the height of a hatch you may see fish taking adult flies, know you're fishing with the right size and color, and know that your presentation is OK—and still get refusals. This is the time to switch from a standard hackled dry to a thorax fly, no-hackle, or comparadun, something with a slightly cleaner silhouette. The change to a different pattern of the same size and color will often fool a difficult surface-feeding trout.

Returning mayfly spinners or egg-laying caddisfly adults can cause intense feeding by the trout, but this situation can be misleading. Because the spent insects are lying prostrate on the surface, nothing sticks up above the water and they're difficult to see. The secret is to look up. Aquatic insects can hatch over spread-out periods of time, but they must all mate at the same time. They form mating swarms, which hover and dip above the stream, starting at treetop level and gradually working their way down to the surface of the water. If the flies are still pretty high and the fish are rising, it's probably to something else, but when the flies get lower peer closely at the surface. You should be able to see the dying flies lying with their wings spent, half spent, or fully upright.

Trout may prefer the spinners with either upright or fully spent wings —I've never seen them actually selectively feeding on half-spent flies. If you can't see what they're taking, it's probably a spent spinner; if you see flies disappearing into the rises, they're taking the insects whose wings haven't collapsed yet. The one hallmark of fish taking spent flies is a very steady, deliberate rise. The trout seem to sense that the flies won't get away and they can take their time. The only exception is at the very beginning of a fall of spent insects, when overeager trout (usually smaller ones) slash at the flies just as they touch the water. Small trout may even clear the water in an attempt to catch the flies in midair—a popular theme with calendar art, but in real life the big sockers wait until the flies are trapped in the surface film and are an easy meal.

Mayfly spinners with wings that are still upright or caddisflies or stoneflies that have landed or are dipping and laying their eggs are easy to match—just use a standard adult pattern of the correct size and color. After the flies are spent, though, not only are size and color critical, but the fly must lie flush in the surface film. This is the time for a spent-wing dry fly such as a hackled spinner or polywing spinner. In a pinch you can also trim all the hackle from the top and bottom of a standard dry fly with a pair of scissors or your angler's clips.

There are thousands of different dry-fly patterns. Most aquatic insects are gray, cream, brown, or olive, and if you have one pattern in each of these colors in sizes 10 through 24 you'll be able to match almost any insect hatch in the world. This approach is much less confusing than trying to fill your fly box with hundreds of different patterns, many of them redundant when it comes to imitating a particular insect.

DRY FLIES WHEN THERE IS NO HATCH

You won't see a hatch every time you go trout fishing, especially early and late in the season. This is the time to "fish blind" or "fish the water." The choice is up to you: dry, wet, nymph, or streamer. No one can tell you what will work; there is never a sure thing in any kind of fishing, and that's what makes it so mysterious and appealing.

Dry flies will work when no fish are rising, especially if the water temperature is between 55 and 65 degrees Fahrenheit. Trout are very active within this temperature range and will respond to almost any kind of properly presented fly. If there is no hatch but you saw a hatch yesterday or the day before, try a dry fly that matches that insect. It will be a familiar morsel to the trout, and they should rise to it without much hesitation.

It's generally futile to fish blind with a dry fly smaller than size 16. A trout that is not actively rising needs a juicy morsel to interest him in surface food, one that will make it worth his while to travel all the way to the surface and expose himself to predators. Hairwing or hair-bodied dry flies are best in this situation, because they present juicy silhouettes and are easily visible to the fisherman. Bivisibles and variants are productive in this case for the same reasons. Color doesn't seem to be as important as shape and size when fishing blind, but if one color doesn't work, try others.

From late May through October, terrestrial imitations make excellent "searching" patterns. Land insects are constantly dropping into streams and lakeshores, and after the aquatic hatches dwindle in midsummer terrestrials become a major part of a trout's diet. Terrestrial insects don't fall into the water on a regular schedule, so the trout may be sitting and waiting for an ant or grasshopper to float overhead, even though they're not rising with a regular rhythm.

Although terrestrials may drift and get blown into all areas of a stream, they are usually most concentrated in areas with overhanging trees or weeds that grow right up to the shore. In rocky mountain rivers with wide gravel banks terrestrial flies will be less effective than in small woodland brooks or grassland streams with brush right down to the banks.

Shaking the bushes along the edge of a river or pond will tell you not only what kinds of terrestrial insects are present, it will probably turn up some mayflies, caddisflies, or stoneflies that hatched the day before. These insects can help you make an educated guess for fly selection, because the trout will recognize them as familiar food.

Where deciduous trees overhang the water, ant, beetle, and caterpillar imitations will be most effective. Where grasses and weeds abut the shore, these insects plus grasshoppers and crickets will be available to the trout. A walk through a streamside field will tell you if grasshoppers are present and what color and size imitation you should use. In many streams in July through October grasshoppers are the largest food available to the trout and imitations are taken with great enthusiasm and confidence.

WET FLIES AND NYMPHS

It's often said that a great majority of a trout's food is taken underwater. The proportion of trout taken on dry flies, however, is much greater, because the fisherman can see what the fish are eating—and where they are. Unless the water is clear and you're accomplished at spotting trout

117

before they spot you, most nymph and wet-fly fishing will rely on educated guesses, intuition, and a little luck.

Turn over a few rocks in a stream. Grab a handful of aquatic vegetation in a lake or weedy stream. The insects and crustaceans that you find can serve as models for your subsurface fishing. As with all animals, a trout's diet is based upon familiar shapes, sizes, and colors; the trout develops a "search image" for these items. Boring, perhaps, but safe and secure for the most part. If most of the nymphs in a stream are brown and olive and size 12 or 14, don't expect the trout to turn cartwheels over a cream-colored size 16 nymph. A black size 6 nymph might even scare them.

Most of the nymphs found in lakes and ponds will be slim and tan or olive, to match the aquatic vegetation or sand that makes up the bottom. Scuds are a very common food in lakes, as are damselfly nymphs. Patterns that imitate these insects are good to start with if you have no other guesses.

In streams with lots of big flat rocks the nymphs will be mostly large and flat. Something like a March Brown or Hare's Ear nymph in size 10 or 12 will work well in this kind of water. Rivers with small, fine gravel will contain mostly small, skinny nymphs, because the big ones have no place to hide from predators. Slow, clear, weedy streams or spring creeks are also homes for these slim, tiny nymphs. This water should be fished blind with a slim, lightly dressed nymph like a Pheasant Tail or Blue Quill Nymph in sizes 14 through 18.

The fuzzy outline of the Hare's Ear nymph gives the fly a flattened look when it gets wet.

Nymphs and wet flies have their greatest potential early in the season, when no flies are hatching. There are always insect larvae on the stream bottom because of the seasonal succession of insect hatches, because some insects live two or more years underwater as larvae, and because crustaceans such as sow bugs and scuds live their entire lives underwater. Hendrickson nymphs, for example, are too tiny for catchable-sized trout to bother with after their eggs hatch in May, but by fall they will be finding their way into trout stomachs. Is an imitation of the Hendrickson nymph useless in June after the Hendricksons have hatched? Definitely not. There are other nymphs that look like the Hendrickson nymph but don't hatch until late June or July.

Wet flies are less slavish imitations of subsurface food than nymphs, but trout take them just as eagerly. The same suggestions for choosing wet-fly patterns hold for nymphs, plus a few more. Wet flies are excellent imitations of drowned or drowning mayfly duns and spinners, and caddis and stonefly adults. Not all the insects that attempt to hatch make it. Some get drowned in fast water; others just fail to crawl out of their nymphal shucks. After a hatch is over, a wet fly fished through the riffles will often add a few bonus fish to your catch. Just match the approximate size and color of the insects that were emerging.

Wet-fly selection often involves just plain chuck-and-chance-it luck. Try a big black one. Try a little olive one. Color in wet flies may sometimes be more important than shape and size, especially in streams where there is little food and the most visible pattern gets the nod from the trout. Bright yellows, reds, and whites may work well in wilderness waters where the relatively gullible brook or cutthroat trout abound, but the more somber, lightly dressed patterns are much more popular in today's heavily fished trout waters.

In the last century and for the first half of the twentieth century, the accepted way of fishing wet flies was to fish three, four, or as many as seven flies on a single leader, using droppers for each fly. This method lacks the delicacy of presentation needed for most of today's sophisticated trout waters, but fishing two or three different flies at the same time will often tell you which one the fish favor. You can add an additional wet fly to your leader by leaving the heavier tag end of the barrel knot closest to your tippet a little long. Just tie the additional fly to this piece. Keep the dropper short and no finer than 3X or .008 inch, or else it will tangle with the rest of the leader.

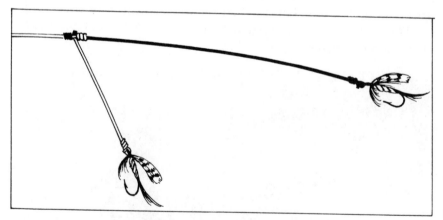

The wet-fly dropper system. You can also fish two or three nymphs this way.

In streams, large wet flies, sizes 8 through 12, work best when the water is fast or discolored. In pools and under clear water conditions the smaller 14 through 18 wets are more effective. I really don't know why. I can see where the larger flies are more visible in riffled or dirty water, but I'm not sure why it's necessary to switch to a smaller fly when you get to a slow pool. Ah, if only trout could talk...

STREAMERS

Trout that live in large lakes may never eat an insect after they reach a foot or so in length; instead, they feed on abundant baitfish like alewives or smelt. Smelt and alewives are gray-green in color with silvery white bellies. Streamers and bucktails that incorporate these colors in sizes 2 through 8 are popular in New England ponds, in the Great Lakes, and in large western reservoirs where large salmonids feed on these forage fish.

On the other hand, Dr. Robert Bachman, the noted brown-trout behaviorist, never once saw a trout eat a minnow in over three thousand hours of observing a wild, undisturbed population of stream trout. Why? Trout in streams often take our streamers and bucktails. The answer lies in the words "never once *saw*."

Bachman is sure that the trout fed upon minnows after dark and when the water became high and dirty after a rainstorm. Under normal water conditions a minnow is just too fast for a large trout and the trout expends too much energy at too great a risk. After dark or during a flood minnows become disoriented, and a trout has the edge.

Trout-stream minnows fall into three broad categories: long and thin with a horizontal black stripe (dace and shiner), slightly deeper in the body with vertical bands (darter and sucker), and short and stubby fish that are flattened horizontally (bottom dwellers like sculpin). An investigation of shallow areas will tell you what kinds are present and what size they are.

A sparsely dressed bucktail with bands of white, black, and brown hair like the Black-Nose Dace or one of the Thunder Creek Series will imitate the various dace and shiners. If the minnows show vertical bars you might select a streamer tied with barred Plymouth Rock chicken hackles like the Gray Matuka, or a bucktail with hair that has a vertical barring—the Squirrel Tail is a good example. Finally, bottom-dwelling fish like sculpin are best imitated by a Muddler Minnow or one of the new Sculpin variations.

A sculpin minnow and two imitations: a Muddler Minnow (top) and a Matuka Sculpin (bottom).

Even though trout in streams seldom take minnows under normal, clear water conditions, streamers are surprisingly effective. A large trout will seldom pass up a crayfish, and such bulky patterns with some brown and yellow in them as the Yellow Matuka or the Dark Edson Tiger may be taken for a crayfish fleeing from a potential predator. Tiny streamers in sizes 8 to 12 may also look to the trout like stonefly nymphs, damselfly nymphs, or leeches.

Streamers reach their full potential when there is absolutely no activity on a trout stream—early season when the water temperature is too cold for insect hatches, slack periods during the season, late in the season after the hatches are over. At these times streamers may be just lures—large, nonspecific chunks of something that's alive and good to eat.

If the water is dirty or has some "color" to it, bright streamer patterns usually draw the most strikes. The reds and yellows of a Mickey Finn bucktail, a Yellow Marabou streamer, or the contrasting black and white of the Black Ghost bucktail will catch the fish's attention. Larger sizes, 2 to 6, are a good bet when visibility is low. Because Muddler-type flies with their deer-hair heads seem to produce a vibration that fish pick up with their lateral line, you might want to stack the deck and fish a big Yellow Marabou Muddler.

Under clear water conditions, trout may chase big, bright streamers but will usually turn away without striking. Something less flashy, on the order of a size 10 or 12 Black Nose Dace bucktail, appears to be large enough to be noticed but subtle enough to be inhaled.

Big rivers and fast water will require larger streamer patterns to attract a trout's attention. On the Madison River in Montana, for instance, fly-fishermen use big, sizes 2 and 1/0, Marabou Muddlers to fish for fall-spawning brown trout. A streamer this big on a small, infertile mountain stream where growth is slow may actually be larger than the majority of the fish population. A streamer bigger than a size 10 or 12 might frighten trout that aren't used to seeing large minnows or crayfish.

A crayfish and its imitation—a top fly for smallmouth bass.

BASS FLIES

When we talk about selecting flies for freshwater bass, it's important to make a distinction between the largemouth bass, which inhabits warm, weedy waters with silty bottoms, and smallmouth bass, which will be found in clear lakes and rivers with rocky bottoms and cooler water temperatures. The redeye and spotted bass, close relatives of the smallmouth that occupy a limited range in the southern United States, can be lumped with the smallmouth as far as fly selection is concerned.

Smallmouth bass often live in trout streams and will feed upon insect hatches side by side with the trout. It generally takes a heavy hatch of insects to interest smallmouths, though, and you'll seldom find them feeding on mayflies or caddisflies that are smaller than size 16. Standard trout wets, nymphs, and dries will work during hatches, although smallmouth, unlike trout, can often be taken with a small popper or hair bug even when they're feeding on insects that are much smaller.

The larger the smallmouth, the less inclined he will be to feed on insects except the largest ones. Big smallmouths prefer to ambush their prey, and minnows and crayfish rate very high on their menu. Hellgrammites, large black larvae of the dobsonfly, are also found frequently in smallmouth stomachs.

Streamer flies and nymphs in sizes 4 through 12 should be included in your fly box if you're after smallmouths. The Crayfish bass fly or a brown streamer will imitate these crustaceans, and you should also have a large black nymph like the Montana, especially in streams where hellgrammites are present. A good selection of imitator-type streamers for the various minnows will round out your selection. Two you shouldn't be without are the Muddler Minnow and the Black Matuka.

Smallmouths also take brightly colored attractor-type streamers. White, black, yellow, red, and combinations of these colors in sizes 4 through 12 are popular with smallmouth fly-fishermen. The fish often show a decided preference for one color over another, so finding the right fly is often a matter of trying different patterns until you discover the right color combination.

Early mornings and evenings in lake shallows and in the tails of pools on rivers are times to try floating bass bugs or poppers. Smaller bugs, sizes 4 through 12, are best for smallmouths, in black, brown, yellow, green, chartreuse, and red-and-white. Where the water is clear you should lean toward the smaller sizes that make less commotion on the surface, like hair bugs or bullethead minnows. In murky water you'll be able to catch their attention better with the large poppers with concave faces, ones that make enough noise to be noticed.

Largemouth-bass flies are generally larger than smallmouth flies. Although small largemouths will occasionally eat insects, individuals over a foot long prefer larger food like frogs, mice, and minnows. Largemouths can swallow prey that is quite large, and have even been reported to take water snakes and small muskrats.

Flies used for largemouth bass should reflect their habitat. Largemouths prefer to ambush their prey from the protection of heavy cover like submerged weed beds, lily pads, and sunken logs, so flies used for largemouths should incorporate some sort of weed guard to keep your flies from catching on weeds and other obstructions. You'll find working your streamer or bug outside a weed bed to be futile, yet if you drop it into the center of the weeds and work it though open spots you'll catch bass. Common types of weed guards include keel hooks, which ride upside down, and monofilament loops, or the wing of a fly may be tied so that it covers the hook point.

Choosing flies for largemouth bass depends less on matching their food than on the mood of the fisherman and his quarry. Of course there are hair bugs that look just like frogs and mice, but you're hardly going to see a bass sipping mice selectively, one right after another. Nor are you going to wait for a bass to eat a mouse, then toss your fly to him. You want to appeal to his ambushing instinct—show him something that looks like a juicy morsel.

Largemouth bass flies: a hair mouse, a noisy popper, a floating/sinking Muddler-type streamer, and a fast-sinking streamer tied with a wiggly strip of rabbit hair.

Surface lures, bugs and poppers, are the most exciting way to catch largemouths. Bass will take surface lures whenever they're in shallow water—usually at dawn and dusk, and all day long during the spring spawning season. If there is a lot of cover or structure, like logs or lily pads, there may be bass lurking in shallow water all day, but they seldom stray far from deep water or structure when the light is bright.

Surface lures for largemouths are more effective in the larger sizes, 4 through 4/0. Don't rule out tiny size 12 bluegill bugs, though, when you're sure the bass are in shallow water but they refuse everything else. Green, yellow, black, and brown are the most popular colors.

I like to start with a standard cork popper in size 1/0 or 2 in one of the above colors. If the bass strike short or boil under the popper without taking it, I'll switch to either a smaller popper in the same color or a softer, more subtle hair bug. Often a small hair bug in natural brown deer hair will do the trick when the traditional bright-colored bass bugs fail.

123

Bass visibly boiling near shore and among aquatic vegetation may mean they're feeding on frogs or minnows; largemouths boiling in open water almost always means they're herding schools of minnows near the surface. This is the time for a Keel Bug, Prismatic Muddler, or Marabou Muddler. These flies, with their streamer-like wing and deer-hair head, look like crippled minnows struggling just under the surface.

When the surface water is cold (below 60 degrees) or very warm (over 75 degrees), bass will be found in deep water. At these times you'll want to use one of the large streamers tied for bass. They are usually weighted or tied with bead-chain eyes to get them down quickly. Most use wings of marabou, which gives them a wiggling, pulsating action, much like the plastic worms that bait and spin casters use. For subsurface lures, the darker colors—black, brown, and olive—work best, although white is sometimes effective, especially in murky water.

PANFISH FLIES

Selecting flies for panfish is quite easy—they're always eager to take anything that vaguely resembles a small minnow, insect, or crustacean. Bluegills are so easy to catch on flies that a small one will often impale itself on a huge bass popper, although the really big bluegills are a little more cautious and it may require some observation to see what they're feeding on.

Study the feeding habits of the panfish you're after before selecting flies for them. Even though bluegills get larger than other sunfish, they feed almost exclusively on small insects and crustaceans. Thus, a tiny popper, dry fly, or nymph will catch more bluegills than a streamer. Rock bass and crappie, on the other hand, prefer small minnows, under two inches in length, so streamer flies in sizes 8 through 12 are the most productive flies for these fish.

A small selection of trout dries, nymphs, and streamers, plus some tiny cork poppers or sponge-rubber bugs in various colors, should be all you'll need to catch all species of panfish.

Even though they grow quite large, walleyes are often considered to be panfish. Walleyes are almost exclusively minnow feeders and have a decided preference for red-and-yellow flies. The best fly for walleyes I've ever used is a large Mickey Finn bucktail in sizes 2 through 6. If walleyes are herding minnows on the surface, a black or yellow popper will take them as well as any surface lure. Black is especially good after dark, since it's most visible silhouetted against the night sky.

SALMON FLIES

Most of the Atlantic salmon caught on flies are taken on large wet flies, sizes 5/0 through 12. Where sizes 4 and 6 were considered to be the standard sizes for salmon, there is a growing tendency, especially in Iceland and North America, to use the smaller 10s, 12s, and even 14s. The larger flies are more effective in high, fast, or dirty water; the smaller sizes are used during midsummer or when the water is low and clear.

For example, if you arrive at a salmon river when it's in flood stage you'll probably see most of the fish caught on large flies, sizes 3/0 through 2. The next day, as the water drops, 4s and 6s may take the most fish, and by the end of the week, it if doesn't rain, you may have to go to 10s and 12s to raise fish. You may also stroll out into a salmon river during low water with a big size 1/0 and take the biggest fish in the pool—but that's salmon fishing, never predictable.

To be most effective, the salmon should see a wet fly broadside, and the wet fly seems to be most effective when it's a foot or two under the surface. Single-hook wet flies may tumble in broken water or skim across the surface in fast water, hence the double hook: doubles ride hook down even in the most broken currents, so they show the fly broadside to the fish more often. In addition, the extra weight of a double hook will keep the fly riding a little deeper. There doesn't seem to be any strict rule as to when you should use doubles or when to use singles, but a switch from a single to a double in the same size and pattern may rise the only salmon of the day.

When salmon don't respond to traditional wet flies, experienced fishermen often try nymphs as a change of pace. The drab colors and different silhouette of a nymph pattern are so far from the traditional bright, flashy salmon patterns that they may work when nothing else does. Nymphs seem to work best under low, clear water conditions and in smaller sizes, 8 through 12.

Low-water flies are another option when a small fly is needed. Because they occupy only half to three quarters of the hook shank and are very sparse, you can present a small fly to the salmon with the hooking and holding advantages of a larger hook. A size 8 low-water fly, for example, is equivalent to a size 12 standard wet fly. The salmon seem to ignore the extra hook sticking out beyond the fly.

Color in salmon flies is a matter of great controversy. Most authorities agree that you should have bright flies, something with green or yellow or orange in them; light flies, with silver tinsel bodies and light wings; and dark flies, with black bodies and wings. The general rule is "bright day, bright fly—dark day, dark fly," and it seems to work under most circumstances.

Every salmon river has its preferred colors, and the fish seem to be consistent about their choice of colors. The color of the water and the bottom may affect the visibility of particular colors. For example, flies with yellows and greens are most visible in tea-colored water—and they catch a lot of salmon in this kind of water.

It's a good idea to use a fly of the same size and color that has been catching fish, or one that has been recommended by your guide. If the favorite doesn't work, experiment with flies that haven't been shown to the salmon in a while, something with a totally different shape, like an Ingall's Butterfly or a Salmon Muddler.

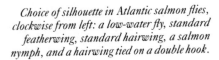

Choice of silhouette in Atlantic salmon flies, clockwise from left: a low-water fly, standard featherwing, standard hairwing, a salmon nymph, and a hairwing tied on a double hook.

Salmon will rise to large dry flies, especially when the water temperature is between 60 and 70 degrees. Below 60 degrees they may take dries, but wets are much more productive; above 68 degrees salmon are difficult to take on any type of fly. Dry flies used for salmon are bushy, high-floating flies in sizes 1/0 through 12. The Wulff and Irresistible patterns are popular, along with big bivisibles and hairwing flies like the MacIntosh. As with wet flies, high water calls for big patterns that are easily seen by the fish, and low water may require dries as small as size 12. A size 12 Black Gnat is an excellent salmon dry fly during low-water conditions.

In some rivers, especially those in northern Maritime Canada, most salmon are taken on dry flies. In others, notably Icelandic and European rivers, salmon never rise to dry flies—in fact, salmon dry flies are almost unknown in Europe.

Color seems to be of little importance with salmon dries, but shape and especially size are critical. Try various sizes. If a salmon rises to inspect your dry but doesn't take it, try a smaller size.

STEELHEAD FLIES

As with salmon flies, steelhead flies must be visible for long distances to be effective. The fish are not actively feeding and must be attracted to the fly, so in a raging torrent the fly should be large (up to size 1/0), and in low, clear water it may be effective to fish flies as small as size 12 or 14. Average steelhead flies for normal water conditions are sizes 4, 6, and 8.

Steelhead and lake-run rainbows have a penchant for bright colors. The traditional West Coast wet flies, incorporate red and white, and such patterns as the Thor and Skykomish Sunrise are still among the most popular. Fluorescent greens, reds, and oranges are being used more and more for steelhead; it seems that the high visibility of these colors in deep, dark steelhead rivers will draw strikes when standard flies go unnoticed.

If the standard bright colors fail to entice steelhead, a change-of-pace fly should be tried. The Skunk, a black and white pattern, is one of the best.

Most steelhead fishing is done with hairwing wet flies, and unlike salmon, steelhead take flies more readily near the bottom. To get down to the fish, steelhead flies may use bead-chain heads, like the Comet series, or heavy wire bodies, like the Brass Hat and Paintbrush patterns. Many fly-tiers avoid the use of lead wire to weight steelhead patterns, preferring a fast-sinking line and short leader to get down to the fish. (Steelhead fishermen often cast long distances at very high lines speeds,

Variation in steelhead flies: a Two-Egg Sperm Fly, a single-egg fly, a standard steelhead wet fly, a wet fly with heavy bead-chain eyes, a spey fly for low water.

and a weighted fly under these circumstances can be a dangerous projectile.)

In streams with runs of Pacific salmon, flies that imitate eggs or clumps of eggs are devastatingly effective for steelhead. Such patterns as the Two-Egg Sperm Fly, Babine, and Glo Bugs in fluorescent red, pink, and orange, fished right along the bottom, will simulate loose salmon eggs. The same patterns in bright green or chartreuse work well in streams that have spring runs of steelhead, because the fish will feed on bright green sucker spawn.

Large nymphs that imitate stoneflies or burrowing mayflies are reported to be very effective on the steelhead that migrate into streams in the Great Lakes area of the East and Midwest.

127

Steelhead that are holding in pools during low-water conditions in summer can be taken with small wets, flies fished "damp" or just under the surface, and occasionally on dry flies. Damp flies are tied with buoyant deer-hair heads or wings so they ride just under the surface. Common examples are the Grease Liner, Muddler Minnow, and Dragon Fly. If a river is very low and clear and the steelhead are holding in pools, a dry fly may be effective. Steelhead dry flies are very similar to those used for Atlantic salmon, with hair wings and lots of hackle for good flotation.

PACIFIC SALMON FLIES

Like Atlantic salmon and steelhead, Pacific salmon feed little when on their spawning migration and are more easily caught on flies just after they have entered a river and the memory of feeding is still fresh.

There is a substantial sport fishery for Pacific salmon in the estuaries of spawning rivers, before the fish have begun their migration. Pacific salmon readily take large streamer flies in estuaries in the Pacific Northwest, and in the Great Lakes where they have been introduced. Patterns should be large, sizes 1 through 3/0, and should imitate the baitfish on which the salmon feed. Much of this fishing is done by trolling, so large tandem streamers are often used. The Herring and Candlefish bucktails are the most popular flies on the West Coast, and are named after the baitfish they imitate. These patterns have silver bodies with green and white or blue and white wings, and any large streamer pattern that has these colors should work. The same streamers will also work for Great Lakes salmon, because the alewife, the predominant baitfish there, has the same coloration.

Once Pacific salmon have been in the river for a week or so, they are difficult to take on flies, although large steelhead wet flies or big white or orange streamer flies can be effective in certain rivers.

PIKE AND PICKEREL FLIES

The same flies used for largemouth bass will catch pike and pickerel, especially large streamer patterns and large poppers and hair bugs. Salt-water streamers like Lefty's Deceivers and the Blonde series also work well. The best colors are red and white, red and yellow, or all white, and a tinsel body seems to add some attraction.

Bucktails and cork poppers rather than streamers and hair bugs are usually used, because the sharp teeth of these species can cut a less durable fly to shreds.

Sizes 3/0 through 2 are best for pike, but the smaller pickerel may take size 4, 6, and 8 patterns more readily.

Occasionally a duller pattern will work better for pike and pickerel, especially on very bright days or in very clear water.

SHAD FLIES

Shad ascend freshwater rivers on the East and West Coasts in the spring months. While they are moving they seldom stray far from the bottom of the river; thus, quick-sinking, simple wet flies tied on heavy hooks or on weighted hooks are used. Shad do not feed before spawning, so highly visible colors are used, notably reds, whites, and yellows. The best sizes are 4, 6, and 8, with the larger flies used in fast water and the smaller ones in slow, clear water. Red glass beads are sometimes strung on the tippet before the fly is tied on, for extra color and to get the fly deeper.

In June, after the shad have spawned and they are working their way back to the ocean, they will feed and can be taken on nymphs, wet flies, and even dry flies.

LANDLOCKED SALMON

Landlocked salmon are Atlantic salmon that do not have access to the ocean. They live in cold, clear lakes in the northeastern United States and move in and out of streams and rivers that feed these lakes.

During the spring and summer months landlocked salmon may feed on insect hatches in both lakes and rivers. Flies should be chosen just as you would for trout, although landlocks are not as selective as trout.

During spring and summer landlocks feed heavily on smelt, and streamer flies with smelt coloration—greens, grays, blue, and whites —are by far the best flies. The Gray Ghost, Nine-Three, and Supervisor are good examples of landlocked-salmon streamers.

Most flies used for landlocked salmon reflect the size and shape of their most important food—smelt. This pattern is called the Magog Smelt.

Landlocks also have a strong attraction for yellow flies, and the Dark Edson Tiger bucktail and Yellow Marabou account for many landlocks, especially in the fall, when the fish spawn in rivers that feed their lakes.

SALTWATER FLIES

Saltwater fly selection is relatively simple. With a few streamer or bucktail patterns in a couple of colors and three or four sizes, two sizes of poppers, and half a dozen large wet flies, you can catch almost any saltwater fish that can be taken on flies.

All saltwater game fish feed on baitfish at one time or another, from the bottom-feeding bonefish in the shallows right up to sailfish in the open ocean. Length is the most important consideration when saltwater fish are actively feeding on baitfish, so fly size can be critical. Small striped bass are about the most selective fish in salt water, and if they're feeding on two-inch baitfish a streamer that is four inches long may go untouched. If the fish are herding baitfish near the surface you'll see the baitfish clearing the water, trying to escape; it's an easy matter to estimate their size and choose your fly size accordingly. If the fish are feeding in deeper water you may have to determine the correct size by trial-and-error fly changing.

This large tarpon streamer is used in shallow water, so it is tied with lots of hackle to slow down its sink rate.

The depth at which you retrieve your fly is also important. How deep your fly is presented is determined to a great degree by the density of floating, intermediate, sinking, or fast-sinking fly line, but different kinds of flies have various sink rates. The larger the fly, the quicker it will sink; thus, bonefish, which are generally caught in very shallow water, may be taking a size 6 Horror while permit in the same vicinity might require a size 2. Permit feed in deeper water than bonefish, and a size 6 may not sink quickly enough to get a feeding permit while he's still visible. The tarpon flies used in Florida shallows have a lot of bushy hackle wound around them to retard the sink rate of these big 4/0 patterns. Fly fishermen using sinking lines in a deep Costa Rican estuary may use the same patterns for tarpon, with the addition of beadchain eyes to sink the flies quickly.

If you can see the color of the baitfish the fish are feeding on, it's always a good idea to match them as closely as possible. Most saltwater baitfish have dark backs—blue, black, or green—with silvery white bellies, sometimes with a black medial stripe. The Lefty's Deceiver patterns in blue and white, green and white and black and white should handle all the baitfish imitating situations you'll ever need.

These same patterns in all-white, yellow, yellow and white, and red and white can also be used as attractors. Bright colors are best when you don't know where the fish are or what they're feeding on. Simple bucktail patterns like the Platinum Blonde and the Honey Blonde also work well as attractors, and these sparsely tied flies sink quicker than the more bulky Deceivers. Certain saltwater species, like tarpon, snook, and crevalle, seem to prefer bright colors regardless of what they're feeding on. The redfish, a popular fly-rod fish in southern coastal waters, has such poor eyesight that brightly colored streamers are almost a necessity.

Poppers increase the enjoyment of saltwater fly fishing, because all the action is in full view. You can see your fly all the time, and you can see the fish with its open mouth charging your fly. Poppers can be used when species like bluefish or stripers are herding baitfish at the surface, and big 7/0 poppers are used after such giant fish of the open ocean as sailfish, amberjack, or cobia are chummed or teased close to the boat. More so than any other kind of fly, poppers call attention to themselves by making noise and throwing spray out in front of them. A bluefish that is charging a school of baitfish will be drawn to a noisy popper more quickly than to a streamer that is competing with all the other baitfish in the school for attention.

Poppers can also be used as attractors, drawing stripers or bluefish out of ten feet of water to investigate the commotion. Redfish,. with their weak eyesight, are often brought to the surface by a small popper. Experienced fly-fishermen say that the sound a popper makes resembles the noise a frightened shrimp makes when it scoots to the surface.

Sometimes a bullet-minnow type of popper is effective, especially for fish like striped bass that are easily spooked. This type of popper gives the impression of a wounded baitfish struggling on the surface, without the commotion of a standard popper.

As with saltwater streamers, the best colors for poppers are all white, red and white, blue and white, and yellow and white.

Bottom-feeding fish that cruise the tropical flats—bonefish, permit, and redfish—require the use of relatively small (in relation to other saltwater flies) streamers that are nymphlike in appearance and function, since they imitate crustaceans. These fish feed on small crabs, shrimp, worms, and baitfish, rooting them out of aquatic grasses and crevasses in rocks. They seldom feed anywhere but right next to the bottom. Flies for these species are designed to sink quickly, as the fish are on the move constantly when feeding. Bonefish flies are usually tied upside down, with the wing covering the hook point. They can then be

131

fished right along the bottom without catching on rocks or fouling on aquatic vegetation.

Color is also important with these flies. Redfish, with their poor eyesight, respond best to bright yellow, red and white, or pink flies. Bonefish and permit occasionally prefer bright-colored flies like the pink shrimp, especially in deep or discolored water. Bright flies may also spook these fish. The best rule of thumb for selecting flies for bonefish is to match the color of the bottom. Bonefish feeding over a sand bottom should be tried first with tan-colored patterns like the Horror or Brown Snapping Shrimp; when they're feeding in grasses, best bets are green patterns like the Green Mantis or yellow ones like the Golden Mantis. Apparently, the crustaceans that live in each habitat are carefully camouflaged and a fly that is too bright or too dark in relation to the backgroud sounds an alarm.

Small saltwater flies used for bonefish and permit. The bottom two flies ride upside down to prevent fouling on rocks or aquatic grasses.

WHEN TO CHANGE FLIES

How do you know when to change flies, and how long do you stick with a particular pattern? Generally, if the fish are visible and they ignore your fly or chase it without taking, you can do two things: either change flies or change your presentation slightly.

If you're fishing to a rising trout and he either splashes at your fly or ignores it, you know something is wrong. Catch another natural insect and make sure your imitation is correct. Watch the rise form. Is he really taking insects on the surface?

At the other end of the scale, if you're fishing blind and don't know where the fish are, you might want to keep the same fly on your tippet for hours. Atlantic salmon may ignore your fly for ninety-nine casts and take the fly on the hundredth. You may be fishing a nymph deep on a sinking line in a trout lake, not knowing where the fish are. Here, you might keep moving, covering the water thoroughly. If the nymph you're using is a proven favorite, why switch?

FILLING YOUR FLY BOX

Let's say you're taking a fishing trip and have a recommended list of flies from a guide or fishing lodge. How many of each should you have?

I feel naked without at least four flies in each size of each recommended pattern. This may sound like an inordinate amount, especially if your recommended list is quite large. Look at it this way—even a proficient fly caster expects to lose at least two flies in the trees or on submerged logs or rocks during a day of fishing, plus one fly lost by striking a large fish too hard. If you only have one or two of the pattern that's working and you leave them in the trees, your long-awaited fishing trip is going to be spoiled. Flies are cheap compared to gasoline or travel expenses.

When you first start fly-fishing you may have trouble identifying hook sizes and patterns merely by eyeballing them. This will come in time; there is no shortcut. I suggest that you keep patterns and sizes together in a fly box and attach a sticky label to the top of each compartment of your fly box, writing on it the pattern and size in pencil. Not only will you learn fly names more quickly, it will make it much easier to reorder your favorite patterns.

RECOMMENDED FLY LISTS

The following are lists of flies that should be useful for the favorite fly-rod fish we've discussed. Like all such lists, they have the inherent drawback of my own biases on fly selection, but they're a good place to start if you have no other source of information.

TROUT—EASTERN U.S.	SIZES
Dry Flies	
Adams	10–24
Light Cahill	10–24
Blue-Winged Olive	14–24
Hendrickson	12–16
Quill Gordon	14–18
Ausable Wulff	10–14
Black Ant	14–20
Black Midge	20–24
Tan Elk–Wing Caddis	14–18
Rusty Spinner	12–18
White-Black Spinner	20, 24
LeTort Hopper	8–14
Nymphs	
Hare's Ear	8–16
Zug Bug	10–16
Olive/Gray Scud	12, 14

Blue–Winged Olive	12–16
Speckled Sedge	12–18
Early Brown Stone	10, 12

Wets

Hare's Ear	10–14
Light Cahill	10–14
Leadwing Coachman	10–14
Blue Quill	12–16

Streamers and Bucktails

Muddler Minnow	6–12
Black-Nose Dace	6–12
Gray Ghost	6–12
Black Ghost	4–10
Black Marabou Muddler	6–10
Squirrel Tail	6–10

TROUT—WESTERN U.S.

Dry Flies

Western Green Drake	10, 12
Pale Morning Dun	10–20
Adams	10–20
Blue–Wing Olive	14–22
Tan Elk–Wing Caddis	12–18
Royal Wulff	10–14
Yellow Humpy	10–14
Rusty Spinner	14–18
Olive Spinner	14–18
White/Black Spinner	20, 24
Henry's Fork Salmon Fly	6, 8
Irresistible	10, 12
LeTort Hopper	8–12
Black Ant	12–20
Rusty Emerger	14–18

Nymphs

Black Stone	4–8
Bitch Creek	4–8
Hare's Ear	8–14
Pheasant Tail	12–18
Speckled Sedge	12–16

Wets

Black Wooly Worm	6–12
Leadwing Coachman	12–14
Hare's Ear	10–14
Dark Cahill	12, 14
Light Cahill	12, 14

Streamers and Bucktails

Brown Matuka Sculpin	2–6

White Marabou Muddler	2–12
Muddler Minnow	2–12
Olive Matuka	6, 8
Black Leech	4–8

SMALLMOUTH BASS

Floating Flies

Sneaky Pete Popper	4, 8
Yellow/Black/White Bass Getter	4
Natural Bass Getter	4
Black Bluegill Bug	12

Streamers and Bucktails

Muddler Minnow	4–12
Black Matuka	6–10
Black-Nose Dace	6–12
White Marabou Muddler	6–12
Crayfish	4–8
Yellow Matuka	6, 8

Nymphs

| Montana | 4–12 |
| Hare's Ear | 8, 10 |

LARGEMOUTH BASS

Floating Flies

Black Minnow Popper	1/0
Yellow Minnow Popper	1/0
Kicker Frog	2, 4
Hair Mouse	2
Sneaky Pete	4
Yellow Keel Bass Bug	4

Sinking Flies

Black Marabou Leech	4
Florida Muddler	4/0
White Marabou Muddler	1
Silver Prismatic Shiner	2

ATLANTIC SALMON FLIES

Wet Flies

Green Butt	2–10
Cosseboom	4–8
Rusty Rat	4–8
Silver Rat	4–8
Blue Charm Low-Water	4–8
Salmon Muddler Double	4–8
Green Highlander	4–8

Dry Flies

| Buck Bug | 4–8 |
| Royal Wulff | 4–8 |

STEELHEAD—WEST COAST OCEAN RUNS

Wet Flies

Thor	4–8
Comet	4–8
Skunk	4–8
Silver Hilton	4–8
Golden Demon	4–8

Dry Flies

Royal Wulff	4–8
Grease Liner	4–8

STEELHEAD—LAKE-RUN FISH IN GREAT LAKES AND ALASKA

Wets

Babine	4–8
Glo Bugs (Orange, Red, and Chartreuse)	6
Royal Coachman	4–8
Fall Favorite	2–8

Streamers

Gray Ghost	4–8
Cardinelle	4–8

Nymphs

Montana	4–8
Hare's Ear	6–10

SALTWATER FLIES—OPEN OCEAN SPECIES

Blue/White Skipping Bug	2/0
Yellow Skipping Bug	2/0
White Deceiver	2/0, 2
Sailfish Streamer	4/0
Blue/White Deceiver	2/0, 2
Yellow Deceiver	2/0, 2

SALTWATER FLIES—INSHORE SPECIES

Pink Shrimp	2–6
Brown Snapping Shrimp	4, 6
Permit Fly	1
Green Mantis	4, 6
Horror	4
White Deceiver	2/0, 2
Blue/White Deceiver	2/0, 2
Chase Tarpon	4/0
Gold Cup	4/0
Yellow Skipping Bug	2/0
Blue/White Skipping Bug	2/0
Honey Blonde	2, 1/0, 3/0

8
Stream Tactics

Current adds mysteries and challenges to fishing. Resident trout and smallmouth bass don't move around much in streams, preferring to find a spot that offers them easy meals without costing them a lot of energy. A knowledge of the needs of stream fish plus a basic understanding of stream hydraulics will enable you to "read the water," which is a fisherman's term for being able to predict where trout and bass hold in streams.

THE STREAM ENVIRONMENT

Before we can discuss finding fish in a stream you should understand the following terms in relation to moving water:

Pool. A pool is a relatively deep area in a stream, generally with fast water at the upstream end, or head, a broad flat expanse of slow water, or middle, and a narrower, gradually faster area of current, known as the tail. Pools can be anywhere from three feet long in a mountain brook to half a mile long on big rivers.

Riffle. Riffles usually separate one pool from another. They are areas

Aerial view of a typical pool, with the tail at the far left, the middle in the center, the head, and the tail of another pool in the upper right-hand corner.

of more rapidly descending topography than pools; the water is shallower, faster, and the surface of the water is more broken.

Runs. Runs are midway in depth between pools and riffles, and narrower than either pools or riffles. The water, at least on the surface, is faster than in a pool.

Pocket water. Pocket water is a run or deep riffle with big rocks or boulders on the bottom, causing the surface of the water to be frothy and heavily broken.

Undercut bank. An undercut bank is formed in a pool, riffle, or run when the current erodes the bank under the surface of the water, making a pocket of water that is overhung by rocks or soil.

TROUT ENVIRONMENTS

Trout in streams need water temperature of the proper range, a place to feed where they won't expend more energy than they obtain by feeding, a place to run and hide when predators threaten, and proper spawning habitat. An understanding of all of these except the last will help you find fish in a stream. Trout will move out to spawn sometime between late fall and early spring, depending on the species, but they'll

138

Fishing a nice looking run that flows along the bank of a Vermont stream. Percy Gilbert

return home when you begin to fish for them next spring.

Fish, unlike mammals, are cold-blooded and cannot regulate their internal temperature. They need a narrow range of temperatures for survival, and also have an optimum temperature range in which feeding levels are at their highest and growth is fastest. For trout, the survival range is from 35 to about 75 degrees Fahrenheit; the optimum range for feeding (and for fishing!) is from 50 to 68 degrees for brown trout and rainbows, the most common species. Brook trout and cutthroat require slightly colder water temperatures for optimum growth and feeding.

Below 45 degrees, trout feed little and are almost in a state of suspended animation, not expending much energy and requiring little food. Above 68 degrees they will feed somewhat if the water is broken and has sufficient oxygen concentration. It isn't actually the heat above 75 degrees that kills trout. As water gets warmer it can hold less oxygen, and if the water gets too warm the trout simply suffocate.

During the winter and early spring trout will hold in slow deep areas where they don't have to fight the current to stay alive. As the water warms above 50 degrees in the spring they will be found almost anywhere—in riffles, pools, and runs. The temperature everywhere is well within the optimum range. Some trout streams never get over 65 degrees, and the fish will stay in the same places until spawning time, but on those that get too warm the trout will seek colder, more oxygenated water. Springs and small feeder streams are almost always colder, so look for trout below incoming streams and spring seeps during the summer. You can use a stream thermometer to find these spots. Other places to find trout in midsummer are shaded areas of fast, broken water. Even though the water temperature in fast water may be above 65 degress, there will be sufficient oxygen to support trout here. When the temperature of the stream gets above 75 degrees trout will move to cooler areas; if they can't, they'll die.

Much has been written in trout literature about "cover": the old brown trout under a rock, the brookie next to a log, or the cutthroat holding beneath an undercut bank. Recent studies have shown that trout prefer to live wherever they can obtain food easily, and that they only need the protection of a rock, log, or undercut bank nearby, somewhere they can bolt to when frightened. Of course, their feeding stations may be near these obstructions, but they may also be right out in the middle of a flat, open pool.

Trout need a place where they can wait for their food to drift by, a place where the current overhead is fast enough to bring an endless supply of food but where they can rest while waiting for it.

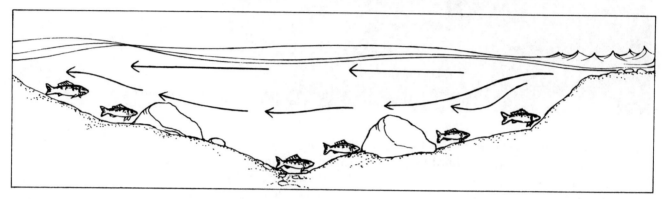

Vertical cross-section of a pool, showing places that may hold trout.

Trout must face upstream, because that's the way they're built. If a fish faced broadside to the current or downstream, he'd be pushed away by the current. The streamlined design of trout enables them to rest their heads on the stream bottom almost effortlessly. When they see an interesting morsel drift by they merely tip their fins upward and the current carries them up to intercept the food; then they tip their fins down to return to the bottom. The current carries them downstream in the process of feeding; the only time they have to work is to return to their spot, swimming back upstream.

Not all places on the bottom are used by trout. A small depression in the stream bed or the shape of a particular rock may afford a trout a place where he can rest his head. These "seats in the restaurant" are used from year to year unless floods scour the bottom and move things around.

Stream trout are territorial and live and feed in a very small area. They will defend their seat against other trout. If you catch a good trout from a spot this year there will most likely be another good one there next year. If you release him the same fish will often be there, as trout live to be up to ten years old and will use the same territory from year to year, unless forced out by a more aggressive fish.

We can't really predict where these favored spots can be, but we can certainly narrow things down a bit.

Wherever moving water encounters an object it will be slowed down, due to the friction between a hard surface and water molecules. The surface of a stream in the middle of a straight stretch of water is always faster than water near the bottom or near the banks. Where the current meets a rock on the bottom of the stream there will be areas of dead water in front of, behind, and on the sides of the rock. This phenomenon allows such tiny, almost weightless animals like aquatic insects to move freely in the gravel in a stream bed without being swept away. It also gives trout places to live.

Looking at a piece of very fast pocket water, we often think, "How can a trout live in there?" Upon closer examination, we see many different currents, fast in some areas and almost motionless in others. There is an old saying about there being "a trout behind every rock," and in some of the best trout streams there will be a trout behind, in front of, and even on the sides of many rocks. The more varied a stream bottom,

*From a distance, this rainbow trout's shadow
will be easier to spot than the fish itself.*

the more trout it has the potential to hold. In a good trout stream with adequate temperature and food supply, the only limiting factors to trout abundance will be feeding sites and fishing pressure.

Look for trout in places where they have a spot to rest that is in or immediately adjacent to the main current or currents in a stream. You can spot the main current because it will have the fastest water flow, generally the most depth, and it will be the area that carries the most bubbles and debris—and food—downstream. Trout will seldom be found in extremely slow areas of a stream, simply because these places do not provide enough food. Trout may move in and out of these areas occasionally to ambush minnows, but they won't stay there for long.

You will seldom be able to see a trout in a stream, even if he is ten feet away. Trout are well camouflaged against the bottom of a stream, and they can change their skin shading from light to dark in a matter of days. I've caught brown trout that were feeding alongside a rock or log, and the side that was in the sun was light, while his other side was a couple of shades darker. A trout's camouflage is so good that it's easier to spot fish by their shadows than by trying to see them.

The best time to spot trout is when they are rising. A trout cannot

141

The best way to spot trout is when they are rising. Bob Bachman

take an insect off the surface without making some kind of disturbance, however subtle.

The following are places that almost always hold trout:

A typical pool, showing where you can expect to find trout.

Near rocks. The classic situation to find trout is in the slow current behind rocks. There is also a spot of slow current in front of rocks and, to a lesser degree, along the sides of larger rocks. Trout will use rocks

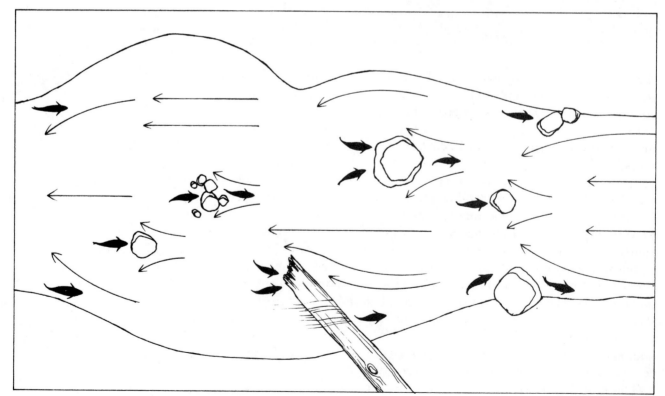

Trout will be found just in front of this mid-stream rock and in the plume behind it.

anywhere from the size of a grapefruit to half the size of a house.

Where riffles meet pools. Where a riffle runs into a pool there will be a depression formed where the faster water has dug into the bottom. Trout can sit in this depression with little effort, waiting for insects that live in the riffle to drift into the pool. Although adult trout are seldom found in shallow riffles, keep your eye out for slightly deeper depressions in riffles. A good trout can sit in this trench and feed to his heart's content, passed up by most fishermen.

Tails of pools. Tails of pools are shallower than the middle, and as the current quickens at the tail there will be a slow area formed along the bottom as the water from the pool hits the shallower tail. Tails of pools are great spots for trout, because they are generally narrower than the middle, so the drifting food is more concentrated here.

Near the banks. Many streams have a main current flow along the banks, and the banks will break the current enough for trout to have a perfect feeding spot. Trees and bushes that overhang the water also provide trout with a steady supply of terrestrial insects, and trout will take up feeding stations under and near them. Overhanging trees provide protection from predators such as ospreys, herons, mergansers, and kingfishers. Other than man, avian predators are a trout's major cause for alarm.

In many large western rivers, most of the large trout will be found a few feet from grassy banks; the center of the rivers are mainly populated with small trout and whitefish.

Near downed trees. Trees that have fallen into a river, whether they are logs lying parallel to the current or "sweepers" (trees still attached to the bank, lying 90 degrees to the current), provide a break in the current and protection for the trout.

Flats. Areas of flat water with moderate currents and a depth of one

143

The downed trees along the bank and on the bottom of this stream provide havens for trout.

Smooth flats like this may hold an unbelievable number of trout. Percy Gilbert

to three feet are among the finest trout habitats you'll find, as long as there are rocks or other obstructions on the bottom that provide places for the trout to rest.

Where fast currents meet slow water. Where there is an interface between fast and slow currents you'll find trout. The fast current carries the food and the slow current holds the trout where they don't have to move very far for their food.

Where feeder streams enter a larger river. These spots are especially important in large rivers that get warm during the summer, and trout may move from their normal positions to congregate in unbelievable numbers below these sources of cool water during hot spells. Trout do most of their spawning in feeder streams, so look for browns and brookies here in the fall and rainbows and cutthroats in the spring.

Anywhere in spring creeks. Spring creeks, as opposed to rocky (freestone) trout streams, derive their flow mainly from subsurface springs rather than groundwater. They are constant in temperature, stable, and slow-flowing, with a profusion of aquatic plants. Because of a rich food supply, slow current, and the profusion of weed beds, trout will hold almost anywhere in spring creeks.

From the trout's point of view, objects that don't protrude above the surface of the stream are just as good as those that do. Sometimes you'll be able to see them with polarized sunglasses; other times the surface of the stream will give you clues. Wrinkles or boils on the surface indicate turbulence from submerged objects. In two equally fast pieces of water, you can bet that the one with a broken surface will hold more trout than the one with a smooth surface.

A TROUT'S SENSES

Trout are very nervous fish. The fisherman who strolls into a trout stream without caution may never see, much less catch, a single trout in an entire day's fishing.

Trout are constantly on the alert for predators. Most of them come from above: herons, mergansers, kingfishers, raccoons, and mink. Otters and such large fish as northern pike are predators that attack from below the surface, but they are much less common, and a trout will tolerate a man swimming with scuba gear much closer than a man looming above him.

Trout perceive danger through two of their senses, visually and through their lateral line system, a network of nerves that senses vibrations in the water. Both senses are extremely acute. To catch trout consistently you must be aware of their scope and their limitations.

Trout can't see objects that are very far away underwater. Because even the purest water has some suspended matter in it, light entering the water from above is diffused, much like car headlights in a fog. You can probably wade to within ten feet of a trout without his seeing your legs.

The upper part of your body is a different story. Trout can see very well above the surface of the water, judging by the fact that they can leap out of the water to catch a caddisfly in midair. Because of the refractive properties of water, though, a trout can see only a portion of what surrounds the surface, a phenomenon known as his "window."

The window is a cone that occupies a 97-degree angle above the fish's head. Because light that strikes the surface of the water below 10 degrees above the horizontal is reflected and does not enter the water, a fish sees 160 degrees compressed into 97 degrees. Consequently, there is some distortion of objects, especially on the lower edges of the window.

What does this mean to the fisherman? Looking at the diagram, you can see that the lower you keep your profile, the less likely it is that a trout will see you. A trout in shallow water is less likely to see you than one that is holding in deep water, because the 10-degree and 97-degree angles remain constant—the fish takes his window with him as he moves up and down in the water.

A fish can see on both sides and straight ahead, and because of the physiology of his eyes can see in all directions at once, except directly behind him. In a stream, where a trout is facing upstream, you can approach him quite close from downstream. If you are upstream or to one side of the fish, you should stay farther away or cast from a kneeling or crouching position. This is one great advantage of wading—when you are in the water your profile is lower.

Why the preoccupation with trout seeing you? Does a trout naturally fear man?

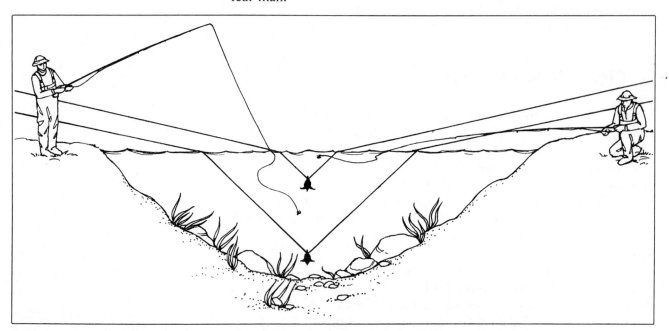

A trout's window. Note that the kneeling fisherman is less visible and that a trout in shallow water sees less than one in deep water.

A trout has an instinctive fear of anything moving above the water. If he sees you or your fly rod moving back and forth, it's likely that he will become frightened and spook. If a trout is rising steadily and stops abruptly, you can assume that your approach has not been careful enough. This is called "putting him down."

Spooking has a number of degrees. A cast that splashes on the water might just make the fish a little nervous. What he'll do is stop feeding, sink slowly to the bottom, and stay motionless for anywhere from a minute to a half hour or more. The best thing to do in this situation is move quietly to the bank, sit down, and wait for him to resume feeding. Approach him more carefully next time.

An overt move on your part, such as entering his window or actually walking near him, will cause the trout to bolt for the cover of a log or rock, and in that case he's probably finished for the day and won't feed until tomorrow.

A trout's vision is not the only thing you have to be concerned with. More trout are spooked because they hear our approach through vibrations in their lateral line than actually see us. I'd be willing to bet that even the most careful fly-fisherman spooks at least half the trout in every pool he fishes.

A trout can hear anything that sets up vibrations in the water, and can detect your presence from much farther away this way than by seeing you. By careless wading I've spooked trout that were over sixty feet away.

Many things can cause frightening vibrations. Most of them can be avoided by a careful approach. On streams with sod banks, heavy footfalls will warn trout of your approach long before you know that they are rising. The sound of rocks knocking against each other will carry incredible distances underwater; try it sometime when you're swimming. Splashy wading, noisy line pickups, and sloppy casts will also decrease your success.

In very still, slow pools even wading too fast will form ripples that warn the trout of your approach. The solution here is to wade very slowly, moving your feet only inches at a step and taking breaks between steps. On one Catskill stream that I fish it may take me fifteen minutes to wade the fifty feet necessary to get within casting range of the fish.

Water conditions, the weather, and how preoccupied the trout are with feeding will determine how closely you can approach a rising or nymphing trout. In riffled water, not only will the background noise of rushing water cover your approach, the broken surface also distorts the trout's window. In broken water you can come up behind a trout, approaching him from downstream, sometimes as close as ten feet. If you're upstream of him, of course, he can still see you, although not as well as in flat water.

The placid surface of a pool will require much more stealth. Not only does the trout have a relatively good window on the outside world, your wading or careless casting can send ripples through the water that will tell him something is amiss. In a pool with a smooth surface but relatively swift current these ripples will be dissipated quickly, but if the current is slow as well your ripples can carry up to sixty or seventy feet away. Watch the water in front of you. If the ripples threaten to carry themselves all the way to where you think a fish is or where one is rising, slow down.

Cloudy weather or early morning and late evening decrease a fish's ability to resolve individual objects, so they are easier to approach. When the sun is high in the sky it's much easier for a trout to spot you silhouetted against the skyline or against streamside foliage. Allowing your shadow to fall across a spot where you suspect a fish is sitting is definitely taboo; trout are instantly spooked by shadows from above.

You can also use bright sun to your advantage. A trout is blinded by bright sun, just as we are, and if you can approach the fish so that the sun is behind you but your shadow is not falling on a likely-looking spot, all the better.

Some fly-fishermen go to the extent of wearing dark green or camouflage fishing vests so that they blend in with streamside foliage. I've never been able to quantify the difference between wearing light

You can get quite close to trout in riffles and pocket water. Percy Gilbert

and dark clothing, but I suspect that if you are careful about the direction from which you approach a fish and move slowly, clothing color is unimportant.

Rain on the water makes trout lose their caution, probably because of a combination of lower light levels and the distortion on the surface of the water caused by raindrops. Many insects hatch more readily during rain or cloudy weather, and increased feeding activity by the fish also makes them easier to approach.

A trout that is feeding with a steady rhythm is always easier to approach than one that is feeding sporadically or not at all. A combination of factors are at work when he's taking an insect every ten seconds or so, including the fact that he's probably preoccupied with feeding and

Four ways of approaching a trout. At A, the fisherman is in the trout's blind spot and can get very close. As he moves upstream to B, C, or D, he is visible to the fish and must stay farther away.

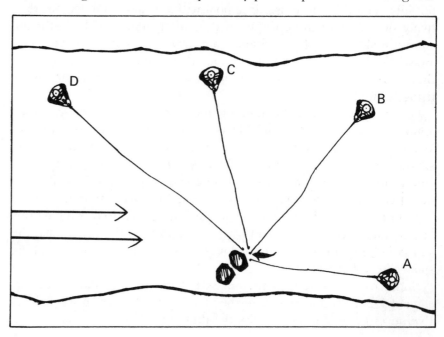

doesn't have his guard up as he normally would. A trout that is actively feeding will be hanging close to the surface. His window is smaller, so you can approach him closer without his seeing you, plus he's focusing his eyes on objects that are close to him, so his depth of field is very shallow.

WADING

Wading is as much a skill as fly casting, not only for a careful approach, as we've seen, but to keep from taking spills or going over the tops of your waders.

Long strides are out when you're wading, unless you're crossing a shallow riffle where you won't be doing any fishing. When wading, you should use your feet to feel your way across the bottom, never lifting your feet more than a foot or so off the bottom—something like a slow shuffle.

The two most important things to remember when wading are that it's always easier to wade downstream than upstream and it's easier to move your body facing sideways to the current than broadside to it.

Suppose you're trying to cross a river of unknown depth. You don't know where the deep spots are. The best thing to do is find the spot that looks most shallow, either a riffled area or one that appears lighter in color. The tail of a pool is usually a good bet. Start at the downstream end of the shallow area and walk carefully upstream at an angle to the current that's comfortable. If the water becomes too deep, you can always retrace your steps. If you try to wade straight across a fast river, the current may push you downstream into a deep hole, forcing you to take a bath. Wading directly downstream presents the same problem —you may find yourself being pushed into a hole, and the current may make it physically impossible to retrace your steps.

When wading fast water or around slippery, round rocks, take care to always have one foot planted firmly on the bottom while the other feels its way forward to find a second firm purchase. Always wade between rocks and boulders, never on top of them. The tops of rocks are weathered smooth by the current, and are unwise places to plant your feet. There is usually an area of sand or gravel just behind and sometimes in front of midstream boulders, giving you both relief from the current and a firm place to plant your feet.

If you're wading in water that's thigh to waist deep and start to lose your balance, you can use your fly rod to right yourself. Plunge the rod into the water. It should give you enough support to regain your balance. As long as the water is deep enough and you don't bang the rod on a rock, you won't have to worry about breaking it.

A wading staff is a great boon to those who are not confident wading fast water or who are unsteady on their feet. A staff can help with your balance and to find hidden obstructions and deep spots. Always use the wading staff on your downstream side, pushing forward and slightly

149

upstream as you use it. A convenient emergency staff can be made from a streamside stick.

Wading in shallow water is potentially more dangerous than wading in deep water. There is a temptation to be overconfident and wade quickly in shallow water, increasing the chance that you'll trip on a slippery rock or log. A fall in deep water will give you a bath and a little swim at worst, but a fall in shallow water can cause bruises or broken bones.

If you do lose your footing in deep water and take a plunge, remain calm, try to keep your head above water, and try to keep your feet in front of you so your head doesn't bang against rocks. The current will carry you to shallower water, and it's better to ride out the current than to struggle and swim to shore. If you're a confident swimmer you may want to swim to shallow water; a fairly decent dog paddle can be done while wearing waders. The old story about a man in waders tipping upside down because of trapped air in his waders is absolutely untrue.

One final word on wading that may save you a spill or two: turning your body around in deep, fast water is best done by rotating in an upstream direction and leaning into the current slightly. Turning downstream will suddenly place your body broadside to the current, with an irresistible temptation to begin walking downstream. Once your momentum gets going it's tough to stop moving, and you may find yourself being pushed into a deep hole.

DRY FLY FISHING

Before you begin to approach a rising trout you should understand the effects of currents on your fly, fly line, and leader, and the concept the fly-fishermen call "drag." Drag is responsible for as many trout refusing flies as the wrong size, shape, or color of your imitation.

If you cast directly across a current of uniform speed, your line and leader will always move faster than your fly. Imagine yourself directly across from a rising trout. You cast your dry fly 90 degrees to the current, about two feet above the rise form. The fly starts to drift directly downstream over the trout, but because the line and leader are moving more quickly than the fly, they begin to pull the fly across and downstream. A tiny V wake appears behind the fly. This is drag, and it is very apparent from below the surface of the water. Natural insects skip and flutter across the surface of the water, but they don't leave wakes behind them. Drag will ordinarily cause a trout to ignore or refuse your fly.

The effects of drag are heightened when your fly line and/or leader falls in faster currents than your fly, which is a typical situation because trout are usually in spots that are slightly sheltered from the current. Casting directly downstream on a tight line will cause your fly to drag immediately.

One solution is to approach a rising trout from directly downstream. Not only are you approaching him from his blind spot, but you'll be

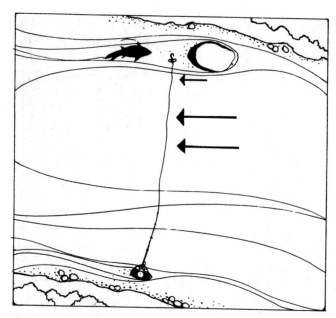

A fly is cast directly across the current, just above a rising trout.

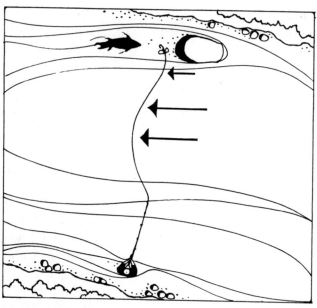

The faster current in the middle of the stream puts a belly in the line almost immediately.

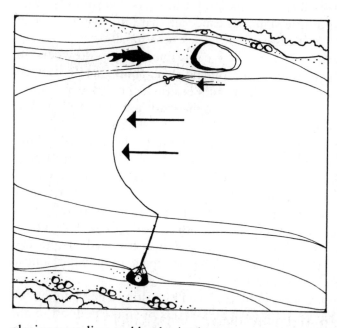

Drag develops as the line pulls the fly across and downstream.

placing your line and leader in the same current as the fly, so the danger of drag is greatly diminished.

To present a dry fly to a fish that is rising directly upstream of your position, begin to false cast, working out a little line on each false cast until it looks as if the fly will land a foot or two above the rise. On the last false cast, follow through and lower your rod tip. Immediately start stripping line just as fast as the current brings it back to you. The line should be coiled neatly in your stripping hand, but if the current is extremely fast you may not have enough time to coil the line. In that case, just strip in the line and let it fall to the water at your side.

If slack develops below the rod tip, you're stripping too slow. If the fly moves downstream faster than the current, you're stripping too fast.

Allowing slack line to accumulate below the rod tip causes a couple of problems. A trout will eject a fly almost immediately when he senses its artificiality, and you have to set the hook as soon as you see his rise. Too much slack line prevents you from setting the hook promptly. Second, slack line will be washed downstream, around your legs and behind you, causing tangles when you want to make another cast.

It's best to wait until the fly passes well below the fish before you pick up to make another cast. Ripping the line off the water right below a trout may spook him. Try not to pick up more line than you have to. If you're casting to a fish that is thirty feet above you, let the fly drift until is is fifteen feet above you, pick up, then make several snappy false casts to dry the fly, shooting about five feet of line with each false cast by letting it slip through your fingers. If you were right on target on the first cast, there's no need to adjust your line length. If the first cast was too short or too long, put some line back on the reel or strip some off accordingly.

Can you see the problem with casting directly upstream? With this strategy, your leader and possibly your line will land right on top of the trout's head. It's possible to spook a trout this way, known as "lining" him. A cast that is a little sloppy is especially harmful from this angle, and even the very best casters blow a cast occasionally.

Speaking of blown casts, the worst possible thing to do when you make a bad cast is to rip the line off the water immediately. Let the whole mess drift well below the trout's position, then pick up and try again. Don't get caught off guard, though—bad casts have fooled some magnificent trout.

A straight upstream cast is OK in riffled water, where the added disturbance won't alarm the trout, but on smooth water I prefer an alternative angle that has all the benefits of an upstream cast and less chance of spooking the trout. It's called a quartering upstream cast, and it involves moving your position just a few feet to the right or left of the fish. You'll still be taking advantage of a relatively drag-free float and the trout's blind spot, but only the fly will pass over his head, if your cast has been accurate. Presentation and line pickup are exactly the same as with the straight upstream cast.

The same presentation can be achieved by casting a curve to the left or right, which also keeps your line and most of your leader off to one side of the trout. As I stated in the casting chapter, though, curve casts are inconsistent and few of us can use them properly on a regular basis.

The quartering upstream cast is the best way to present a dry fly to a trout, but there will be times when this cast is impractical. One instance is where a trout is rising in front of an obstruction like a rock or log. Another is where a trout is rising in the almost dead-calm water behind a rock or next to the bank. If you approach a trout rising behind a rock from below, the fast water to the side of and behind the rock will whisk your line and leader downstream quickly, dragging the fly. In these instances you might try a quartering downstream cast, either cast-

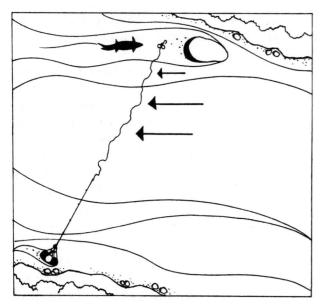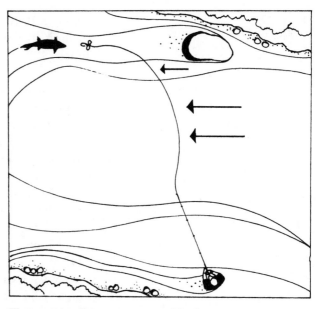

The quartering upstream cast is one of the best ways to present a dry fly. The fisherman has thrown slack into his line because of the fast midstream current.

The quartering downstream cast can either be used with an upstream curve, as shown here, or a slack line cast.

ing slack into the line or using an upstream curve to prevent the fly from dragging immediately.

Here's a typical example: a trout is rising about six inches from the bank, in very slow water. There is an area of fast current just out from the bank. You've tried him with a quartering upstream cast, but the fast current between you and the trout puts a belly into your line that drags the fly almost immediately.

Carefully move sideways, away from the trout, and wade upstream of his position. Remember that the trout can see you now if you approach too closely, because you're out of his blind spot, so you'll have to stay farther away and use a longer cast. Let's say you've moved about ten feet upstream of his position, and thirty feet away from him in a line diagonal to the current.

False cast a little over thirty feet of line, aiming for a spot about two feet above his position. On the final false cast, check your rod at about ten o'clock and pull back on the rod slightly, then drop the rod to waist level. Slack line will be formed, slack that will allow your fly to float drag-free over the trout.

You can also use a side-arm cast, forming an upstream curve that will have to be inverted before the fly will drag. In contrast to the upstream presentation, you don't retrieve line as the fly is drifting.

After the fly floats over the fish, don't pick it up immediately. Point the rod tip directly downstream, allowing the current to pull the fly and leader off to the side and below the trout. You can then retrieve and pick up your line for another cast without disturbing him.

In the situation where you have to cast from directly upstream of a trout, where a fish is rising just in front of a low bridge or brush pile, use the same tactics but throw an even sloppier cast for added slack. To prolong a drift, you can even point your rod tip directly downstream, wiggling it gently from side to side, feeding slack line through the guides.

On many large rivers, especially in the Rocky Mountains, the quartering downstream cast is used for dry-fly fishing extensively. It's said that this presentation is more effective because the fish sees the fly before he sees the leader, but I'm willing to bet it has more to do with the way the fly drifts than whether or not the trout sees your leader.

When float or drift fishing a river from a boat, the quartering downstream presentation is the best method to use, because as the boat floats downstream a dry fly cast upstream or directly across will drag almost immediately. With a good man at the oars and a cleverly presented downstream cast, it's possible to get a drag-free float of twenty feet or more.

Drag can be very subtle, so subtle that you can't see it from twenty feet away. If you present a dry fly to a steadily rising trout and he refuses it time and again, drag, rather than your fly pattern, may be at fault. Try a slight change in your position, or even try the trout from the other side of the river. Often a change in position will place your cast in different currents, currents that will allow you to obtain a drag-free float.

How long should you work over a rising trout before changing flies or giving up and moving on? That depends on your temperament and your confidence. Some fly-fishermen will work over the same trout for hours, especially if he's a good one, changing flies and positions until the trout is either hooked or spooked. Others may only try a few dozen casts before moving on to find another feeding fish. If there are a lot of fish feeding, changing fish rather than changing flies is not a bad idea, because trout are individuals and what one refuses the next one may inhale eagerly.

A trout's rise rhythm is important when you're fishing dry flies. When there are many natural flies on the water and a trout is holding just below the surface to take advantage of the abundance of food, rises will be deliberate and paced at regular intervals. If you can determine the time between rises, try to pitch your fly to him when you think the next rise is due.

A trout may also rise at infrequent or irregular intervals. Here, the best strategy is to cast to him as soon as he rises, while he's still looking at the surface.

It's always best to cast slightly above a trout's rise form. The force of the current as a trout rises will push him downstream of his observation position, and casting directly to the rise may place your fly in his blind spot. In fast water where the fish are not easily disturbed, I like to cast one to two feet upstream of the rise. In slow water, try to lead the rise by at least two feet or more so that the disturbance of the fly and leader landing on the water are well above your target.

If you're unsure of your accuracy or exactly where the trout is, always try to err on the short rather than the long side. A cast that's too short will only put the fly behind or off to the side of the trout's vision, so he'll ignore it. A cast that is too long may put the leader, or, even worse, the line, right on top of him.

How much of a drag problem a particular position presents may determine how far above the trout's rise you cast your dry fly. In some spots, especially those with swirly, conflicting currents or when a trout is rising in slow water adjacent to very fast water, you'll be able to get a drag-free float of only a couple of inches. This may be enough. If it isn't, you'll have to resort to something else.

One solution, the one I like least, can be used when you're directly across from a trout that is rising in slow water and there are fast currents between you and him. Holding your rod tip high helps to keep the fly line out of the fast water so your fly isn't whisked away immediately. The problem here is that it's very difficult to set the hook in this position. In addition, holding the rod high tends to put a belly of line between the rod tip and the water that gravity will pull toward you, dragging the fly anyway.

The fisherman holds his rod high to keep the line out of the fast current between him and a rising fish.

A midstream obstruction like a rock or log can sometimes be used to advantage. If you can cast so that your line drapes over the obstruction, it may hold your line upstream long enough to permit a drag-free float.

Throwing an extra amount of slack into your cast is probably the best way to conquer very tricky drag situations, and there is a way to exaggerate this effect. Reel in your line, clip off your fly and tippet, and add a new tippet of the same diameter—but longer. Adding a foot or so to your tippet will cause the last part of your leader to land in loose coils, giving you a foot or so of extra drift before drag sets in.

Mends can be used to help avoid drag, but I don't like to use them because they are difficult to accomplish without moving the fly as well as the line and leader. Remember to let some line slip from your hand as you mend to help alleviate this problem. I usually use mends only at

155

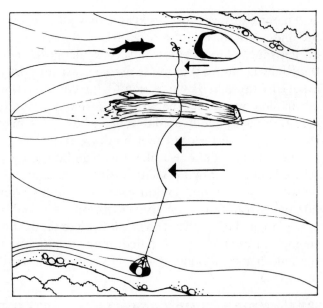

Using a midstream log to avoid drag.

the end of a drift, when the line starts to belly and drag is imminent anyway.

There are a few times when you'll want your fly to plop into the water with a distinct splat that the trout will notice. This technique is especially useful when fishing terrestrial imitations like ants, beetles, and grasshoppers, food that drops into the water. Trout are attracted to the sound of something falling into the water, especially during the summer, when terrestrial insects are abundant. Another time this technique is useful is when large, egg-laying stonefly adults are returning to the water, especially on the salmonfly hatch.

To make your fly drop onto the water with a tiny splash, just overpower your cast slightly and point the rod tip at the spot where you want your fly to land, rather than aiming high as you usually would.

There are instances where drag is a necessary addition to your presentation, but it must be controlled drag. Caddisfly adults, large stonefly adults, large mayflies, and grasshoppers may move across the surface of the water in a series of hops and flutters. Adult midges may careen across the surface like tiny motorboats.

If you notice trout taking the flies that are moving and ignoring those that are drifting motionless, it's time to add some controlled drag to your presentation. This drag must always occur in an upstream or across-stream direction, and you should position yourself across from or upstream of the trout.

For flies that are skittering across the surface of the water at a steady pace, most often seen with caddisflies and midges, try a skittering presentation. To do this, cast above and slightly beyond the rise, keep your rod tip high, and strip in line at a steady pace while wiggling your rod tip slightly. Your fly must stay above surface of the water and should not be pulled under, so choose a good floater with lots of hackle. Variants, spiders, and the various hackled caddis dry flies are all good choices. To help keep your fly on top of the water, you might also try greasing your leader with line dressing or silicone dry-fly paste.

Another technique is the slight upstream twitch followed by a drag-free drift, developed and aptly named "the sudden inch" by Leonard Wright. The sudden inch was developed for caddisflies and mayflies that flutter or twitch slightly, then ride the water for some distance. It's an attention-getting device that signals to the trout that your fly is alive and is ready to fly away at any moment.

To perform the sudden inch you'll need to cast either an upstream curve or a downstream slack-line cast. Your fly should land a few feet above the trout, and you should also be upstream of the trout's position.

As soon as your fly hits the water, raise your rod tip and move it in a quick upstream and upward motion until you see your fly twitch upstream for an inch or so. Then quickly drop your rod tip and let the fly float over the fish in a drag-free manner. The upstream curve or the slack line you've thrown will let the fly drift unhindered until it passes below the trout and out of his vision.

Whether your leader should float or sink when fishing dry flies is a subject that too many people put too much emphasis on. It's true that a floating leader does cast a bigger shadow on the bottom than one that is below the surface, but trout have sticks and blades of grass and other debris floating over them all day long. I do use a commercial leader sink called Mud under delicate conditions, especially in low clear water, but I use it more because it removes the shine from my leader than because it makes the leader sink. Natural debris doesn't reflect much light, and the flash from a shiny leader may spook trout.

When trout are taking drifting caddis or midge pupae, or emerging mayflies with that characteristic dimpling rise, you may want to grease all but the last foot of your leader and use an unweighted nymph. Your fly will drift just under the surface of the water, right where the natural flies are. You can get the same effect by using an emerger or floating nymph pattern, or even a standard dry fly that has not been treated with silicone fly dressing.

Even if you're blessed with 20:20 vision, you won't always be able to see your dry fly. It's hard to see a size 18 Blue Dun dry fly in a riffle from thirty feet away. Yet we fish tiny dull-colored flies in fast water, in the rain, and at dusk and after dark. How?

There's no secret. Just cast your fly above the rise, and even if you can't see the fly, strike when a rise occurs in the general area. You can almost always see the rise during the daytime, and at dark you can often hear it, especially in slow water. With practice, you'll be surprised at how well you can track your fly's drift, even when you can't see it.

What do you do when you rise a fish and either you fail to hook him or he refuses it at the last minute, splashing at your fly? The best thing to do is watch him for a while; see if he continues to rise. If you pricked him with the hook he'll probably stop feeding, but if he just refused the fly or rejected it before you tightened up, he may continue to rise. Rest him for a couple of minutes. Watch his rise form. What kind of insect is he really taking?

The most productive tactic for me in a situation like this is to change to a fly that is one size smaller and perhaps slightly different in shape. For example, if I rise him initially on a size 14 Hendrickson I might switch to a size 16 Red Quill. There is also a philosophy that says show him something radically different, but the fact that he showed any interest in your original offering means that you weren't far off.

A last minute refusal can also mean that your presentation wasn't quite right. Drag might have been setting in just as he rose to the fly. Try changing your position slightly.

Blind fishing dry flies, or fishing dry flies when no rises are seen, is a game of imagining that there is a trout rising in a particular spot. Remember those spots trout like best, along the banks, in depressions, and around rocks? Cast to likely spots, taking care that you approach them just as carefully as if a trout were rising there.

When temperatures are right, trout feed all day long, both below and on the surface. If the water is cloudy, very fast, or very deep he probably won't see your fly, but under clear water conditions, in water that is a foot to three feet in depth, blind fishing can be very productive.

Blind fishing is best in riffles or pocket water. Because you don't know exactly where the fish are, and you can approach them much closer in broken water, you'll spook fewer unseen fish here. Choose a visible fly, one with lots of hackle like a variant, or white wings like a Royal Wulff. Work upstream, hitting every fishy-looking spot within your casting range, then walk a few feet upstream and try some new water. A half dozen casts to each spot is usually sufficient—either there's nobody home, you've spooked him, or he's just not interested.

The only time I've found blind fishing to be productive in flat water is during the summer or fall when terrestrial insects are abundant. You have to be especially careful with your wading, moving very slowly, trying not to riffle the water. Pitch your terrestrial imitation to places where insects might fall into the water—under overhanging trees and along grassy or shrubby banks.

WET FLY AND NYMPH FISHING

Wet flies and nymphs can be fished upstream, downstream, across stream, and anywhere in between. Although trout sometimes prefer to take wet flies and nymphs drag-free, or dead drift, drag is not as much of a problem, because those little wakes aren't created underwater, and many aquatic insects and crustaceans do swim against or across currents.

The traditional and most common way to fish subsurface flies is to cast directly across stream, about 90 degrees to the current flow. The current pulls on the fly line, leader, and fly, causing the fly to swing across and downstream in an arc. In slow currents the arc will be fairly open and the fly will swing slowly across the current, even breaking the surface and skimming across the water. Your rod tip should point to where the line first touches the water and should follow the line as it drifts downstream.

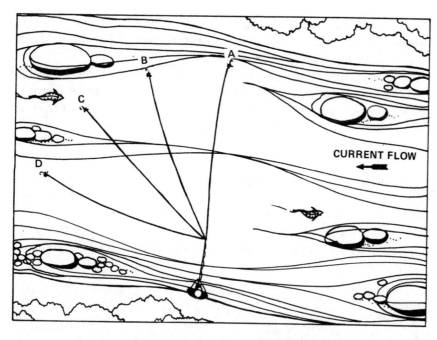

CURRENT FLOW

The standard wet-fly drift.

Strikes can occur almost anywhere in the drift and will show up as either a twitch or unnatural tightening of the line. If there is no slack in the line you will actually feel the strike as an electrifying jolt. On a tight line, especially if the fly is hanging downstream, the current's force on the line will set the hook for you. If there is slack in the line, you must strike immediately. The tightening of the line can mean only one thing —something has grabbed your fly. If you hesitate, he'll eject the fly before you have a chance to set the hook.

Fishing wet flies or nymphs in this manner, without any manipulation by the fisherman, is an effective way to cover a lot of water, especially if you fish two or three flies on droppers. It's also a relaxing way to fish. You're wading downstream, which requires a lot less effort, and the current is doing all the work for you. All you have to do is take a few steps downstream after each cast and make another cast.

Your line length remains constant, and you don't even have to false cast. In fact, you should false cast as little as possible, so that your flies stay wet and sink as soon as they hit the water.

Most strikes will appear toward the end of the drift, just as the fly begins to swing across the current. The fly begins to sink as soon as it lands, and keeps sinking until the belly that forms in the line begins to draw the fly across the current and toward the surface. Apparently this looks much like an aquatic insect rising to the surface.

After the fly completes its swing and is hanging directly downstream from you, it's a good idea to strip in line, a few inches at a time, for a couple of feet. Sometimes a trout will follow your fly and hesitate as it stops; the fly swimming back upstream triggers his instinct to strike. On a very long cast you'll want to retrieve some line anyway, so that you can pick up for another cast without working too hard and disturbing the water.

When bringing a subsurface fly directly upstream against the current, keep the rod at a 90-degree angle to the line, to act as a shock absorber against violent strikes. Your line is so tight under these circumstances that it's easy for even a small fish to break your tippet.

Although a wet fly drifting with the current on a tight line is usually effective, you may want to try manipulating the fly slightly as it swings. You can either twitch your rod tip slightly throughout the drift or use short strips or a hand-twist retrieve. Some nymphs swim quite rapidly just before they hatch, and the trout may be on the lookout for this type of behavior.

The problem with the standard across-stream presentation is that, all too often, the fly moves too fast and doesn't get deep enough. A trout is especially reluctant to pursue something that is moving a bit quicker than everything else he's been eating. Why chase something that might get away when a sure meal will drift along soon?

There are a number of ways to slow things down and get your fly

If the line is not mended, fast currents in the center of the stream will put an arc into the end of the fly line, causing the fly to whip around at the end of the swing.

deeper. One is to switch from a floating line to a sinking or sink-tip line with a short leader. Lines that are under the surface help keep the fly under, of course, but they also drift slower, because the subsurface currents are always slower than the surface currents.

Another is to hold your rod tip high, about 45 degrees above the surface of the water, following the fly's drift with the rod tip. The more line you keep off the water, the less the line will influence the swing of your fly.

Mending line in an upstream direction is a tactic many wet-fly fishermen use to get a better drift. As soon as the line hits the water, mend a loop of line upstream, letting the line that you flip upstream slip from the line you are holding in your stripping hand, rather than from the line that is already on the water. Every time the line begins to belly downstream, mend again, repeating the process throughout the drift.

A slack-line cast is a very useful tactic to use when trout are following emerging insects to the surface. Cast some slack exactly as if you were casting a dry fly directly across stream. The slack will allow the fly to sink and drift downstream naturally; as the line begins to tighten, the fly will rise quickly to the surface, mimicking the behavior of the natural insects.

You don't always have to cast wet flies or nymphs across stream, and changing the angle at which you cast can radically change the behavior of your fly as it drifts.

A quartering downstream cast with wet flies and nymphs produces a drift that has less drag because the line doesn't have a chance to belly as much, but it gives a drift that is fairly shallow. You can use mends or a slack-line cast to get the fly a little deeper. This presentation works best when trout are taking emerging caddis pupae and mayfly nymphs.

A quartering upstream cast lets your fly sink deeper before the line bellies and pulls the fly to the surface. It also allows you to use a deadly

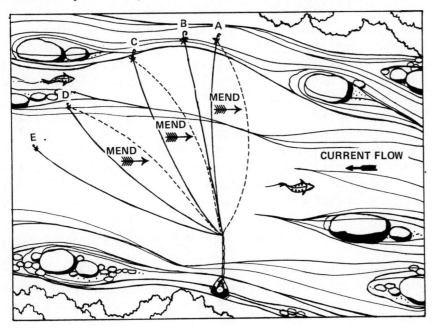

Mending line throughout a wet-fly drift will keep the fly swinging at a slow, uniform speed.

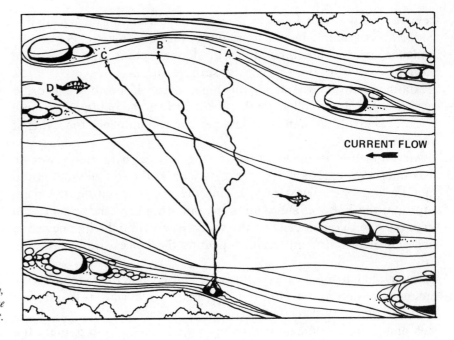

The slack-line cast, when used with a wet fly, will cause the fly to rise to the surface at the end of the drift.

tactic on a fish that has been spotted splashing at emerging nymphs just under the surface—the Leisenring lift. It is performed like this: cast well above the fish, letting the fly sink on a dead drift as it moves downstream. Follow the fly with your rod tip high as it drifts. When you think the fly is just upstream of the fish, stop following it with the rod tip. The line will belly quickly, drawing the fly to the surface right in front of the fish's nose. A similar presentation can be achieved by following the fly with a low rod tip, raising the rod at the same point, just above the fish.

You can also fish subsurface flies directly upstream, dead drift, just like a dry fly. This presentation produces the most insectlike drift, so it's usually done with nymphs, which are more realistic imitations of natural insects. Upstream nymphing is also the most demanding way of fly-fishing, both physically and mentally. You seldom see the fish, you almost never see your fly, and strikes can't be felt because of the slack line. Your only indication of a strike will be a twitch or slight upstream motion of your floating line.

Upstream nymphing requires some special tackle and tactics. Because you must watch the tip of your line, sinking lines are out. It's a way of fishing nymphs deeper than any other method, and to help get them right near the bottom, weighted nymphs or a couple of small split shot on the leader about a foot above the fly are often used. A common strategy is to start with a weighted nymph, adding split shot to the leader until the fly hangs bottom occasionally. A fly that isn't ticking bottom once in a while is probably not getting deep enough to interest the fish.

A word of caution when using heavily weighted flies or split shot: your cast won't behave as it normally would, because the extra weight slows things down and brings the fly dangerously close to your ear. It's best to stick to short casts, lobbing them sidearm rather than trying a standard overhead cast.

Fishing weighted nymphs upstream is a deadly tactic to use with stonefly or large mayfly nymphs in fast pocket water. Use short casts, hitting the pockets behind and in front of the rocks, striking instantly when the line jumps or hesitates. Keeping your rod tip high also keeps more line off the water, giving you a more lifelike, drag-free drift.

Upstream nymphing to visible trout in spring creeks and slow, clear pools requires sharp eyesight and stealth. You should be equipped with a long, fine leader, a small weighted mayfly nymph or scud imitation, a floating line, and polarized sunglasses.

You may see the trout move to take a nymph; you might spot his shadow, or see him as an indistinct shape on the bottom. Seldom will you get a good look at the fish, and often you'll fish to a stick or light-colored rock before you realize it's not a trout.

The procedure here is to sneak up quietly to the fish and cast your nymph far enough upstream so it is at his level when it passes his nose. Remember that the farther upstream you cast, the deeper your fly will get. Try to watch both the fish and your fly line at the same time. If the fish opens his mouth or so much as wiggles his fins as the fly passes near him, set the hook! If the tip of the fly line or the leader twitches, do likewise. A strike indicator, such as a tiny piece of cork painted red and strung on the leader, or a tiny piece of red yarn tied to the leader, may help you detect strikes. Takes will not be vicious, and seldom will you see the fish turn or dart for the fly.

A clever strategy to use when nymphing to visible trout is the induced take. Just before the fly reaches the fish, strip in a little more line than is necessary to gather the slack or raise your rod tip slightly, drawing the nymph toward the surface. This will often take a sullen trout that refuses a standard dead-drifted nymph.

FISHING STREAMERS

Streamers can be fished just like nymphs and wet flies—across stream, upstream, and downstream. Streamers will take all of these ways, even dead-drifted directly upstream. They are most effective, however, when you give them some manipulation, either by stripping in line as they drift or by pumping the rod tip to give them life.

Streamers are usually used when nothing else will attract the trout's attention, in high, dirty water, in the cold water of early season, and in very fast, broken water where smaller flies aren't visible.

You can cover a lot of water with streamers, because a trout will usually take your streamer on the first drift, or at least make a pass at it. If he's not interested, no amount of repeated casting will make him strike. If he swirls at your streamer but doesn't take, try one of a different color or one that's slightly smaller than the one you're using. Some fly fishermen

163

also use streamers to locate trout, returning later with a standard dry, wet, or nymph.

A popular way to fish streamers is to cast directly across the current to the far bank, stripping in line in foot-long pulls as the fly swings around in the current. This is one of the most effective ways of float-fishing large western rivers. Strikes to this kind of presentation will be quick and vicious, and the fish will usually hook themselves because of the tight line.

In rivers with very fast currents, you should angle your cast downstream to slow the swing of your fly. Just as in nymph and wet-fly fishing, casting slightly upstream or using a sink-tip or sinking line will also make your fly ride deeper and slower.

A deadly method of fishing streamers, although one that isn't used very often, is fishing them directly upstream. Try to retrieve line just slightly faster than the current, so that your fly darts along the bottom in little fits and pauses, just like a sculpin or crayfish darting from one rock to another.

Streamers will also work cast directly downstream. You can just let your fly hang in the current, using the current to give it life. You can also flip your rod back and forth, making the fly swim from side to side in the same spot. If this presentation doesn't work, try retrieving your streamer back upstream by stripping in line. Try short quick pulls, long steady pulls, or even erratic strips. One of these approaches may appeal to the trout.

UPSTREAM OR DOWN?

Older fly-fishing literature tells you that "the dry-fly fisherman always works upstream, and the wet fly, nymph, and streamer man works downstream." We've seen, however, that you can fish a dry fly downstream or a nymph upstream. Before you start to fish, decide whether you're going to use an upstream or downstream presentation and then move in the same direction as you fish. Otherwise you'll be fishing in water that you've just walked through, and the trout will probably be spooked.

If you've just covered a pool working upstream with a dry fly, should you turn around and try it with a wet? That depends on the size of the stream. In a small stream, you've just walked near all of the trout in the pool and spooked them. In a large river, however, you probably stayed to the shallow side and didn't get near any of the trout on the far side. They may not even know you're there, so why not give them a whirl with a wet fly.

NIGHT FISHING

On a moonlit night you can often extend the time you fish an evening hatch. Find a flat stretch of water and get into a casting position where

Large brown trout like this may feed almost entirely after dark.

the moon reflecting off the surface of the water will illuminate the rise forms. You probably won't be able to see your fly; just strike when you see a rise in the general vicinity of your fly. This isn't true night fishing, though.

Real night fishing means returning to the stream when it is pitch black, when every tree becomes a clutching, invisible obstacle and even the smallest rock on the bottom is dangerous.

Why night fish at all?

Most trout are daytime sight feeders and don't eat at night. In every population of brown trout, however, there are a few individuals who, when they grow to over fourteen inches, become meat hunters. They seldom feed when the sun is on the water, and forgo the traditional aquatic insect diet for minnows, crayfish, and large night-flying moths and beetles that fall into the water. My fish-biologist friend calls them "sharks."

Never night fish in an unfamiliar stretch of river. The best night fishing occurs on nights with no moon, and a flashlight shone into the water will spook the fish. You need to know every rock on the bottom.

Night fishing doesn't require long, fine leaders. A seven-and-a-half-foot leader with a 6- or 8-pound tippet is about right. The flies will be large and so will the fish. Fish smaller than twelve inches are rare after dark.

Flies should be large and bushy. Large dries like salmon dry flies or hair bass bugs are good, as are unweighted streamers like the Muddler Minnow or Picket Pin. Palmer-hackled wet flies like the Wooly Worm will also produce after dark. The pattern doesn't seem to matter as long as it is bushy enough to produce vibrations in the water. Night-feeding trout use their lateral line hearing to find their prey.

The best places to night fish are shallow heads and tails of pools. Unlike daytime drift feeders, night-feeding trout leave their positions and hunt for their food, especially in shallow areas rich in crayfish and minnows.

Your casts should be short, no more than thirty feet, and you should work quietly and slowly downstream. Cast straight across the current and allow your flies to swing in the current. Occasionally a steady hand-twist retrieve throughout the swing will help, especially in slower currents.

Strikes will not be hard; they'll be felt as a sudden deliberate tightening of the line. Nighttime is no time to baby a big trout—play it as quickly as the heavy leader will allow, as you never know exactly where the snags are after dark.

Best times to night fish are hot, humid, still nights during the new moon, anytime from midnight until dawn.

TIME OF YEAR AND TIME OF DAY

Streams change with the seasons. Fly-fishing is always better when there are insects hatching, and there is a general rule that says that the best time of the day for insect hatches is when the temperature is most comfortable for you. In April and May in the East, the best time is the middle of the afternoon, when the sun warms the water and the air. From late May through August, the most pleasant time of day for us is evenings and mornings, and this is when you'll find the fish feeding most actively. In the fall, we return to the midday feeding schedule of early spring.

In the Rocky Mountain region, nights are almost always cold, even in the middle of summer. As a result, there are seldom any hatches in this area until the middle of the morning. Best fishing at this high altitude occurs throughout the daytime hours, although you may see some feeding fish in the evening after an unusually hot day.

BIG AND LITTLE TROUT STREAMS

Don't let big rivers intimidate you, and don't be afraid of trying to fly fish tiny brooks. Big rivers, with their varying currents, are just a bunch of little rivers running together. Divide a big river up into little streams in your mind and fish each little river as though it were a separate entity.

Tiny brooks that look totally impossible for fly-fishing can be surprisingly easy. There may be spots that are so brushy you'll have to pass them up, but you'll usually be able to find areas where there is plenty of room behind you for a back cast, even though the banks may be brushy. Fishing straight upstream in tiny brooks is probably the best idea anyway, because casts will be short and you may spook most of the fish trying to work downstream. In a small bubbly stream you can sometimes approach the fish so closely that you'll barely have to cast more than your leader.

SMALLMOUTH BASS IN STREAMS

Smallmouth bass will be found in streams that warm to over 60 degrees Fahrenheit in the late spring. They occupy places in streams that are similar to places where you'll find trout, but smallmouths aren't as streamlined as trout and prefer the eddies that occur behind rocks and logs, on the edges of fast currents, along rock ledges, and especially in the tails of pools. In large, slow rivers smallmouths will be found on the edges of weed beds along the banks. Bass will also be found in backwaters and eddies that would be too slow to hold trout.

Smallmouths aren't as selective as trout, nor are they as spooky. You can't splash a lot of water around, nor can you step right on top of them, but you don't have to be as cautious as you would with a wild brown trout.

When smallmouths are feeding on hatching insects you can use the same tactics you'd use for trout. When they're surface feeding, though, they'll take almost any floating fly. You might want to drop a small popper in front of a feeding smallmouth, twitching it slightly as it drifts in front of him.

If you can't see any smallmouths feeding on insects or chasing minnows, choose a strategy that allows you to cover as much water as possible. This usually means working downstream, either wading or in a slow-drifting boat. Use either a streamer or a popper, casting to rocks, under overhanging branches, and alongside logs.

Smallmouths usually prefer a fast retrieve, especially with streamers. Steady foot-long pulls will keep your streamer moving fast enough, although you might want to slow down your retrieve if no strikes are forthcoming. With poppers and hair bugs, cast them just upstream of where you think the fish is and make the bug pop by using hard, short strips. You should pull hard enough to make the popper blurp and throw a few bubbles each time. About one pop per second is about right, although slower or faster retrieves may produce more results on some days.

When fishing for smallmouths, try to avoid slack line and using your rod tip to give the fly action, which also produces unwanted slack line. Smallmouths have harder mouths than trout and seldom hook themselves, so you must maintain a tight line and strike harder than you would for trout.

The Crayfish fly, fished on a sink-tip line, is a deadly way to catch smallmouths in streams. It is especially deadly in deep, slow pools when smallmouths are reluctant to chase poppers or streamers. Cast across and slightly upstream, letting the sinking tip pull the fly down. Then retrieve with short strips with pauses in between.

If smallmouths don't respond to these proven techniques, there are a number of things you can try. One is to fish a hair bug or big salmon dry fly upstream, dead drift, just as you would for trout. This is especially productive in tails of pools.

When the water is shallow and clear, switch from a standard popping bug to a bullethead hair bug or feather minnow, something that doesn't make as much noise. Smallmouths often hide in slow, shallow water, places where you'd never expect to find bass of any size. They wait in these areas to ambush schools of minnows.

You may have days on smallmouth rivers where they chase your streamers or poppers all the way across the river but never actually strike your flies. It's a frustrating experience. The best solution I've found when they're behaving like this is to throw them tiny trout-sized dries or nymphs, sizes 10 through 14. Cast to the spot you last saw the bass chasing your fly, then twitch them slightly to attract attention. Strikes to this kind of presentation will be slow and subtle, more like the way a big brown trout would inhale your fly.

OTHER FISH IN STREAMS

Largemouth bass, walleye, pike, and pickerel as well as panfish may also be found in streams. All of these fish prefer very slow water and will be found mainly in backwaters and eddies. Because these fish will be found in miniature still-water environments within a stream, they can be caught with the tactics discussed in the next chapter.

Migratory fish like salmon and steelhead have different needs than trout because they are moving and not feeding, so they are discussed in Chapter 10.

9
Still Waters

When most people think of fly-fishing they think of moving water and trout and salmon, yet lakes, ponds, and reservoirs present fly-fishing opportunities that far surpass those of rivers and streams.

Fly-fishing, at least fly-fishing that is efficient and fun, is limited to shallow-water fishing. We can fly-fish to about thirty feet under the surface of a lake; after this depth fly-fishing would be limited to trolling with lead-core line. Even with an extra-fast sinking fly line, fishing depths of more than twenty feet is a lot of work, and it's tough to cover a lot of area with flies in deep water.

Fortunately, bass, panfish, and pike do most of their feeding in shallow water. Even such deepwater dwellers as lake trout and landlocked salmon, which generally reside in the cool depths of sixty feet or more, can be taken right near the surface on flies during the spring and fall when the water temperature near shore is under 55 degrees.

Water temperature is as important in still waters as it is in streams. Shallow ponds that warm above 65 degrees and don't have any cool-water depths or spring holes will not support trout. Instead, you'll find warm-water species like bass or panfish, which can tolerate water temperatures above 80 degrees. Alpine lakes that never warm above 60 degrees may have trout in them and nothing else.

169

Many large lakes and reservoirs, bodies of water that are deep enough to stratify during the summer, are what are called "two-story" lakes. In the early spring, just after ice-out, you'll find trout in the shallows; when the water warms in the early summer, the trout retreat to deeper water, out of reach of the fly-fisher. The fly-rodder shouldn't forsake these lakes, though, because just as the trout go into deep water, warm-water fish like bass, pike, and panfish become active in the shallows. If the water warms even further during the summer, bass retreat to the depths during the day, but they usually return to the shallows in early morning and evening to feed. And the panfish are always there.

In streams you use the current to help you deliver flies. The current helps you determine where the fish will be. It sometimes even sets the hook for you.

In still waters, unless you're fishing inlet or outlet streams, you don't have the current to help you. Slack-line casts, curve casts, and a high rod tip are not only unneeded, they're undesirable. Whether you fish wet or dry, your line must always be tight, and except in instances where you have trout or bass cruising the surface for insects, your fly must be kept in motion. This is especially important when fishing sub-surface flies—a fish may take your sunken fly in still water when it's not moving, but you'd never know it. Fortunately, stillwater insects do more swimming than their swift-water counterparts, so a fly that is swimming looks realistic to the fish.

Because fish in still waters seldom stay put for long, you'll probably want a greater variety of fly-line types, unless you fish only shallow ponds, where you can do all of your fishing with a floating line. You'll want at least a sinking-tip line for times when they retreat to the depths, and for very deep (up to thirty feet) fishing, if you choose to chase them that far, you'll need a full fast-sinking fly line. Although shooting heads sink quickly, they are not as desirable in still waters. Because you'll be doing a lot of line handling, the thin running line becomes a problem, as it tangles more easily than the thicker diameter of a regular fly line.

You can fly-fish from the shore of a lake, but you're fairly limited to the water near shore, and if the banks are lined with trees you'll be restricted to the roll cast or a forward cast that is parallel to the shoreline. You'll be better off getting into the water somehow. Wading will get you around in a lake, but again, you're limited to the shallow water.

Belly boats are becoming very popular for still-water fly-fishing. They consist of an inner tube covered with a nylon protective shell that includes a seat, and may also have pockets for fly boxes and other gear. The belly-boat user wears stocking-foot waders and either swim fins or paddle pushers on his feet. Swim fins push you backward and have the advantage of moving you around fairly quickly; paddle pushers move you forward, but they're slower than swim fins.

Belly boats offer advantages over conventional water craft. Since you're sitting low in the water, you can sneak up quietly to feeding fish that might be spooked by the higher profile of a fisherman in a boat or canoe. Belly boats are very stable. Fly-fishermen who chase big rainbows and cutthroats in large western reservoirs prefer them, even dur-

A belly boat, showing seat, accessory pouches, and swim fins.

ing winter storms. They ride with the waves and are almost impossible to tip over. Belly boats can also be toted uninflated into remote lakes, where it would be impossible to carry a boat. Once at your destination, you can inflate your boat with a CO_2 cartridge or hand pump.

You can fly-fish in any kind of boat, from a rowboat to a fancy bass boat with swivel seats and a depth finder. The small boats—canoes, punts, and rowboats—are preferred, however, because they are more maneuverable and can be brought within range of a rising fish with less disturbance.

As with wading in streams, the less you disturb the water, the better. Getting upwind and drifting into an area where fish are feeding is preferable to rowing or paddling.

There is no special trick to fly-fishing from a canoe or belly boat, except that your movement will be somewhat restricted. If a trout rises directly behind you, it may require a little more care in turning around than when you're standing in a stream. Remember that in all cases, fly casting should involve only your wrist, forearm, and a little upper arm. It's especially important when fishing from a canoe. Too much body English can send a series of waves out from your canoe, spooking cautious fish.

Because you will be sitting very low to the water, a longer rod helps to keep your back cast high. I would never fish from a canoe or belly boat with a rod shorter than eight feet.

TROUT IN LAKES

A trout lake or pond is often an intimidating prospect to a stream fisherman. Here, trout may be around logs or weed beds, but they could just as soon be in open water. They use the security of deep water, rather than rocks or logs, when they are frightened by predators.

Where do you start? The first thing to do is look for rises. The trout have given themselves away at this point; you *know* where at least a few are. Binoculars are essential on very large trout lakes.

Streams entering lakes are always hot spots for trout. Streams bring cooler, more highly oxygenated water to lakes, carry in aquatic and terrestrial insects, and often have concentrations of baitfish around their mouths. Smelt and other baitfish spawn in streams, and trout will cruise the area where a stream enters a lake, waiting for baitfish to ascend or descend.

Where a stream enters a pond or lake is always a hotspot for trout.

Trout often use inlet streams for spawning. Browns, rainbows, and landlocked salmon *must* spawn in moving water, so at some time of year they'll be in or near these streams. Look for brook trout, brown trout, salmon, and domestic (hatchery-raised) rainbows here in October and November. Most strains of rainbow and cutthroat spawn in the spring, anytime between March and June.

Brook and lake trout have the unique ability to spawn in lakes and ponds, but they must have a gravel-bottomed area with springs near it; otherwise they spawn in tributary streams, like the other species.

The influence of a stream can extend hundreds of feet out into a lake. There is often a deep channel where the trout can hide while having a plentiful supply of food. A nymph or streamer fished through these channels will often produce trout all day long.

Streams often enter lakes underground, in which case they're called springs. They can be found by taking water temperatures at various spots. The area near a spring will be noticeably cooler than the surrounding water in the summer, warmer during the early spring and late fall. Springs may also show up as light-colored patches of sand in clear water.

Be careful when fishing spring-fed lakes or high-altitude lakes, places where shallow water stays comfortable for trout throughout the season. Don't fish out in the middle. The shallows are where you'll find aquatic plants and algae, and thus the insects and baitfish that trout feed upon. The depths may often be barren because sunlight can't penetrate to the bottom.

Outlets of lakes are often good places for trout, because some species will spawn in them, and many baitfish also spawn there. If the outlet has enough current you'll want to fish it just as you would a stream.

Shoals, drop-offs, islands, points—any interface between shallow and deep water will hold trout, especially in the spring and fall.

If you've ever been out on a lake on a windy day you've probably seen long lines of foam that run perpendicular to the wind direction. These are called wind streaks, and are points between waves where turbulence is at a minimum. Foam, debris, and insects become trapped in these areas. If you look carefully at wind streaks, you'll often find trout cruising along the line, picking up drowned and hatching insects.

Trout have the same foods in lakes as they do in streams, plus a few more. Caddisflies and mayflies will be common, stoneflies much less so except in windswept rocky shores. Dragonflies, damselflies, scuds, leeches, midges, and baitfish are perhaps the most important trout foods in lakes, so you'll want to imitate these with appropriate fly patterns and fishing techniques. What do trout do in still waters? Do they feed the same way they do in streams?

In shallow, clear, spring-fed ponds, trout, especially brook and brown trout, behave much the same. They sit on the bottom, waiting for food to swim by, rising up to grab a morsel and returning to their spots. When food is really abundant, as in a midge or mayfly hatch, they'll cruise for their food.

It's fascinating to watch a cruising trout, or "gulper," as they're called in the West. Trout will swim along, gulp two or three or maybe six insects in quick succession, then swim along without feeding, then gulp again. Or they'll feed with evenly spaced gulps. They may cruise in a straight line. The may even cruise in a circle or a figure eight.

Rainbow trout always cruise, whether they're eating or not, and so do the other species in large lakes. Trout that are exclusively baitfish eaters cruise constantly, on the move for schools of baitfish.

You can see that if you're fishing a shallow pond you might want to stay put, but if you're in a big lake and not catching fish, you might as well move around until you find some.

Dry Flies

Dry flies are less useful for trout in lakes than they are in streams. Still waters have hatches, of course, and you shouldn't leave your dry flies home, but many of the stillwater food forms don't hatch; leeches, scuds, and baitfish live their entire lives underwater. Dragonflies and damselflies and many species of mayfly and caddisfly crawl out on vegetation to hatch, so the fish don't have a chance to get to them as they hatch. These insects have to return to water to mate and lay eggs, though, so spinner falls and mating flights can be important.

Fish in still waters get a long look at your dry fly; unless the surface of a lake is riffled, they get a *very* good look at it. Your leader should be as long and as fine as you dare—a twelve-footer is standard. You might even want to extend your leader to fifteen feet by making the butt section and tippet longer. Too long a leader will also defeat your purpose, however, because if the tippet lands in a big pile around your dry fly, a trout may shy away. You might be able to get away with this in the broken water of a stream, but not in a pond.

Fishing a dry fly blind in a lake is a futile gesture, so you should look for rises. As in streams, dimpling rises mean small flies or spent spinners, splashy rises mean big flies, caddisflies, or emerging nymphs, and bulges mean emerging nymphs or ones that swim just under the surface, like water boatmen or back swimmers.

Rises that are sporadic or erratic should be hit immediately with your fly, while he's still looking at the surface. This can be a frustrating experience—you don't know if it's one fish, cruising and rising once in a while, or a bunch of them feeding occasionally. My best results have come from casting a dry in the center of the activity and letting it sit there, even for three or four minutes.

Do you just sit there and stare at your dry fly? Usually. Take all the slack out of your line, without moving the fly, and wait for the strike. Keep your rod tip low, not only to get the line tight so you can strike, but also to keep the wind from blowing around that portion of your fly line between the rod tip and the water.

Sometimes a subtle twitch will make the trout notice your fly, especially if they're only rising occasionally or there are so many natural flies on the water that the trout ignore yours. Try one twitch, about an inch or so, then let the fly sit motionless again. Try another if you don't get any response. Your fly should be well dressed with fly flotant if you're going to twitch it, and your leader should be greased as well, so that when you twitch the fly it moves lightly across the surface, like the naturals.

When the trout are taking caddisflies or adult midges you can sometimes use a steady retrieve with great success, making the fly skitter steadily across the surface of the water. Six-inch strips of line with very little pause in between will give you a good steady pace.

When trout are gulping, or feeding steadily and predictably, sit somewhere out of range and observe them. You can usually pick up a pattern. Paddle or drift quietly to a spot where a trout will intercept you. Cast

Fishing to a rising trout. The fisherman sits in the canoe and waits until a cruising trout comes into range.

your fly well ahead of him and wait for him to come to the fly. The worst thing you can do in this situation is try to chase a gulper, because you'll usually succeed only in putting him down. You'll sometimes have to wait quite a while for a gulper or group of gulpers to return, but the wait is well worth it.

Wet Flies and Nymphs

Wet flies, other than the soft-hackled wingless variety, are seldom used these days in still waters. The trout get a very good look at your fly when there's no current, and the more representative nymphs are far more successful in still waters. There are many patterns of nymphs that were developed especially for still-water fishing. Because there is no current to make your nymph look alive, soft, pulsating feathers like marabou, ostrich herl, and soft webby bird hackles are commonly used to give stillwater nymphs "action."

Nymph fishing in still waters involves casting the fly and retrieving it back to you by stripping in line. It's as simple as that. A trout may take your nymph as it's sinking, before you begin your retrieve, but these strikes usually go undetected. You need to have a tight line and a moving fly to detect strikes. You'll see your line or leader twitch, or if you're stripping fast or the trout hits hard you'll feel the strike.

It is very important to keep your rod tip low when working a nymph in still waters. With a high rod tip you'll miss strikes because of the slack line between your rod tip and the water. That low rod tip is also important because of line control.

When your rod tip is hanging in the air the line doesn't drop straight to the water, it hangs in an arc. If you strip six inches of line, the arc straightens and the fly moves six inches toward you. Then, however, gravity takes over to put that arc back into the line and the fly moves again toward you, this time out of your control. With your rod tip close to the water, the fly moves exactly as fast as you strip in line. You have complete control over what your fly is doing, even though it may be forty or fifty feet away.

Besides fly pattern, two things are important in still-water nymphing: depth and the speed at which you retrieve. Depth can, of course, be controlled by the type of fly line you use, and the fly can be weighted to get it deeper more quickly. The amount of time you wait before you begin the retrieve will also control the fly's depth.

A good way to find the correct depth is called the countdown method. Count to ten before you begin your retrieve on the first cast, fifteen on the second, and so on until you catch a fish or hang up on the bottom.

The type of fly line you use will determine how "flat" your nymph rides in the water. A weighted nymph fished on a floating line will gradually rise toward the surface as it is retrieved, good when aquatic insects are hatching. The same nymph fished on a sinking line will swim in a straight line or actually get deeper as you retrieve it—good for leech and crustacean imitations.

The speed at which your fly swims is controlled by your stripping hand. Unless you know what worked yesterday or exactly what the fish are feeding on or what speed the guy in the boat next to you (who is catching lots of fish!) is using, it's going to be a matter of trial and error.

I like to start with steady six-inch pulls of line. This is a pretty standard retrieve and will often produce fish. If not, try fast foot-long pulls, long, slow, steady pulls, or even use a hand-twist retrieve for an extra-slow, steady retrieve.

Leeches and dragonflies are fairly quick swimmers, so if any of these critters are in evidence try a fast retrieve. Dragonflies move in quick spurts, as they are jet-propelled—they expel water through their abdomens when they want to go somewhere in a hurry.

There is one type of nymph that is either not retrieved at all or is drawn along slowly, just under the surface. This is the emerger or pupal imitation, and it should be fished just as you would a dry fly, with a long, greased leader and floating line. Strikes will be visible as a boil in the vicinity of your fly.

Streamers

The same techniques used to fish nymphs are used to fish streamers, except that in most cases a fast retrieval or an erratic one is all you'll need. You're either trying to imitate a wounded or scared bait fish or just trying to catch a trout's attention. In either case, a fast retrieve will get the nod more often than a slow one.

Streamers are more effective than nymphs in very large lakes, especially if you're some distance from shore. There are few aquatic insects in deep water, so if the trout are there they will be eating baitfish.

On big water, streamers are often trolled. Although it's not fly casting, you are still fishing with a fly and a fly rod, and it's a good way to cover a lot of water. Once the trout are found, you can stop the boat and cast to them.

Trolling is usually done with big, long streamers, size 2, 4, or 6; or even tandem streamers, which may be three or four inches long. Using a long, level leader, usually a piece of 6- or 8-pound monofilament, about sixty feet of fly line is trolled behind the boat, and the boat is driven or padded in a zigzag pattern off rocky points, islands, and stream mouths. It is a deadly way to catch trout and landlocked salmon just after ice-out, when the fish are near the surface, and is especially popular in New England.

BASS

Catching bass, both largemouth and smallmouth, on a fly rod is a matter of finding them when they're in relatively shallow water. Bass will be found in the shallows, spawning, when spring water temperatures reach the high 50s, and they'll be there all day long. As long as the water temperatures in the shallows remain below 75 degrees you'll

Good largemouth water in the early morning mist.

continue to find them in shallow water all season long, but when the water gets too warm they'll retreat to deeper water, at least during the day. Because the supply of minnows, frogs, insects, and crayfish is pretty slim in deep water, the bass won't stay there all the time. In the early morning and late evening they'll cruise into the shallows to feed.

Look for largemouths around lily pads, brush piles, cattails, or any other structure that provides shade and protection for both the largemouth and his prey. Largemouths seldom feed out in the open, so your casting should be as accurate as possible, striving to place your fly as close as possible to these areas. I've seen bass ignore a popper that was cast a few feet from their log, yet pounce on the same fly when it was dropped right next to the log.

While the largemouth likes mud or silt bottoms, you'll almost always find smallmouths over rocky bottoms. The two species may sometimes feed side by side over sandy shoals in the evening, but other than that their habitats are segregated. Smallmouth bass prefer crayfish over any other kind of food, and crayfish are most abundant along rocky shorelines. Rocks anywhere from the size of bowling balls to big boulders are preferred.

A look at the shoreline will give you clues to where the smallmouths are. Smallmouths like drop-offs, so if the banks are steep, chances are there will be a drop-off close to shore. A light-colored bottom shading

Even a small largemouth can consume large prey. This one took a deer-hair bug.

into an area of darker water anywhere in a lake also indicates possible smallmouth habitat. Cast your flies into the area where the shallow water ends and the deep water begins.

Both species of bass will eat insects such as mayflies and dragonflies, especially smallmouths. When they're feeding on insects, use the same nymph and dry-fly strategies you'd use for trout. Poppers and streamers, however, are the most consistent producers of fly-rod bass.

Unlike trout, you don't have to see rising bass to catch them on surface lures. They'll be waiting to ambush prey, and if the water is shallow and clear enough they'll find your popper or hair bug—and attack it with a vengeance.

The usual strategy with a popper is to cast it into a bassy-looking spot and let it sit for a few minutes without moving it. I don't mean a few seconds, either—wait at least a full minute, or until all the ripples made by the popper landing on the water dissipate. While you're waiting, carefully remove all the slack from your line by stripping until the line is tight. Don't forget to keep the rod tip low to the water.

Strikes will often come at this point, so you should be ready to set the hook at any time. Bass may eyeball a popper for a long time, inches from the fly, suddenly lunging for it with a tremendous swirl.

If nothing hits your motionless popper, give it a little twitch. With a tight line and a low rod tip, strip in enough line to barely move the popper. Let it sit again. Try another twitch. Then strip hard enough to make the popper gurgle. Let it sit again. Try three or four pops in a row. By fishing this way you can see which strategy produces strikes, and you can then use that method exclusively.

Sometimes a steady retrieve, with foot-long pulls starting as soon as the fly hits the water, will work better than the sit-and-wait method. Try all kinds of retrieves until you draw strikes, but avoid using the rod tip to give your popper action. Using the rod tip throws slack into the line and makes it very difficult to set the hook.

179

It's best to fish poppers until they're fifteen or twenty feet from the boat. Bass may often follow a popper for a long time before they decide to take it. Besides, the shape of a popper makes it difficult to pick up for another cast, especially with a lot of line out. When the popper is close to the boat, you can lift it straight out of the water.

Fishing a popper in the thick stuff.

In general, smallmouths prefer a faster-paced retrieve than largemouths. With both species, deep or murky water usually calls for loud, hard pops, while clear or shallow water requires gentle twitches and longer pauses in between.

Hair bugs and bullethead minnows are fished in the same manner. Although they don't pop as loud as hard-bodied poppers, you should still experiment with fast and slow retrieves and hard and gentle pulls.

When fishing for smallmouths, cast right next to protruding rocks and on top of submerged boulders. If the water near shore is deep, don't be afraid to cast your bug right onto shore and then work it back to you. Check your hook point often when doing this to make sure that it hasn't glanced off a rock.

In largemouth country you should toss your bugs as close as possible to logs, brushy banks, and beds of cattails. When fishing large expanses of weed beds, use a weedless popper or hair bug and cast right onto lily pads or mats of floating weeds. Twitch the popper into openings between the weeds and let it sit motionless. Twitch it across the opening, back onto the weeds, and repeat for the next opening.

Streamers can be used for bass in the same place as poppers. Fished with a floating line, they can be crawled over weed beds, next to logs, and over submerged brush piles. Use a fast retrieve for smallmouths and a slower speed for largemouths.

Streamers are more useful than bugs over the whole season. They can be used in the shallows, and they can also be fished on sinking and sink-tip lines when bass are in deeper water. Bass will be in twenty to thirty feet of water in the spring and fall, when the water temperature is in the 50s, and also during the summer, when surface water temperatures are above 80 degrees. When bass are in deep water, they're fairly sluggish, and a slow retrieve should be used for both largemouths and smallmouths. Use the countdown method and fish your streamers just off the bottom.

The muddler-type bass streamer is an interesting fly that can be fished either deep or right on the surface. The hollow deer-hair head will keep the fly just under the surface. Fished on a floating line, it imitates a struggling minnow. Try both steady retrieves and a stop-and-go presentation.

The same fly can be used on a sinking line. The buoyancy of the fly makes it ride above the bottom, but the sinking line keeps it swimming deep. You can fish over logs and rocky bottoms without hanging up, as your fly line will slide along the bottom without snagging on obstructions.

Streamers have another big advantage over poppers and hair bugs. The long, slim shape of a streamer is much easier to cast than an air-resistant popper or bug. If you have to cast into the wind, you'll find a streamer to be more manageable than a bug or popper.

PIKE AND PICKEREL

Pike and pickerel feed actively throughout the winter, so they are some of the first fish available to the fly rodder in the spring. They can be found in shallow water most of the spring, near submerged weed beds, drop-offs, and near sluggish tributary streams. When the water warms to over 60 degrees, pike will retreat to twenty or thirty feet, returning to the shallows in the fall. Pickerel will stay in very shallow water all season long.

Just after ice-out, fish a very brightly colored streamer on a sink-tip line in two to six feet of water. You should retrieve it slowly in early spring, because a pike's metabolism is in low gear then and he won't chase a quick-moving fly.

The most exciting time to catch pike and pickerel is when the shallows begin to warm and they are actively feeding. Use a floating line and fish streamers and poppers with a very fast stripping motion, just as fast as you can retrieve them. Strikes will be vicious, and because of their sharp teeth you'll want to use a foot of 30-pound monofilament as a shock tippet.

181

A small pike caught on a streamer.

Pike can be taken on streamers when they're in deep water during the summer. Use a full-sinking line, cast out about fifty feet, and let the line sink almost to the bottom. Then strip like mad.

Unlike bass, pike and pickerel feed actively throughout the day, so they can fill in some otherwise unproductive hours on weedy lakes and ponds.

PANFISH

Bluegills. Bluegills, pumpkinseeds, rock bass, flier, green sunfish, and other small members of the sunfish family can be taken on almost any small fly. They will be found in warm, shallow water, around weed beds, overhanging trees, docks, and pilings.

The best time to catch sunfish is while they're spawning, when the water temperature approaches 65 degrees. You'll see saucer-shaped beds around silty or sandy shallows, usually right out in the open. Anything that lands near these nests will be attacked, and no method is more fun than using a small rubber-legged popper or sponge-rubber bag.

Cast your bug right over a nest. It will often be pounced on immediately; if not, give it a twitch or two. Don't move your fly too fast, as the larger sunfish prefer a slowly retrieved bug to one that is skimming across the surface.

Later in the year they will move to shaded areas near the shore. Sunfish may move into deeper water. Try a wet fly or nymph retrieved slowly and steadily on a sink-tip line.

Sunfish will sometimes get a little selective about their food, especially later in the year. If they refuse your standard bluegill bugs, try a small dry fly on a 4X or 5X tippet. The pattern doesn't seem to matter, just the more delicate presentation and profile.

White bass, white perch, yellow bass. These closely related species are favorite targets for a small streamer. Look for them in estuaries, shallow bays of large lakes, and channels between lakes, and around warm-water discharges of power plants.

Traveling in schools, these spirited fighters herd baitfish near the surface mornings and evenings. When you find a school, toss a streamer or small popper into the area and retrieve it with foot-long strips. During the day they can be taken near drop-off areas and shoals with a streamer fished on a sink-tip line.

Yellow perch. Yellow perch are another panfish that travel in large schools, usually over weed beds in two to twenty feet of water. When you catch a perch, stay put—there are bound to be more in the area. They may come to the surface to inspect a popper, but will seldom strike one. Small wets, nymphs, and streamers fished very slowly near the bottom produce the best results.

Crappie. These are voracious minnow feeders that feed in and around weed beds and brush piles, usually over a silty bottom. They seldom pass up a small streamer fished on a sink-tip line in four to eight feet of water.

Walleye. Walleyes are deep-dwelling fish that avoid bright light. They congregate to spawn around large inlet streams in the early spring. At this time they're easy to take on large, brightly colored streamers.

After spawning, walleyes will be found near large sand or gravel bars. During the day you'll need to fish your streamers slowly on a full-sinking line, but on gloomy days or at night walleyes can be caught near the surface on streamers and poppers.

Because lakes and ponds have more diverse fish species than streams, fly-fishing with a universal fish-taker like a streamer can be an interesting proposition. In the spring it's possible to catch a trout, a bass, a pike, and half a dozen species of panfish on consecutive casts. The mystery of not knowing what kind of fish will take your fly next adds a lot to the pleasure of fly-fishing in still waters.

10
Salmon, Steelhead, and Saltwater Fly-Fishing

Atlantic salmon, steelhead, and the various saltwater species are the big game of fly-fishing. They all require a lot of persistence, usually heavy tackle, and large flies. The same rod, something around nine feet long for a 9-weight line, can be used to fish for all of them, except large tarpon, billfish, or tuna, which require a 12-weight outfit.

This chapter requires a familiarity with many of the techniques discussed in Chapters 8 and 9, so I would recommend you read those chapters first even if you don't intend to fish for trout and bass.

ATLANTIC SALMON

The Atlantic salmon is tailor-made for fly fishing. It takes a fly well, perhaps better than any other kind of lure or bait. Salmon are superb fighters, their leaping ability surpassed only by the tarpon's. There are few rivers in North America where you can legally catch sea-run Atlantic salmon on anything but an unweighted fly.

Yet, in our anthropomorphic way of assigning intelligence levels to fish, the Atlantic salmon is one of the dumbest fish that swims. When they are in a taking mood, you can wade clumsily, run a boat over them, and turn around and catch one on the most unlikely fly, with a cast that barely straightens.

You can also fish over a dozen salmon "laying in" in a clear pool for hours without drawing a rise.

Salmon do not need to feed on their spawning runs, so they never *have* to take a fly. They feed voraciously as young parr for one to eight years before they run to the ocean, then grow quickly on a diet of shrimp and capelin. When they return to freshwater rivers to spawn, anywhere from one to three years later, they have plenty of energy stored up, enough to run a hundred-mile river, fight an angler's hook, spawn, overwinter, and return to the sea the following spring. Yet we can elicit a feeding reflex from the salmon with our flies.

A nineteen-pound Atlantic salmon caught in Iceland on a small wet fly. Tony Skilton

Adult Atlantic salmon are divided into two groups: grilse and salmon. A grilse is a fish that has been to sea for only one year and weighs from three to six pounds; a salmon has spent at least two years at sea and weighs from seven to over forty pounds upon returning to the river. Unlike Pacific salmon, Atlantic salmon can survive the rigors of spawning and may spawn two, three, or even four times.

Adult salmon return to freshwater rivers any time from May through October in rivers from the Connecticut north to Labrador. Some rivers are "early run," others are late, and some rivers have a multiple run: grilse at one time and salmon at another. The cue appears to be proper water temperature. Before you plan a salmon-fishing trip, be sure that your vacation time coincides with a likely time for a run of fish.

Salmon will enter a river on a rise of water or high tide, then make tracks for the vicinity of their spawning grounds. Early fish may hold in spring-fed pools for a month or more; late arrivals have been known to travel over twenty miles a day in their haste to mate. Nature times things so that they all arrive in the headwater spawning areas at about the same time, usually in late fall. Laws prohibit fishing over salmon that are actually on the spawning beds, closing the season before the fish begin spawning and sometimes closing upper areas of rivers to fishing.

The best situation for salmon fishing is when a large group of fish is moving on a moderate rise of water. Heavy, dirty floodwater makes fishing difficult. When a river is low, clear, or warm they show less enthusiasm for taking flies, although special flies and tactics have been developed for these difficult periods.

Salmon will rest above and below areas that require energy to pass, such as falls and rapids. They will be found anywhere near the main flow of the river, because their purpose is to use that flow to guide them upstream. They'll seldom be found in back eddies or side channels, but may rest in very shallow water if it's near the main flow. Anything that breaks the current—rocks, points, ledges, depressions in the stream bed, tails of pools, the intersection of two currents—may hold salmon. During periods of low water, salmon will be concentrated in deep still pools.

Salmon can often be seen leaping clear of the water, especially in the morning or evening. This does not necessarily mean they will take a fly, but it at least gives you a clue to where one or more fish can be found. A salmon will sometimes do a slow porpoising roll, with his head, dorsal fin, and tail breaking the water. This usually indicates potential interest in a fly.

Most salmon fishing is done with wet flies, especially early in the season, when the water is high and cold. In most currents, the fly is merely cast across or quartering downstream and allowed to swing below you. Unless a salmon is spotted, you'll want to cover as much water as possible. The best way to do this is to make a short cast, thirty feet or so, then extend your line a few feet on the next cast. Keep on extending your line until you near the far bank or reach the maximum distance you can cast. Take three or four steps downstream and repeat the process.

Your fly should not swing so fast that it skims across the surface (except in special circumstances), nor should it drift so slowly that it sinks. To keep your fly swinging at the proper pace, cast directly across the current in slow water, angling your casts more in a downstream direction in faster water.

Unlike trout and winter steelhead, salmon will come up for a fly, even if they are lying in six feet of water. Your fly should be swinging from three inches to a foot below the surface. If the water is very high or cold, a sink-tip line may be effective, but most salmon fishing is done with a floating or intermediate-weight line.

With standard wet-fly fishing for salmon, you do not want any slack in your line or leader. Your fly should be under tension at all times, and it is effectively fishing as soon as it hits the water. Slack will not allow the fly to swing properly, and if your leader doesn't straighten immediately you'll lose some effectiveness on the first part of your drift—until the current puts some tension into it.

Salmon in shallow water are not very spooky, and you won't alarm them unless you block their access to deep water. Make sure that you cover the shallow water near the bank before you lengthen your casts.

Salmon will rest and take flies in traditional holding pools and spots that remain the same from year to year. A good guide is an asset, not only for fly selection but to make sure you fish the right pools. Areas on a particular river that look great to a stranger may be devoid of fish, even though they look like holding water.

You should try to watch your fly (or where you think your fly is) all the time. A salmon that has risen is one that can usually be taken. If a salmon boils or flashes at your fly but does not connect, rest him for a few minutes by standing quietly, or else casting to another spot. Keep the same length of line and cast to the exact same spot or a bit above it after you have rested the fish. If you rise a salmon he will usually come back to the same fly; if he doesn't, try a different pattern or size, usually a smaller one.

Salmon take flies best after a rain has raised the water level a few feet, and in the early morning and evening when the water is at normal or low levels. They can also be taken during the day, even when the water is low and clear, by using special techniques designed to raise sullen fish.

One such technique is the greased-line method, which presents the fly broadside to the current (and to the salmon) throughout most of the drift. The greased-line method also swings a fly with a uniform speed, instead of speeding up at the end of the swing, and may provoke a rise when nothing else will.

The greased-line method is performed by casting across or quartering downstream and mending line every time the line bellies. The rod tip should follow the fly's drift throughout the swing, staying just upstream of the fly. Line is usually mended in an upstream direction, except when you are standing in slow water and the fly is in fast water, in which case you should mend in a downstream direction. In a nutshell, the line between the rod tip and the fly should be kept as straight as possible.

The greased-line method is usually used in conjunction with small, sparse flies such as low-water flies or salmon nymphs.

Another way to raise uncooperative salmon is to use a riffled fly. This technique can be used with any wet fly, and is performed by first taking a half hitch with the leader around the head of the fly, behind the eye, so that the leader emerges from the side of the fly rather than the front.

The riffling hitch makes the fly skim along the surface of the water,

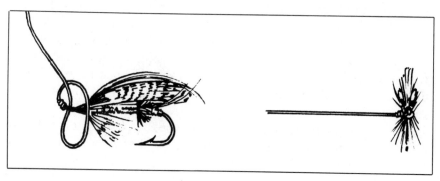

The riffling hitch.

and may draw explosive strikes from the salmon. It works better on some rivers than others; in certain rivers in Newfoundland and Iceland it is used most of the time. The hitch should be changed depending upon which direction the current is flowing. If when you are facing directly across the river the current flows from right to left, the leader should stick out from the right side of the fly as you look down the shank of the hook with the eye facing you.

If the fly throws spray as it swings, it is moving too fast and you should use an upstream mend to slow it down. If it sinks you should speed up the swing—increase the line tension by mending downstream.

During periods of low water, salmon will hold in large, slow pools that have such a slight current they resemble ponds. In order to obtain the proper wet-fly speed in a situation like this, you should strip in line as the fly swings, just as you would fish a streamer for trout.

A salmon can also be enticed with the "patent" method, which is merely casting a salmon fly upstream on a slack line. The fly should pass dead drift over the fish. This method cannot be used to cover a lot of water, and the fly loses its effectiveness when it sinks too deep, so it is used for a salmon that has been spotted on the bottom or one that has risen to a fly.

Dry flies can be used for salmon anytime, but are most successful when the water is low and over 60 degrees. A salmon that has been located should be tried first by presenting the fly upstream, dead drift, exactly as you would for trout. This method can also be used to fish blind, but it's tiring because you're wading upstream and will need to false cast more than with a wet fly.

If an upstream presentation doesn't work, try casting a dry across stream as you would a wet, and allow the fly to drag violently across the current. This method is especially successful with palmer-hackled deer-hair flies such as the Bomber and Buck Bug, and will draw violent, slashing rises from the salmon.

Nova Scotians use an interesting technique that combines both wet- and dry-fly presentation on a single cast. They use a sparsely tied dry fly that has a slanted hackle, so it looks like a wet but floats when cast upstream. They cast the fly quartering upstream and fish it dry until it drifts just below them, then pull on the line so that the fly sinks. The fly is then fished wet until the line straightens below, then it is picked up for another cast.

Salmon, especially big salmon, move for a fly slowly, and you should resist the impulse to strike immediately. An experienced trout fisherman, who is used to setting the hook as quickly as possible, may hook fewer salmon than the novice, whose reactions are slower. With a wet fly, make sure you feel the salmon before tightening the line; many times with a wet fly the tension on the line will set the hook for you. With a dry fly, wait until you see the fish turning toward the bottom before striking.

The best salmon fishermen are those who are persistent and like to cast. The more your fly is in the water, the better your chances of hooking a salmon.

STEELHEAD

Steelhead are rainbow trout that live in the ocean or large fresh water lakes and return to freshwater rivers to spawn. Actually, any rainbow that lives in a lake will use a freshwater river to spawn, as they must have moving water to perpetuate the species. "Steelhead" usually indicates the race of rainbows that are silvery, quite large, and may migrate up river hundreds of miles to their spawning ground.

In any population of trout that has access to the ocean, certain individuals will become anadromous, dropping down into the ocean and returning to spawn. In the United States we have sea-run brown trout in a few rivers on Long Island and Cape Cod, sea-run brookies in Maritime Canada, and sea-run cutthroats in the Pacific Northwest. These fish, however, have very limited ranges, and the sport fishery for them as compared to steelhead is limited. They may be caught in estuaries, where they spend most of their time, on streamer flies that imitate prevalent baitfish. When they ascend rivers in the fall to spawn they are usually caught on standard trout streamers, wets, and nymphs.

Steelhead mate in shallow gravel beds on the stream bottom, where the fry hatch. The fry soon mature into tiny replicas of their parents with dark oval or crescent-shaped parr markings on their sides; they are called parr. They remain in their natal rivers for one to four years, finally changing into silvery smolts and dropping down into the ocean. They will be six to nine inches at this time.

Adult steelhead, after growing fat on ocean baitfish and crustaceans, return to the same river they were born in, by some method of navigation that is not entirely understood but is thought to involve the chemical signature of their river, which the steelhead can smell. In general, the longer a steelhead has remained in the ocean before spawning, the larger he will be.

Steelhead may enter a river at any time of the year, but the most

Steelhead rivers, like this one in British Columbia, are often fast and deep. John Merwin

common times are spring and fall. There are many distinct races of steelhead, and the time that they are available will vary greatly from river to river. One river may also support more than one race of steelhead, and may have more than one run per year.

Timing and knowledge of local conditions are essential in steelhead fishing. The fish take a fly much better when they are silvery, fresh from the ocean or lake. Steelhead feed very little when they migrate, and as they ascend a river they become less and less inclined to take a fly. Stale fish, or those that are penned up in a pool, waiting for the proper time to spawn or a rise of water to move upstream, are the most difficult to take on a fly.

Because steelhead are moving but not feeding, you must cover a lot of water in order to find the fish. The pool you're fishing might contain ten fish today and none tomorrow. Unless you have weeks or months to fish a particular river, a guide or someone who has fished the river before can be invaluable. Steelhead will rest in the same spots from year to year. These spots, unless changed by flooding that alters the stream bed, will contain steelhead, while spots that look exactly the same to us will be devoid of fish.

Steelhead will most often be concentrated above and below obstructions that require some energy expenditure to pass. A low waterfall or a long stretch of fast water will hold fish that are either waiting to scale the obstacle or are resting after passing it. This makes heads and tails of pools logical places to fish.

Steelhead will also be found in the middle of pools and in long expanses of flat water, but they will be more spread out and difficult to find, requiring a lot of movement on your part and many casts over unproductive areas.

Look for steelhead above and below rocks on the stream bed, on the edge of fast currents, close to the bank in tails of pools, and just under the lips of waterfalls or at the head of a pool. They will seldom be found far from the main current in a river, because even if they're not moving at the present time, they have one purpose: to get upstream as easily as possible. Water that has a smooth flow is usually more productive than water with lots of eddies and conflicting currents.

The various races of steelhead can be lumped into two groups for fly-fishing purposes: summer- and winter-run fish. The tactics used for each group are quite different.

Winter-run fish are steelhead that run a river from late fall through early spring. The water in steelhead rivers at this time is high, fast, and cold, and the steelhead will be found on or near the bottom. They will seldom rise to a fly that is more than a couple of feet above them. The most eagerly taken flies are those that are drifting at about the same speed as the bottom currents. They will also attack a fly that is drifting just off the bottom and suddenly rises toward the surface, perhaps an instinctive reaction to something that is getting away.

Bright flies are necessary, both to provoke a steelhead and because the water is often dark and cloudy, as is a sinking line of some type. It will be a rare occasion that a floating line with a weighted fly will get

An eight-pound summer steelhead. John Merwin

deep enough, except in small, shallow streams.

A fly line presents a problem when you are trying for a slow, deep drift. Because the current is always faster in a stream near the surface, the thick fly line between you and the fly will pull the fly away from productive water. Fishermen who use spinning- or bait-casting tackle and lead weights can get their lures near the bottom quicker and keep it there longer, because monofilament line slices through the current and is less likely to be pushed toward the surface. With fly-fishing gear, as soon as the fly is put under tension by the line it will be pulled toward the surface.

The classic steelhead cast is a quartering upstream cast, using either a sink-tip or a full-sinking line. As soon as the fly and line hit the water they begin to sink, because they are not under tension yet. With a sink-tip line, the floating portion should be mended upstream every time it begins to belly downstream, so that the fly sinks as deeply as possible. The fly will be at its deepest point when it is quartering downstream from you; hopefully, it will be near the bottom. Strikes will usually come at this point and will be signaled by a tightening of the line. A steelhead guide once told me, "With fly-fishing gear, you probably have only a couple of feet of drift on each cast when the fly is at the proper spot—when it's quartering downstream." At any other point in its drift the fly is riding too far above the fish to be noticed.

You should be hanging bottom frequently when fly-fishing for winter steelhead, otherwise you're not getting the fly deep enough. To get the fly deeper, you can cast farther upstream, change to a heavily weighted fly, or change to a fly-line type that sinks deeper—from a sink-tip to a full-sinking line, for example.

A trick that is often used to extend the productive drift of a fly is to point your rod tip downstream at the end of the drift, just before the line starts to belly, and feed line through the guides.

A fast-sinking shooting head is the best way to cover a lot of water.

Because of the thin-diameter running line, heads can be cast quartering downstream, where they will sink the fly to the proper depth very quickly. All of the unproductive time spent casting upstream to sink the fly is eliminated. To cover a pool thoroughly with a shooting head you should start at the head of a pool, casting just above areas that look as if they'll hold steelhead. After the fly completes its swing, take a few steps downstream and repeat the process. The next cast will cover the area just downstream of the previous drift.

Summer steelhead enter rivers from late spring through early fall, when the water is usually low, slow, and clear. They will be found in riffled water and in pools that have some cool spring water coming into them. Unlike winter steelhead, summer-run fish can be teased into taking a fly that is drifting just under the surface, and will even take dry flies if the water is very low and clear.

Summer steelhead are sometimes visible as dark shapes on the bottoms of pools, and you can fish for them with dry flies just as you would for trout, although it may take repeated casts to interest them. If they aren't visible, just work upstream with a big (size 6–12), bushy dry fly, covering as much water as you can.

Summer fish will also rise well to small, lightly dressed wet flies fished across and downstream with the greased-line method, or with a riffled fly, identical to the way you would fish for Atlantic salmon. Summer-runs present a great opportunity for the fly-caster, as fly tackle can be used as efficiently as any other kind of gear under these conditions.

SALT WATER

Saltwater fly rodding can be easy if you find fish feeding near the surface. Finding fish is the key, as there is so much ocean that merely trying to cover the water with your flies is a fruitless proposition.

A guide can save you weeks of unproductive searching. They know where and when to find the species that you're after. Good saltwater guides are also adept at spotting fish like bonefish on shallow flats or the subtle ripple or different color a school of bluefish make when they're near the surface. Many of these signs are overlooked by the untrained eye.

If you're on your own, either on land or in a boat, you can look for clues that indicate good fly-fishing. Stripers, bluefish, bonito, king mackerel, and other species that herd baitfish on the surface can be found almost anywhere. When they're near the surface you may actually see the water frothing, with baitfish jumping clear of the water. Gulls are good indicators of this activity. If the gulls are wheeling above the water without landing, there may be a school of baitfish present; when the gulls begin to drop into the water to pick up dead and crippled baitfish, you can be sure that some potentially good fly-fishing is close at hand. Get to that spot in a hurry, because the school may sound as quickly as it came to the surface.

If the surface of the water is calm, look for protruding fins, ripples or wakes that don't look like they're formed by the wind, or dark discolorations on the surface that may indicate a school of cruising fish.

Certain places will concentrate baitfish, so the quarry you're after will be waiting in ambush. Estuaries contain some of the most productive ecosystems in the world. Their nutrient-rich waters support huge quantities of baitfish and crustaceans, and the constant flux of the tide moves food in and out of channels and bays. Look for feeding game fish on the outside of channels and bays on an outgoing tide, on the inside of these areas on an incoming tide.

Tropical and subtropical flats are among the most consistent sources of fly-rod sport. They host a wide variety of bottom feeders, including bonefish, permit, redfish, barracuda, snapper, sharks, and tarpon. Flats are perfect for fly-fishing, because the water is shallow enough to present a fly, regardless of where the fish are, and the fish are usually visible.

Saltwater fly-fishing can be as easy as tossing a popper into a chum line or to a sailfish that has chased a teaser. It may also require all the stealth and accurate casting of trout fishing, especially when bonefish or permit are involved.

The main problem is getting your fly to the fish as soon as possible. Saltwater fish are constantly on the move when they feed, and you'll often have only one chance at a particular fish. Add to this the problem of a big fly and perhaps a strong wind and you can see the case for a big rod that will deliver your fly with a single false cast.

Standard procedure is to stand ready with twenty to thirty feet of fly line out beyond the tip of your fly rod, hanging behind you in the water. Another thirty feet of line is pulled off the reel and coiled at your feet. The fly is held in your stripping hand. You'll use the line outside the guides to form a quick roll cast, then make a single false cast, double haul, and shoot the line that has been pulled off the reel.

It's important that this shooting line be free of obstructions. Anything that protrudes on the deck of a boat should be covered with towels, rags, or, better yet, a piece of nylon mesh with weights tied to the corners. An improvised shooting basket can be made from a plastic garbage pail. If you're wading in the surf, you should have a shooting basket strapped to your waist.

With poppers, you want to cast just ahead of a surface-feeding fish or right in the middle of a school that is herding baitfish. With a subsurface fly, you want to cast just ahead of a cruising fish, so that when he intercepts your fly it will be at his level. Before fishing with streamers, it's best to make a few trial casts where you can see the fly sink, so that you estimate its sink rate.

Most saltwater game fish, with the exception of the bottom feeders, require a fast retrieve. Open-ocean species are fast swimmers, and so are their quarry. Just before they intercept your fly, begin stripping, using one- to two-foot pulls of line, with no pause in between. A tight line is essential, and so is a quick, firm hook-setting motion. The rod

193

tip should be as close to the water as possible, in order to maintain a tight rod-to-fly connection.

If a visible fish doesn't respond to your fly as it passes in front of him, the best thing to do is speed up your retrieve, as if the fly is a panicked baitfish. Predator fish will usually make an instinctive lunge toward a fleeing fish. Slowing your retrieve will seldom draw strikes, except with such cautious species as striped bass or snook. Stopping your retrieve and letting the fly sit dead in the water will usually cause a saltwater fish to turn away and lose interest, except in a chum line, where the fish are picking up pieces of dead baitfish.

Poppers may be fished fast or slow, but they're seldom fished as slow as you would for freshwater bass. A steady retrieve, while making the popper throw up a stream of bubbles and spray, will work best for the species that like a fast-moving fly, such as bluefish, barracuda, marlin, and sailfish. Stripers and redfish may want a popper that barely gurgles, especially when the water is calm.

To get a very fast retrieve with either a streamer or popper, it's sometimes necessary to sweep the rod tip off to the side, using your stripping hand to bring in line and take up slack at the same time. Make sure after each sweep that you return your rod tip in front of you and low to the water, otherwise you'll have trouble setting the hook.

A fast, even violent retrieve with a popper is useful when fish are chasing big schools of bait and your fly must compete with Mother Nature's creations. A noisy presentation can also be used to draw the attention of fish that are in deep water.

There are hundreds of species of saltwater game fish that can be caught on a fly rod. The following four species are the most popular with fly rodders, and should give you representative examples of the opportunities for saltwater fly-fishing.

Bonefish

Bonefish are found in shallow tropical flats throughout the world. The most popular places for fly-fishing are the Florida Keys and Central America, but untapped bonefish fishing exists throughout the world.

Bonefish feed on mollusks, shrimp, and small baitfish, which they root from aquatic grasses, marl, and crevasses between rocks. They seldom feed more than a foot above the bottom. Bonefish travel in schools that average a half dozen fish, but some schools may number twenty to thirty fish. On the Yucatán peninsula, schools of over 200 one- to three-pound bonefish are often seen. The largest individuals, ten pounds and over, may be solitary or travel in twos or threes.

Bonefish do not jump, but their sizzling runs may peel a hundred yards of line from your reel in a matter of seconds. Leaders and line should be as light as possible, because bonefish are very spooky and can be very picky about what they eat.

Look for bonefish in water that is six inches to four feet deep. In very shallow water their tails will stick out above the water as they feed. This is the most desirable way to find bonefish, as they are easy to

A bonefish's first run may peel 100 yards of line off the reel. Leigh Perkins

A large bonefish caught on the Yucatan peninsula. Orvis

approach and to catch when tailing. Bonefish feeding in deeper water may leave trails of mud, which help to spot the bonefish and indicate in which direction they're traveling. Experienced eyes, usually possessed by professional bonefish guides (who are almost essential), can also see their ghostly shapes cruising just above the bottom.

The fly is presented so that it lands two or three feet ahead of a moving fish, or far enough so that he'll intercept it as he moves along. Slow, foot-long strips are then used to interest the fish, although a quick jerk may help to entice a fickle individual.

Fly-rod bonefishing can become quite a cat-and-mouse game, because individuals and schools cruise erratically. A cast that lands too near one may cause the entire school to bolt for deeper water, so it's important to see not only the fish you're casting to but also the others in the school. A fly line that slaps on top of one fish may spook them all.

A great advantage of fly-fishing for bonefish is that if you cast to a moving fish and he changes direction, you can pick up immediately and put the fly back in front of him while he's still moving. A spin fisherman would have to reel in all his line before making another cast.

Bonefish are so sneaky that you may not see or feel the strike. They usually take the fly in the pause between strips, even if the pause is very short. Experienced fly-rod bonefishers say that they watch for the fish to stop and quiver slightly, then set the hook.

Bonefishing is done either from a shallow-draft skiff, poled by the guide or a fellow fisherman, or by wading shallow flats.

Tarpon

Tarpon are the most spectacular saltwater fish. These silvery giants reach weights in excess of 150 pounds and will often clear the water for six feet vertically and fifteen feet horizontally when hooked, throughout a battle that may encompass hundreds of yards. The fight may last for hours. Smaller individuals are played for less time, but the battle is just as exciting.

Tarpon inhabit shallow, warm water from the southern United States to Central America. They travel in schools, feeding on baitfish and crustaceans. Much of their feeding takes place at night, but they can be enticed to take large streamers during the day.

Cold weather will send tarpon into deep water, but when the water temperature rises in the spring they will migrate into shallow bays. Giant tarpon are found in six to ten feet of water, but "baby" tarpon that range from a couple of pounds to twenty pounds can be taken in very shallow water and in the canals that crisscross the Florida coast.

Schools of tarpon can be spotted by their darker shapes or shadows along the bottom, or they can be seen rolling on the surface. A wake of bubbles may indicate a school is nearby. Tarpon have a unique gas bladder that allows them to use atmospheric air to breathe.

It's interesting that a 100-pound-plus tarpon with a bucket-sized mouth will often prefer four-inch flies to large lures. In the Florida Keys, home of giant tarpon of 175 pounds and more, flies are recognized as the most effective way to hook these fish.

An experienced guide may stake out an area and wait for tarpon to cruise by. If you are on your own, try drifting or poling slowly along flats, banks, or mangrove swamps. Baby tarpon in canals can often be stalked from the bank.

As with bonefish, the fly is cast ahead of a cruising fish and retrieved with slow, steady, foot-long strips. Poppers are effective at times, especially at night for smaller tarpon.

Tarpon provide the most exciting aerial acrobatics of any gamefish.

Striped Bass

Stripers are generally a fish of shallow water that feed near the surface on baitfish, so they make an excellent target for the fly rodder. They range from Nova Scotia south to the Carolinas on the Atlantic Coast, and have been introduced on the Pacific Coast, where they can be found from Washington State south to Los Angeles. We still have a lot to learn about their movements, but they spawn in freshwater estuaries in late spring, where they can be found in heavy concentrations. There is also a seasonal migration from south to north in the spring and back south in the fall. Fly-fishermen have trouble finding them in concentrations near the surface during the spring, and the best fly-fishing occurs in September and October, when the schools are larger and more predictable.

Stripers will congregate in the same places during their migrations year after year. Most fly-fishermen look for schools feeding on the surface, then carefully drift along the edge of the school, using poppers or streamers.

Blind fishing for stripers is nowhere near as productive, but they can be taken by fishing large white streamers on a fast-sinking shooting head. Try the edges of channels, reefs, and around large rocks. An

A pair of striped bass taken on a fly rod.
Spider Andreson

experienced fly-rod striper fisherman told me that 75 percent of his fish have been caught in less than six feet of water.

Although you can get quite close to a school of stripers when they're feeding, care should be taken not to run a boat through the school. They'll sound and may not come back up in the same area. Stripers are also one of the most selective feeders—you might have to change your fly pattern or retrieve or fly size three or four times before you hit on the right combination. Stripers aren't as selective when they're taking poppers, because the distortion produced by the bubbles hides the size of the fly.

Although stripers may feed all day long, by far the best times are early morning and evening. In calm water, they are even caught at night on noisy poppers.

Best retrieve speed with both streamers and poppers is a medium pace with foot-long strips, although you might want to try a very slow stop-and-go motion with poppers, especially on very flat water.

The sight of a big striper's tail waving good-bye after he has sucked in your size 1/0 Skipping Bug is something you'll never forget.

Bluefish

Bluefish are among the most voracious predators in the ocean. Traveling in schools of same-size fish, they migrate along the Atlantic Coast from Maine to Florida. Best fly-rod fishing, when schools are feeding near the surface, occurs during June through September in the North and January through March in the South.

Bluefish will be found in the same kind of habitat as striped bass, although they prefer slightly deeper water. Unlike stripers, you'll most likely find schools of blues feeding on the surface at midday, although they may feed anytime.

Bluefish prefer a much faster retrieve than stripers, usually as fast and as hard as you can strip. They will take a popper or streamer equally well, although some fly-fishermen will use a fast-sinking line and a streamer even when schools are surface feeding, as larger individuals may feed below the surface, picking off crippled baitfish that are mangled by the school above them.

There are times when bluefish will eat anything you throw at them, but they can be selective, especially if they're feeding on small sand eels. They will also sound as quickly as a school of stripers if you run a boat through the school.

Bluefish have razor-sharp teeth, and even if you're catching little "snapper blues" of two to four pounds you'll need a wire leader or heavy shock tippet. Watch your fingers, too!

11
Striking,
Playing,
and Landing

Most fish lost in fly-fishing are lost either at the moment you strike or when you attempt to land them. Playing a fish on a fly rod is a relatively simple matter of making the fish work against the spring of the rod until he gets tired.

STRIKING

Striking a fish means tightening the line by raising your rod tip. Most fly hooks are of fine diameter with very sharp points, so the strike requires very little force—in fact, in many instances fish will hook themselves.

Striking with a fly rod should be a firm, immediate reaction to a fish that has visibly taken your fly, or an unseen fish that you have felt telegraphed along the rod. The only thing a fish can grab objects with is his mouth, and if that thing doesn't feel just right he'll eject it quickly. Other than Atlantic salmon, which aren't feeding anyway, a fish will eject an unwanted object within a second. Atlantic salmon may take flies all the way to the bottom before letting them go.

Some large fish, such as salmon, tarpon, and large trout, move slowly toward a fly, almost as if they were in slow motion. Make sure that you wait until you see the fish take your fly before striking. There is no need to hesitate in striking unseen fish, because that twitch you feel along your rod or see in your line means that something has grabbed your fly.

The strike is performed by pinching the fly line tight with your hand and moving the rod tip until you feel the hook hit home. In most cases, you'll be stripping line by pulling it with your stripping hand through the fingers of your casting hand. To strike, merely pinch the line with your casting hand and raise the rod tip at the same time. If you don't pinch the line, it will merely slip through the guides of the rod and no force will be applied to the hook point.

How hard do you strike? That depends on a number of variables. With a heavy tippet, something over 6-pound test, you can strike fairly hard without popping the tippet. With a lot of slack line on the water, you may have to strike hard in order to take up all that loose line. On a long cast, it also takes a harder strike, because moving sixty feet of line takes a lot more force than moving fifteen feet of line.

The greater the arc you move your rod tip through, the more forceful your strike will be. Slack line on the water may require you to raise the tip from 9:00 to 12:00. If you've been using a high rod technique to avoid drag, you may have to go back as far as 1:00.

There are times when fish will hook themselves. A fish that takes a wet fly on a quartering downstream cast and a tight line will most often hook himself; all you have to do is gently tighten the line. In fact, if you strike too hard on a downstream cast you'll often pop your tippet. If you're moving a fly toward you quickly, as with fishing a streamer in still water, the fish has to rush the fly, getting hooked in the process.

Bass, pike, and most saltwater species require a fairly hard strike. The hooks you use for these species are large, and large hooks require more force to set them than small hooks. These fish also have bony mouths, which require some force to penetrate. Some of the real big bony ones may require a second and third strike to ensure good penetration. With some saltwater species you'll have to haul with your stripping hand as well as using the rod tip. Several short, quick strikes are always better than a mighty heave.

There are times when you need a gentle strike. Big fish and light tippets require just a hint of a strike, barely enough to tighten the line. With light tippets you'll be using tiny flies anyway, which don't need much muscle to penetrate. I've often heard people say that they never strike with small dry flies, size 20 and under, but unless there is some tension on the line you'll never set the hook. A tiny fly fished downstream may be set by the tension of the current on the line, but if you're fishing upstream you *must* set the hook, even if it's a barely perceptible motion.

If you're heavy-handed and sometimes break off fish when striking with light tippets, you can use the slip strike, which uses only the friction of the fly line against the guides. As you raise the rod tip, don't pinch the line but make an O with the thumb and forefinger of your line hand, letting the line slip through as you raise the rod tip. The tippet can't break because the tension on the line is so slight.

If the fly is directly downstream from you, try to use a sideways hook-setting motion rather than an upward one. Using a straight upward motion of the rod may pull the fly right out of the fish's mouth. Atlantic salmon fishermen avoid "hanging" the fly below them for this reason. If a salmon is going to take they'd rather have him do it on an across-stream presentation, where he will be securely hooked in the hinge of the jaw.

I've heard fishermen talk about the relative pros and cons of where in his mouth a fish should be hooked and how they strike to get the hook in the upper jaw or the hinge or whatever. So far as I can see, we have no control over this, and hooking anyplace in the bone of his mouth is OK with me. If, while you're playing a fish, you see that he is hooked on the skin outside his mouth, be very gentle when playing and landing him.

Fish are often foul-hooked on the top of their heads or dorsal fins or even their tails. This usually results from a fish that rose to your fly and refused it at the last moment. You see him break the surface so you set the hook, just as he begins to roll under the fly. If this happens frequently you should change your fly pattern or presentation very slightly —something isn't quite right.

PLAYING

It is impossible to break a well-designed fly rod while playing a fish, and it is difficult to break a tippet while pulling a fish's dead weight through the water. Rods are broken if the line-to-leader knot gets caught on one of the last few guides of a rod, putting all the strain on a short section of rod. Tippets are broken when a fish makes a sudden lunge and you don't respond, or if the fish wraps you around a snag.

Small fish can and should be played by merely stripping them in as you would bring in line for another cast. If you can, skip them right across the top of the water, unhook them quickly, and carefully release them. The longer a fish is played, the less chance it has of surviving. Large fish can be brought to shore and lain on the grass briefly for a photograph; they're tough. But to play a small fish for a long time so that the fellow upstream of you sees that you've caught one is a disgusting display.

How do you know when to play a fish from the reel? You won't have any choice. A fish that must be played from the reel will jerk your rod tip down and begin to pull the stripping line from your hand.

The object of playing a fish from the reel is to get any stripping line that you might have out from around your legs, out of your stripping hand, or off the deck of a boat. If he makes a quick run and this line catches on something, you're going to lose your fish, your fly, and maybe your tippet. Using the reel also allows you to play a fish against a smooth mechanical drag instead of against the uneven pressure of your fingers on the fly line. A smooth drag is necessary because a fish puts the most pressure on your terminal tackle when he makes a sudden lunge. At that moment his mass times his acceleration puts a lot more strain on your leader than he actually weighs.

Good reel drags are smooth; they require little inertia to get them started, eliminating a "catch" that might allow a fish to snap your leader. If your reel has an adjustable drag, where should you set it? If you're using a light tippet, say 6X or 7X, put the drag on the lightest possible setting. If your tippet is very heavy, over 10-pound test, set the drag

The flex of a fly rod will protect very light tippets, even with big fish.

fairly heavy. Otherwise, set the drag on its middle setting—if you think the fish is getting away with murder during the fight, tighten it down; if you think he's going to pop your tippet, set it lighter. One thing to remember is that if you're playing a big fish that has taken you into your backing, you should be prepared to lighten up on the drag. The added weight of a lot of line on the water puts pressure on your tippet, plus as your backing goes out it is pulling against a diminishing diameter, which requires more force for each turn of the spool.

Reels with exposed rims can be palmed for additional drag when you want to snub a fish. Use the flat of your palm on the bottom of the reel, keeping your fingers away from the spinning handle. Many fly-fishermen prefer to palm the reel anytime they need drag, so they set the mechanical drag on the reel just tight enough to prevent spool overruns when line is stripped from the reel.

I've seen tests where you can check your drag against a tippet tied to a tree or doorknob or lead weight, but these are static tests and just cannot duplicate the dynamics of a moving fish in the water.

A large fish that makes a sudden run after striking will pull all of the

Palming an exposed-rim reel for added drag.

stripping line from your hand and put himself on the reel. Try to guide the line smoothly through the guides; if the line catches on something, lower your rod tip a little, snub him by pinching the line against the rod with your casting hand, and try to free the line.

If a big fish takes your fly but doesn't take right off, keep the line pinched in your casting hand as you should have done for the strike, and reel in any slack between the stripping guide and the reel as quickly as you can. To give yourself a cushion to do this, you can drop your rod tip and give him some slack. Flies weigh so little that a fish has trouble throwing them, as he has no weight to work against.

Now you're off! In any area free of snags, you should fight a fish with the butt of the rod between 10:00 and 11:00. At this position the fish has to work against the spring of the rod, which cushions the tippet.

By raising and lowering the rod tip you can vary the amount of drag and thus the pressure on your tippet. With the rod held upright, the friction caused by the guides increases the force needed to pull line from the reel. By dropping the rod tip you eliminate this extra drag. If the big fish makes a sudden run, lower your rod tip to decrease the pressure on your tippet. If there aren't any snags, just let him run. When he stops, raise the rod tip back to 11:00 and try to regain some line.

A high rod will protect your tippet from sharp objects on the bottom. Leigh Perkins

Because most fly reels are single-action direct drive, you'll have to let go of the reel handle and keep your hand away from it when the fish makes his run. With antireverse reels you can hold on to the handle at all times.

Lowering the rod tip, or "bowing to the fish," should be done when

205

a large fish like a salmon or a tarpon makes a leap. If the fish lands on a taut tippet he can break it easily. Besides, a fish that is above water has much more weight to pull against your tippet. If he shakes his head above water while your line is tight, you may part company.

Many areas that you will fish will have objects on the bottom that you'll want to keep both your leader and the fish away from. Coral bottoms and sharp rocks can abrade or sever a leader quickly. A fish can wrap your leader around weeds or brush piles and work the tippet against a stationary object instead of the spring of your rod, snapping the tippet easily. Under these circumstances, play the fish with the rod raised as far over your head as you can. Keeping his head up will force him to swim toward the surface rather than toward the bottom.

Fighting a fish in a current requires some different strategies. Always try to get the fish above you, so that he has to work against the current, rather than you having to pull him back up against the current. If a fish runs downstream you can either put pressure on him and hope he eventually turns around and comes back upstream, or you can follow him.

To follow a fish and get below him, your best bet is to head for the bank and scramble downstream until you're below him. Don't worry about keeping a tight line until you're downstream of the fish, but keep reeling as you go so that you're always gaining line or at least keeping things at a stalemate. When you get below the fish, apply pressure on him. He'll usually respond by pulling against you and running upstream.

A last-resort trick when you can't follow a fish is to strip some line off your reel and pay slack into the current. When the line bellies in the current below the fish, he may respond by pulling against it and running back upstream.

A fish can be led away from snags. He has no reverse gear or sideways propulsion, so he has to go whichever way his head is pointing. If you can turn his head before he reaches a snag, you'll have won the battle.

A typical circumstance is when a fish heads for a streamside tangle of

"Leading" a fish using horizontal rod pressure. The fisherman is keeping his profile low to avoid frightening the fish.

brush. Let's say he's running directly across the current. If you keep your rod tip at 11:00, he'll respond by running right to the snag. Try flopping your rod down to a horizontal position in an upstream or downstream direction. The pressure of the rod tip will force the fish's head away from the snag. He'll have to swim in this direction.

You can also use horizontal rod pressure to turn a fish that is running upstream or downstream toward a snag. It's especially useful against an upstream snag, because when he's turned broadside to the current he'll be pushed back toward you.

What do you do if a fish wraps you around underwater weeds or branches? If you can get to him, the best thing to do is to quickly free the leader from the snag. You can use your hand or canoe paddle or even your foot. Some fish get pinned to a snag, especially with a strong leader, and can be netted right then and there.

If you can't get him to the snag, try giving the fish slack. Sometimes he'll work himself free and swim away. It's worth a try.

A fish that has buried his head in weeds that are not rooted to the bottom, such as the filamentous algae that grow in spring creeks, can also be freed by pointing the rod at him and slowly walking backward. A slow, steady pull is always better than jerking on the line.

In waters with surface weeds between you and the fish, play the fish with the rod held as high as you can. Try to get his head above the weeds—the instant you slip his head onto the weeds, skitter him on top of them. If there is clear water in front of you, you can continue to play him there, or you can pick him up off the weed bed with your hand.

The worst thing you can do while fighting a big fish is let him rest. Keep the pressure on—make sure your rod is bending and he can't get a second wind. An old rule of saltwater fly rodding is "If you're more tired than he is when you land him, you haven't been fighting him hard enough."

Salmon, steelhead, and large trout may get on the bottom of a river and sulk instead of fighting. You've got to get him moving! One way is to tap on the butt section of your rod, sending vibrations down the line to frighten him. If you're close to the fish, kick and thrash around in the water, or get a buddy to. A very effective method, although it sounds silly, is to heave a good-sized rock into the water in the vicinity of the fish. Just be ready for a screaming run!

What happens if a fish runs to the end of your backing? The choice is yours. Will the tippet hold? To snub a fish at a point like this, lower your rod tip until it's sticking straight at him and grab on to the line. Your tippet knot will be the weakest link in the system, and most of us would rather lose a fly and a tippet than our fly line and backing.

To get a big fish close to you, it's necessary to pump him. When he finishes his first run, lower the rod tip the instant he stops and reel until the line is tight. Then, holding on to the reel handle, smoothly raise the rod tip to 11:00, drop it quickly, and reel in the slack. If he starts another run while you're pumping, drop the rod tip, let go of the reel handle, and let him go. With a fish like a big tarpon, this give-and-take

207

battle can last for hours, which is why saltwater and salmon rods have butt extensions. The extension is braced against your lower abdomen to help relieve the tension in your arms.

When a fish is ready to land is a subjective matter. Some fly-fishermen use the heaviest tippet possible and horse fish in when they're still thrashing violently. If you can get away with this, it's a good practice if you plan to release your fish. Others will play a fish until he turns upside down, which is usually considered unsporting and is dangerous to the fish if you plan to release him.

It's safe to say that a fish is ready to land when he stops thrashing violently and begins to swim in tight circles.

Most fish will make a final run or two when they see you or the boat. A stream fish will generally head for deep water; just lower the rod tip and try to regain line after he finishes his run. If you're fishing from a boat, he'll often swim for the protection of the underside of the boat. The best thing to do in a case like that is plunge your rod tip straight down into the water and lead him away from motor, keel, or other obstrucions. On a big boat you can walk around to the other side with your rod tip in the water.

A trick used by stream fishermen, especially if they've hooked a big fish on a light tippet, is to kneel down, keep the rod tip horizontal, and sneak the fish into the net or into their hands. If the fish can't see you and you don't make any sudden jerks with the rod, he'll often come in quietly, before he's expended all his energy. This strategy is often used throughout the fight on spring creeks, where big fish, weeds, and light tippets go together. After a gentle strike, they'll nag the fish into the net. It sometimes seems as if the fish doesn't even know he's hooked.

LANDING

Fly-rod fish can be landed by hand, with a net, gaff, or tailer; or they can be beached.

The grip of the rod should remain in your hand throughout the landing process. You still need the flex of the entire rod to protect your tippet; if you begin to hand-over-hand along the rod toward the rod tip you'll be taking a chance. If the fish makes a sudden run, all of his weight will be on the section of the rod above your hands. It's an easy way to break a tip section.

When landing a fish, the butt section of your rod should not go past 12:00. Bringing the rod back to 1:00 or 2:00 when a fish is in close quarters is asking for trouble, because a rod is not designed to be bent over double. That not only puts undue stress on the tip of the rod, it makes you lose control over the fish, because a tip that is bent over double can rotate 360 degrees around the butt section.

To get a fish close to you, it's better to keep the butt at an angle that is below the vertical while bringing it back over your shoulder or holding it over your head.

If you're using a short leader, try to keep the line-to-leader connection outside the tip-top. With a long leader, like a twelve-footer, you may have to reel this connection inside the guides to get the fish close enough. If he decides to bolt and the knot catches on a guide, rotate the rod in your hand quickly so that the knot slips through the guides.

If you choose to release your catch, you can often slide your hand down the leader, grab the fly, and twist the fish free while he's still in the water. If the hook doesn't come free, lift the fish out by the fly and shake him. His own weight is usually enough to work the hook out. The less a fish is handled, the greater his chances for survival.

For flies that don't come out easily, you can use a pair of forceps to get leverage that you can't obtain with your fingers. Clamp the forceps on the shank of the hook, near the bend, and back the hook out. Both your fly and the fish will suffer less damage.

Most fish can be landed by hand. A trout can be landed by gently encircling the middle of his body with your hand. If you plan to release him, keep your hands away from his delicate gills, and don't squeeze too hard, or you'll damage internal organs. A large trout should not be grabbed by the lower jaw, as they have small but very sharp teeth.

You can land most other fish by grabbing them around the middle of the body. You may find it easier to land bass by gripping their lower jaw with your thumb, which momentarily paralyzes them. Be careful of sunfish and others with sharp dorsal spines; grab them ahead of or behind the dorsal fin.

A fish that you plan to release should be handled gently and kept in the water as much as possible.

A landing net is the surest way to land most fish. Never swipe at a fish with a landing net. Always put the net in the water, lead the fish over the net, and lift the net while dropping your rod tip to slacken the line. Lifting the net into a taut leader could break your tippet. The fish will drop right into your net as you are lifting it. If you're wading in a river, get the fish upstream of you by pointing your rod tip upstream

209

and stepping back a couple of feet. Then slacken your line, let the fish drift downstream over the net, and lift when he passes over it. Fish that are going to be released can be kept right in the net while you remove the hook, so that they have a constant supply of oxygen to their gills.

Gaffing saltwater fish should be done in the same manner: put the gaff in the water, lead the fish over the gaff, and gaff him from underneath. Always lip-gaff fish like tarpon that you plan to release.

This large tarpon has been lip-gaffed and can be released unharmed. Leigh Perkins

In rivers with sloping shallows or gravel bars, you can beach a large fish. If you hook a big one and have no net, plan the whole fight so that you'll end up in a shallow area with a gently sloping bank. When you get the fish in the shallows, walk up onto land and slide the fish along with you. His flopping will push him higher onto the bank. This method is best with a fish that has been thoroughly tired, as most of them will bolt when led into shallow water.

Atlantic salmon can be landed by the tail. Salmon have a wide tail and a narrow caudal peduncle, which provides an excellent handhold. Grasp a tired salmon firmly by the caudal peduncle; the broad tail will keep him from slipping out of your hand. Hand-tailing a salmon is a technique that requires some practice, so you may want to use a tailer, which is a stick with a nooselike loop of coated wire at the far end. They are usually spring-loaded, so you can slip the wire over the salmon's tail and pull back until the loop snaps shut. The salmon can then be towed to shore, with the tailer clipped to your wader belt so you have both hands free.

AFTER

If you're going to keep a couple of fish for dinner, you should be prepared to stop fishing, kill them, and clean them immediately. Get them on ice or in a creel that cools by evaporation, unless the temperature is below freezing. Nothing is more irresponsible than to kill a fish and then ignore it, suddenly finding a couple of hours later that your prize has deteriorated beyond eating.

I hope that you plan to release most of your catch. If you've decided to take up fly-fishing you're obviously looking for more than dead fish in the freezer.

Releasing fish is not the key to preserving our lakes and streams for the future; habitat protection is. Lakes and rivers cannot be fished out to the point where natural reproduction can't restock them in a few years. But we're loking for more than a minimum spawning population where we fish. Quality fishing to many of us means as many adult fish as a body of water can hold, and if we kill off all the trophies it will take years to grow new ones.

To release a fish, get him back into the water as soon as possible —you should plan to revive him until he can swim away under his own power. A fish that has been played will be starved for oxygen. Getting fresh water across his gills will replenish this oxygen, and you can do it by holding him upright while moving his body back and forth, forcing water over the gills.

When he's thoroughly revived he'll be able to swim away from your gentle hold with a flip of his tail. If he turns belly up after swimming

Gently revive a fish until he can swim away from your grasp.

away, grab him and revive him again, as a fish that is upside down will not recover his equilibrium and will die. If he bellies up in deep water where you can't get to him, poke him with your rod tip or canoe paddle until he rights himself and swims away.

Never release an exhausted fish in a fast current, as he will never regain his equilibrium and will be battered around by the current. Revive a stream fish in calm water, but near an area of fast water, so that the water you're reviving him in has plenty of oxygen.

A fly-caught fish has the highest chance for survival of any released fish, because the hooks are so small and the fish are usually lip-hooked. Only *single-hook* spinning lures come close. Barbless hooks, made by carefully mashing down the barb of your fly with small pliers or forceps, increase this survival rate even more, because the hook slips out easily and the fish doesn't have to be handled as much. Most fly-fishermen who use barbless hooks are convinced that they hold fish as well as barbed ones.

A fish caught on a fly occasionally swallows the fly or gets it caught deep in its throat or gills. If the fly can't be removed carefully with your forceps, cut off the leader as close to the fly as possible. The area around the hook will ulcerate slightly and the fly will fall out within a week.

Even fish hooked deep on snelled bait hooks can be saved this way. I rose a brook trout to a dry fly this past season that had two large snells protruding from his mouth, and he seemed no worse for wear.

12
Accessories

Caricatures of fly-fishermen often picture them with vest pockets bulging with exotic paraphernalia. There *are* many gadgets available to fly-fishermen, and most of them make fishing less troublesome and more fun. Few are absolutely necessary for success. You *can* fly-fish with only a plastic box of flies, a pair of clippers, and a spool of tippet material, plus a rod, reel, line, and leader.

WADING GEAR

Waders or Hip Boots?

Unless you plan to fish only in small brooks, I'd advise you to buy chest-high waders. One of fishing's most chilling experiences is to go over the tops of your hip boots on an April day.

You may not fish in water that is over hip deep, but there will be times when you'll want to cross a stream to get back to the car or to change your casting position. Even small streams can be over hip deep, especially in early spring.

*Hip boots are appropriate for small, shallow
streams.*

Hip boots can be very nice in summer, however, when the water is low and the weather makes a pair of waders uncomfortable. As of this writing, waterproof and breathable waders have not been developed. If your budget allows, I'd buy both a pair of waders and a pair of hip boots. If you can afford only one, waders will be more useful over the long run.

Boot Foot or Stocking Foot?

Waders come in two types: boot foot, with the boot molded to the rest of the waders, and stocking foot, with feet similar to the pajama bottoms that babies wear. Stocking-foot waders require a separate shoe.

Boot-foot waders range widely in price, but you generally get what you pay for. The inexpensive types are made from stiff, heavy-gauge rubber or nylon. They can be hot and uncomfortable. The more expensive kinds are cut more comfortably and use laminates of rubber and nylon, which make them lighter, more comfortable, and easier to move in.

Boot-foot waders are easier to get into and out of, but they are less comfortable when you're walking long distances. They are also not as durable as stocking-foot waders. If you get five years of use out of even the best, you're lucky.

Boot-foot waders are made with the boot molded to the uppers. Orvis

Boot-foot waders are more comfortable and last longer if they fit properly. They should not be so tight that you cannot raise your knee to waist level, nor so loose that they bag in the inseam. Waders that are too short in the inseam will wear in the crotch area, and waders that are too baggy will abrade on the inside of the legs. Boot-foot waders are sized by shoe size. If you are long-legged or short-legged for your shoe size, you have two options: either buy a pair of custom waders (available only in the most expensive brands) or go to stocking-foot waders, which are more flexible and are sized by height.

Boot-foot waders are available with an uninsulated rubber boot or a felt-lined boot for cold-water wading.

If you don't conform to "average" height and shoe-size proportions, try stocking-foot waders. The waders are sized by your height and the boots by your shoe size, so you're more likely to get a proper fit. Stocking-foot waders are made from lightweight nylon, latex, or neoprene. The lightweight nylon waders weigh only a couple of ounces, so you hardly know you have them on. They're cooler in hot weather, but you'll need to wear long underwear if you use them in the early season. They puncture easily but also patch easily, and they are extremely abrasion-resistant because the nylon is so slippery.

Latex waders are heavier than nylon, but they stretch to the point where you can even do deep-knee bends. They are both puncture- and abrasion-resistant, and are the most durable of all the wader types.

Neoprene waders are thick and have great insulating properties, so they are favored by winter steelheaders and others who fish in cold

Stocking-foot waders are comfortable and durable. These are made from latex. Orvis

weather. Made from the same material as a skin diver's wet suit, they are unbearably hot for late spring and summer fishing.

The only disadvantage of stocking-foot waders is that it takes more time to get dressed for fishing, and after fishing you have a pair of wet shoes and socks to deal with. A special stocking-foot-wader bag or a zip-lock bag will keep your car seat dry.

Stocking-foot wading shoes are more comfortable than the rubber boots attached to boot-foot waders because they are designed like hiking shoes. They come in a canvas sneaker style, which is lightweight, and leather or synthetic leather styles, which are heavier but offer more support for long walks. For real long walks, you can put a pair of stocking-foot waders and wading shoes into a day pack. They weigh less and take up less room than boot-foot waders.

With a stocking-foot wading outfit you need to wear a pair of socks over the outside of the waders. If you don't, sand and debris will get between the shoes and waders and deteriorate the waders by abrasion. The best kind are special neoprene socks that have a cuff that fold over the top of the shoes. These completely eliminate the debris problem. You can also use an old pair of sweat socks, but they don't work as well and will wear out quickly.

With either style of waders I like to wear a pair of wool socks with some elastic in them over my street socks. They help prevent blisters, and you can tuck you pant legs into them so your pants don't crawl up your leg during a day's fishing. Most trout streams are cool even in the heat of summer, so you'll appreciate the insulating qualities of the wool socks as well.

You'll need a pair of suspenders to hold up your waders. Make sure that they are the "H" style, which help distribute the weight of the waders across your shoulders. Some waders have two buttons on each side, some have one. Check that the tabs on your suspenders correspond to the button arrangement on your waders.

Do you need a wader belt? I never wear one, but if you're concerned about getting water in your waders if you take a spill, by all means wear a belt. If you go in over the tops of your waders, a belt will trap a pocket of air inside that will keep you buoyant. You will not turn upside down and float down the river.

The type of sole you have on your waders is very important. Most inexpensive varieties come only in a rubber-cleated sole, which is OK for duck hunting or wading in sand and mud, but worthless for stream fishing. Felt soles and heels are needed for a secure grip on slippery rocks. The felt cuts into the algae layer on rocks and gives a lot more confidence in your footing.

If you already have rubber-soled waders, you can buy an inexpensive kit to glue felts onto you waders. Another option is to buy felt-bottomed or metal-cleated sandals, which can be slipped, laced, or buckled over your wading boots. These sandals are not designed for cross-country treks, though, and should be carried until you get to the river.

For extremely fast, slippery rivers, some waders come with a combination of felt bottoms with hexagonal aluminum studs. You can almost

217

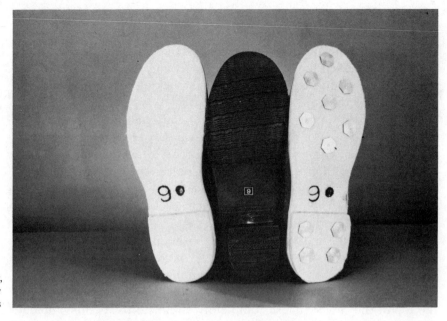

Types of wader soles. Left to right: felt sole, rubber sole, and felt sole with aluminum cleats. Orvis

walk up the side of an underwater boulder with them.

During the summer you can wade "wet," with just a pair of shorts and sneakers. If you fish rivers with slippery rocks, glue some felt or indoor-outdoor carpeting to the bottom of your sneakers. But bear in mind that summer fishing is usually best in the evening, and by the time the sun goes down you may be wishing you had worn your waders.

FISHING VESTS

You should always buy a fishing vest with more pockets than you think you need. If you don't accumulate more fly boxes and gadgets as you go along, you're a rare individual.

Most fishing vests are made from cotton or a poly/cotton blend. The tighter the weave, the longer the vest will last, and the more water- and wind-repellent it will be. Look for bar tacking at all pocket corners and stress points, with the thread stitched back and forth many times to secure the fabric.

Fly-box pockets and pockets that will hold heavy objects that fall out when you bend over, like thermometers or mini-cameras, should have large, smooth, nylon zippers. The zippers should open with one hand, because you'll usually have your rod tucked under one arm when you change flies in midstream.

Smaller pockets should have Velcro fasteners on them. Velcro is secure and durable and makes one-handed opening easy. Don't buy a vest with snap pockets—snaps don't last long and are tough to open with one hand.

Many vests come in two versions, regular or short. The short vest is designed for those who wade right to the top of their waders. It rides high so your fly boxes stay dry. A rusty fly is generally ruined, as the

A well-designed fishing vest has the capacity to carry all this gear. Cook Nielson

Fleece drying patches should be used for wet flies, nymphs, and streamers, but not for dry flies.

wire at the eye and hook point will be weakened.

Vest sizing is not that critical, but you should be able to move freely in all directions. Fill the pockets of a vest before you try it on. If you're going to fish in cold weather, the vest you choose should fit over a sweater and a down vest. It's always better to have one that's too large than one that is constricting when you're all loaded up.

Most vests come with a fleece drying patch, which can be pinned where it's most convenient for you on the outside of the vest. Wet flies, nymphs, and streamers are placed on this patch after using them, so you don't put them away wet. A fly that is put away wet will rust, and may even rust the flies adjacent to it in your box. Dry flies should not be dried on a fleece patch, as this will crush the hackles in a misshapen mess.

Don't economize on a fishing vest. A good one will last for many years. Make sure that the pocket arrangement is convenient for you, and that all the gear you want to take will fit in it, and then some. You can always leave a few pockets empty.

TACKLE BOXES

A fly-fisherman with a tackle box? You bet. I wouldn't go bass or saltwater fishing without one.

It's tough to fit many of the extra-large bass and saltwater flies in fly boxes, and you don't need all those gadgets that trout fishermen carry. The long, skinny trays in tackle boxes are great for big streamers and poppers, and you can put your extra spools, insect repellent, clippers, and other paraphernalia in the bottom of the box. Set it in front of you in the boat and everything is handy.

When trout fishing from a canoe, I still wear my vest, though, because I haven't seen a tackle box that will hold tiny dries and nymphs properly.

FLY BOXES

Your flies should be protected from clothing, gusts of wind, and rain, and they should be kept in some kind of order.

Wet flies, nymphs, streamers, and bass bugs can be kept in any kind of fly box, but delicate dry flies, whose hackle can be easily crushed and matted out of shape, should always be kept loose in individual-compartment boxes. There hasn't been a clip or magnetic arrangement designed that will protect dry flies satisfactorily.

Compartment Boxes

Compartment boxes come in two types: plastic boxes with a lid that opens to expose all the compartments at once, and aluminum boxes

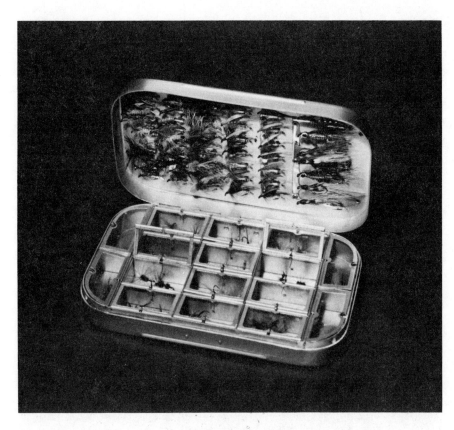

An aluminum box with individual compartments and clips on the lid. Orvis

with clear, individual, spring-loaded lids that snap open individually on each compartment.

The plastic boxes are inexpensive, rugged, and lightweight. They come in all sizes, for midges right up to saltwater poppers. The best designs have lids that fit so tight that tiny midges can't "migrate" from one compartment to the next. These boxes are suitable for all kinds of flies, the only disadvantage being that when you open the lid in windy weather, all flies are exposed to errant gusts that may whisk away some of your prize possessions. Make sure that the compartments are deep enough to hold your dry flies "loose." If a dry doesn't fall out when you turn the box upside down, the compartments are too small. Don't overfill the compartments, either.

The individual-lid aluminum boxes are expensive and heavy, and sometimes the lids get bent out of shape. They are, however, exquisite in appearance and a joy to own. They are not deep or wide enough for a big Wulff or variant dries, and if you try to stuff big dries in these compartments you'll ruin them. The compartments are not designed for nymphs or wets, but the lids usually contain metal clips, magnets, or a foam pad for other types of flies.

Metal-Clip Boxes

Metal clips are used for salmon flies, wets and nymphs, and streamers. They are great for flies larger than size 14, but are not suitable for tiny nymphs.

221

Magnetic Boxes

These are usually combined with metal clips in the lid. They hold flies securely, but sometimes the flies slip around and get out of order.

Coil Spring Clip Boxes

You don't see many of these around anymore, but they are one of the finest designs for holding nymphs and wet flies.

Foam and Foam-Strip Boxes

These are the only kind of fly box that will hold tiny nymphs and wets, size 16 and smaller, without losing them or dulling their hook points. They are also great for any kind of fly except dry flies.

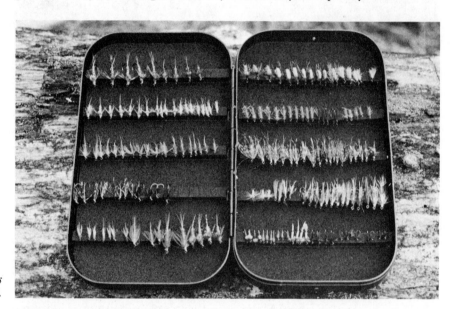

Foam-strip boxes hold tiny nymphs and wets very well.

Fleece-Lined Fly Books

Fleece-lined books are an old traditional design, and they look classy loaded with colorful streamers or salmon flies. Use them with care. If a fly is even remotely damp when you put it in a fleece book, it will rust overnight. Fleece books crush streamer wings out of shape, wings that some poor fly-tier took great pains to set properly. And they don't hold many flies for the space they take up in your vest.

Choose fly boxes that appeal to you, making sure that they will hold the kind of flies you're going to carry. Then put your fly boxes in some kind of order. Put all the cream ones in one corner. Put all the size 20s in one compartment. Keep all your spinners in one box. Whatever system you use, it will eliminate a lot of fumbling around when you need that size 14 Quill Gordon. Less fumbling means less flies dropped in the river by accident. You should be able to pick the fly you want when the last glimmer of twilight is fading.

HELPFUL GADGETS

These are the tools that some of us can't live without, others never use. Most can be kept in small pockets or pinned to your vest on a pin-on retriever reel. If things hanging from the front of your vest bother you, do what a friend of mine does: he pins them on the inside of his vest, so they don't hang out in front every time he bends over.

Clippers or Nippers

These are essential if you plan to stay on good terms with your dentist. Biting the tag ends of your knots removes the enamel from your teeth. Most designs have little pen blades or scissors that come in handy for all kinds of jobs, like cleaning fish when you forget your pocketknife or trimming a fly to make it smaller or sparser.

Forceps

Forceps are essential if you plan to release your fish. They are much more efficient than fingers for backing hooks out of fish. For pike, bluefish, and other toothy species, substitute a good pair of longnose pliers.

Forceps can also be used to make barbless hooks, by carefully mashing down the barb with gentle pressure.

Scissors Pliers

These combine tiny pliers with serrated scissors, and can be used for the same purposes as forceps, plus reel maintenance and crimping split shot to your leader. Dentists look upon using your teeth to crimp split shot to the leader much as they do biting monofilament.

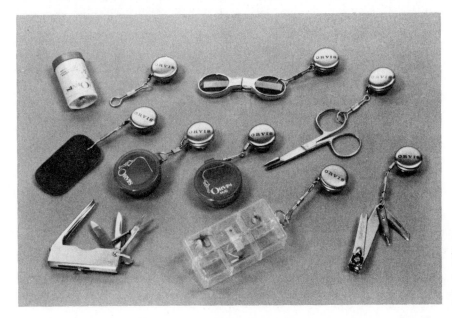

Helpful gadgets. Top: a small flashlight, a pin-on reel that can be attached to any gadget, and a pair of folding scissors. Middle: leader straightener, silicone paste fly dressing, leader sink, and scissor-pliers. Bottom: fisherman's nipper knife, tiny fly box, angler's clips. Orvis

Leader Straightener

Good leader material will straighten when pulled between your hands, but will sometimes cut into your skin. A leader straightener is a leather-covered rubber piece that you can pull your leader through. Pulling your leader through the rubber side while pinching the leather pad around it generates enough heat to take the kinks out of the nylon.

Stream Thermometer

A good stream thermometer should have a metal housing to protect it from bumps. Keep it on a length of old fly line or leader material so you can lower it into a lake or stream without getting your sleeves wet. A stream thermometer will tell you when hatches are due, when fish are spawning, and is indispensable in summer, when the fish are concentrated near cold-water springs.

Fly Threader

If your near vision is going, this gadget can be a lifesaver. It funnels the leader through the eye of a hook, even in the dark.

Knot-Tying Aid

There are various tools designed to make fly-fishing knots simpler. Practice without them first. If you still have trouble, try one of these.

Hook Hone

Hooks lose their sharpness if you catch your back cast on a rock, get your nymph snagged on the bottom, or sometimes when you release a fish by the fly-twisting method. The best hook hones are made from industrial diamond particles, are smaller than a ball-point pen, and will touch up a point in seconds.

Magnifying Loupe

Another handy gadget for those whose near vision isn't as sharp as it used to be. They clip onto your glasses and can be pushed out of the way when you go back to your casting.

Small Flashlight

Essential if you fish in the evening or at night. It should be designed so that it leaves both hands free to tie knots, whether you hold it in your teeth, clip it to your vest, or hang it around your neck.

Insect Repellent

Peak time for mayflies on trout streams is also peak black fly and mosquito time. I don't need to say any more, except get a bottle that fits in your vest so you can reapply it while fishing. Keep it away from all plastics, including leaders, lines, and fly boxes.

Emergency Wader-Repair Stick

This is a plastic that you melt with a lighter and dab onto small wader leaks. It dries in minutes and will stick to most wader materials. If you're going away from home for a day or more, carry a standard wader-patching kit for larger tears.

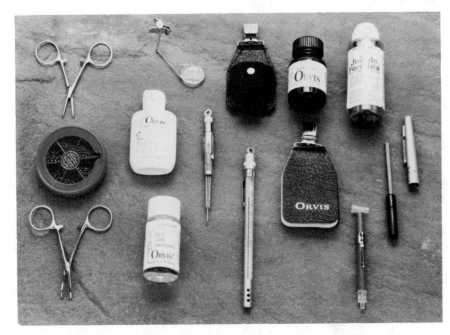

Other useful accessories. Top: forceps, magnifying loupe, accessory-bottle holder, silicone liquid fly dressing, insect repellent. Middle: split shot, silicone drying powder, knot-tyer, thermometer, fly-line cleaner, hook hone. Bottom: curved forceps, fly-line dressing, fly threader. Orvis

FLOATING AND SINKING AIDS

Dry-Fly Flotant

Dry flies should be dressed with some kind of silicone compound before use. Flotants are available in bottle, aerosol, and paste forms. With the bottle version, you dip your fly in after you've tied it to the leader, then blow on the fly to dry the solvent, and false cast a half dozen times. With the aerosol type, you spray the fly and then dry it the same way. If you get the fly into the water before the solvent dries, the silicone will not waterproof the fly properly. With the paste type, you smear a tiny amount on the fly. Use it sparingly—don't gum up the fly. There is no solvent in the paste type, so it doesn't have to be dried.

Silicone Powder

This is sold under such trade names as Dry-N-Float. Once a dry fly has caught a fish, the fish slime that coats it makes flotation difficult. A

225

fly that has been in water will not absorb regular fly flotants, so to redress the fly you shake some of this desiccant powder into your hand, rub it into the fly, and blow on the fly—moisture and fish slime are instantly removed. This stuff saves lots of time spent changing water-logged dry flies.

Fly-Line Cleaner

Modern floating fly lines don't need dressing to float, but do need to be cleaned periodically. Keep a tin in your vest in case your line gets dirty during the day. You can clean an entire line in a few minutes.

Leader Sink

Whether your leader should float or sink with dry flies is a matter for speculation, but it should sink quickly when you're using wets and nymphs. Nylon will float if you get sweat or fly dressing on it, and leader sink removes these. Also, it masks the shine of nylon, which may spook nervous fish.

The most effective one is a special Wyoming mud concoction made by a cowboy friend of mine "from secret ingredients mixed only under a full moon."

Nets, Gaffs, and Tailers

A net will save you lost fish, lost flies, and will enable you to handle fish you plan to release gently. Wading fishermen should use as small a

A wood-handled net and a spring-loaded net retriever. Orvis

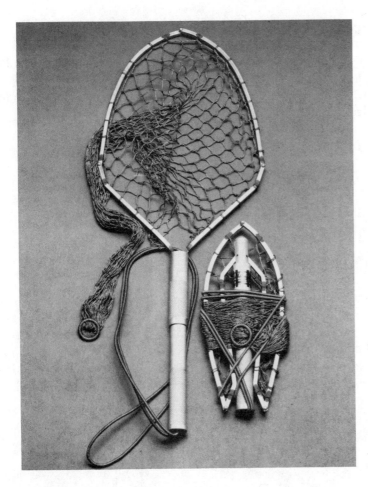

An instant net that springs into shape when you need it. Orvis

net as possible, because a net that is too big only gets in the way. You can always beach a very large fish.

Wooden-handled nets look nice and feel good in the hand, but any small net will work fine. Make sure the mesh isn't too fine, otherwise your leader and fly will get hopelessly entangled.

You can attach a net to your vest with a spring-loaded retriever chain that attaches to the back of the vest, or a French-clip quick release, which hooks onto the net ring under the back of the collar. A squeeze will detach the net from the ring.

There is also a spring-loaded net that folds into a tiny holster and jumps into shape when you pull it out. A net that hangs in front or on the side of you will only get in the way of your stripping line.

Nets used in boats should have longer handles, long enough so you don't have to lean over the side of the boat when netting a fish.

Gaffs are used for saltwater fish. They are hard on a fish if you plan to release him, except for species with wide bony lips, like tarpon, that can be lip-gaffed without injury.

A tailer is a special landing device used for Atlantic salmon. It is a nooselike device that will grip a salmon without injury, because of the narrow rear body and wide tail of the salmon. It requires some practice to use properly.

227

Stripping Basket

On boats or when wading, a stripping basket is used to hold long lengths of shooting line, especially when you're casting with shooting heads. It clips to your wader belt and keeps shooting line from getting tangled around your legs or objects on the deck of a boat.

Creel

If you can't get your fish on ice immediately, a creel is essential unless the weather is below freezing. The basket type is traditional, but it's very bulky and does not cool as efficiently as the canvas varieties, which cool by evaporation.

Wading Staff

For those who are unsteady on their feet in fast water, a wading staff can save the day. They give you something to lean on and can be used to test the water depth in front of you. The traditional wooden type can be clipped to your belt when not in use. The emergency wading staff consists of plastic sections held together by elastic shock cord. It stows into a ten-inch-long holster and jumps into a fifty-inch staff when you pull it out.

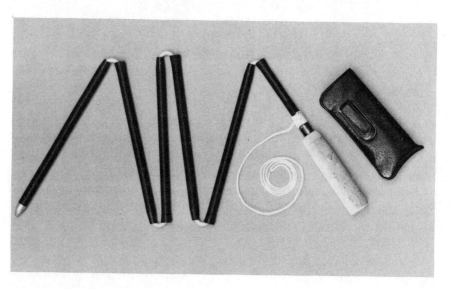

The emergency wading staff folds neatly into a holster. Orvis

Split Shot

Lead split shot is a necessary addition to your leader when you have to get a nymph right on the bottom. It makes casting difficult, so use as little lead as possible. Start with one or two and add more if you're not getting deep enough. Most fly-fishermen crimp split shot to their tippet, anywhere from six to twenty inches above the fly. You can also leave one tag end of the last blood knot in your leader a little long, tie an overhand knot in the end of it, and add your shot here; the overhand knot keeps the shot from slipping off the end. With this method, if the shot hangs up on the bottom you may not lose your fly and tippet.

Tweezers

If you fish with small flies, a pair of tweezers makes it easy to pick through fly-box compartments and select the pattern you want.

Hat

A fly-fisherman's hat is a personal decision and I wouldn't think of suggesting a particular type. Hats protect your head from wild casts, protect you from insects, and keep the rain off your face. One style, with a brim in back and one in front, keeps sun off your neck and face, and is very popular with saltwater fly-fishermen.

Polarized Sunglasses

Polarized sunglasses are essential for any kind of fishing where you are casting to visible fish. They cut most of the glare from the surface of the water and give you a much better view of what is going on below. Gray polarized lenses absorb more light and are used on very bright days; yellow or amber lenses heighten contrast and are better on cloudy days.

If you wear prescription glasses you can obtain prescription polarized sunglasses or inexpensive clip-ons. Most of the clip-ons are made from plastic and scratch very easily. You may go through a couple of pairs a year.

Sunglasses, of course, will also protect your eyes from eyestrain and from (heaven forbid) a back cast that gets blown into your face.

Leader Wallet

Leader wallets are used to keep an assortment of different leader lengths and leaders with different tippet sizes in your vest. They are usually made from vinyl, and each leaf can be written on with pencil so that you can keep track of them. Leaders can be coiled around your hand before they are put away; start with the tippet end, wind around your palm, and then wrap the butt end around the loop a few times to keep the coil from unwinding.

Leader Gauge

Various simple devices to measure the diameter of your leader are available. Most use slots of various sizes that you try to slide your tippet into. A snug but not tight fit indicates the diameter of that particular slot. They are useful when you're using knotless tapered leaders, so you know when the leader has been cut back to the point where you have to add a tippet.

Fishing Mitts

These are wool or polypropylene gloves with the fingertips exposed, so you can tie on a fly or change tippets while keeping most of your hands warm. They are also excellent protection against mosquitoes and black flies.

Rain Jacket

Last but not least. Some of the best fly-fishing occurs during rainstorms; you might as well be comfortable while you're fishing. In a boat, any kind of high-quality rainwear will make things more fun, and the new breathable types are totally reliable and superbly comfortable.

If you wear waders and have a full fishing vest, your ordinary rain jacket will be too long and too narrow in the chest. Specially designed wading jackets are cut short so they don't hang in the water, full in the chest so they fit over a fishing vest.

This short wading jacket is designed to be worn over waders, and even has special pockets for fly boxes. Orvis

13
Care of
Fly-Fishing
Tackle

Modern fly-fishing tackle requires little care. Most of it requires no care at all. Your major investments—rods, reels, lines, and flies—can be kept in perfect working order with a few minutes' time after each day of fishing.

RODS

A fly rod that is broken while playing a fish is rare, and it is nearly impossible to break a well-made rod by casting too hard. Most casters and most fish just do not have enough strength to break a fly rod. The exceptional fly rod that breaks while you are fishing most likely was damaged previously. A hard whack against a rock can cause a tiny fracture that shows up later when stressed, as can a "hook check," which happens when a fly hits your rod on the back or forward cast, making a tiny crack that opens up later.

The most common causes of rod breakage are: catching a rod in a car door (by far the most popular) or station-wagon power window, tripping and falling on a rod, leaving a rod on top of a car and driving off, trans-

Breaking off a fly that is out of reach without breaking the rod.

porting a rod in an airline baggage compartment, and taking a rod apart improperly (not getting a straight pull). Another pitfall is yanking a line-to-leader connection through the guides by pulling the leader down toward the butt section, rather than pulling straight away from the tip-top.

Rods are often broken when you try to yank a fly out of a tree. If you get caught in a tree, first try removing it with a slow, gentle pull. The fly may be wrapped around a twig and not stuck in anything; a gentle pull may remove it. No luck? Then point the rod tip at the fly and slowly walk away. You can't break your rod tip this way.

If you always keep your rod in its aluminum tube and cloth sack when you're not fishing, you will eliminate 95 percent of rod breakage problems. A rod that is left set up at the end of the day rather than taken apart and put away may not only be a prime target for carelessness; it may also be very difficult to take apart when you *do* want to put it away.

Never put a fly rod away when it's still wet. Lay the rod, cloth sack, and tube (with the cap left off) somewhere warm and dry where they won't be disturbed. Overnight will usually do it. Moisture won't hurt the rod blank, but putting a rod away wet may mildew the rod sack and grip, or oxidize metal ferrules. Fly rods should be stored in a cool, dry place, standing upright in a corner. Leave the cap on the tube unscrewed in case a change in temperature forms condensation on the inside of the tube.

Guides eventually wear out. The constant abrasion of fly line against them will form grooves that are sharp and can ruin a fly line in short order. Someone who fishes hard and whose fly line is dirty will go through a set of guides in three years. Another who keeps his line clean and doesn't fish hard may go a lifetime without requiring a new set.

To check your guides, run a piece of nylon stocking through each one. If it catches, it's time to replace that guide. You can buy a new guide set, a spool of thread, and a bottle of varnish and do the job yourself, or send the rod off for repair. Major rod manufacturers do this service regularly for a small fee; they also have pamphlets that show you how to do it yourself.

Cork grips darken with age. This won't hurt the rod a bit, but if it bothers you they can be cleaned with nail-polish remover (don't get it on any varnish windings!) or with very fine sandpaper.

Keep sand out of screw-lock reel seats, as a single grain can bind the threads. Loosen a stuck reel seat by rocking the reel from side to side. If this is a frequent problem, wash the reel seat with soap and water, then lubricate it by nicking the threads a few times with a bar of soap.

All ferrules, whether they are metal or the self-ferrule type, have varnished winds of thread over them for security. The difference in flex between the rod and the stiffer ferrule will cause a tiny crack in the varnish. This happens with all rods and will not present a problem. If it's objectionable to you, take a toothpick, dip it in spar varnish, and run it over the crack a few times.

Any winding that starts to unwind should be sent away for repair or cut off with a razor blade and replaced.

Dirty ferrules will make a rod stick together. To separate stubborn rod sections, first try putting on a pair of rubber gloves, to give you a more secure pull, and pull the sections straight away from each other, without bending the rod. If you have no luck, get a friend to stand opposite you and place a hand on each section of the rod, near the ferrule; then place your hands in the same manner, so that you are both pulling the rod as if you were working alone. Pull the sections apart, being very careful that you are both getting a straight pull.

Ferrules on all high-quality rods are hand-fitted to each other before they leave the factory. This is why if you break a tip section on your rod, the manufacturer asks you to send both the butt and the tip back to him. He can't just send a new tip section to you, because he can't be sure of the proper fit.

Two-handed rod removal. Each tries for a straight pull, as if he were working alone.

Ferrules that stick constantly should be cleaned and lubricated. Clean both the male and female sections with soap and water, using a Q-tip to get inside the female ferrule. Polish the surface of the male ferrule with a soft cloth. After both sections are completely dry, check the fit. If it's still tight, they'll need lubrication, but never use grease or oil and never rub a ferrule alongside your nose or ear. Greasy substances cause suction in the ferrule and also attract dirt particles. Fiberglass, boron/graphite, and graphite self-ferrules should be lubricated with paraffin, metal ferrules with dry soap.

Lubricating the male ferrule of a graphite rod with paraffin.

With years of hard use, ferrules will loosen. A loose ferrule will make the rod sections rock against each other, and can break a rod. Never attempt ferrule repair or replacement unless you are a competent rod maker. Return the rod to the manufacturer or send it to someone who offers custom rod service.

Bamboo rods that are subjected to a lot of strain may develop a "set," which is a slight misalignment of the glue joints. The rod will curve off to one side as you look straight down the rod. A minor set won't hurt a thing, but an experienced bamboo rod maker can realign it by heating the section over a flame and pressing it back into shape. Don't try it yourself.

The blank of a modern impregnated bamboo, fiberglass, graphite, or boron/graphite rod needs no care at all. They are impervious to moisture, extremes in temperature, and saltwater. Varnished bamboo rods should be checked for cracks in the varnish. If moisture gets inside the varnish, a set may result, or if the rod was made prior to World War II and was glued with animal glues, the glue joints may separate. Revarnishing is expensive and time-consuming, but it is necessary to protect your investment.

With a minimum of care, a well-made fly rod should last for several generations. I occasionally use an old bamboo rod that was built in the 1920s.

Lubricating the metal ferrule of a bamboo rod with a bar of dry soap.

REELS

Fly reels used in fresh water should be cleaned and lubricated twice a year or whenever they get dirty. If you don't stick your reel in the sand, and keep it in its case when not in use, you may have to do this only once a year.

Clean your reel in dishwashing detergent and warm water, never with any kind of solvent. A solvent may ruin the finish on your reel and definitely will ruin your fly line. A toothbrush helps to get into tight spaces. Relubricate your reel by applying a light grease to all moving parts, especially the arbor that holds the spool. Heavy grease will gum up the works and may cause your spool to seize up on a fast-running fish.

Reels that are used in saltwater should be washed with soap and warm water and then rinsed several times with fresh water. Take all the line and backing off your reel and rinse them as well. Then apply a light coat of oil to all parts of the reel, including the inside of the spool, except the cork or Teflon pads on disk-drag models. Relubricate all moving metal parts with a light grease. Never use outboard motor lubricant, which is much too heavy.

LINES

Modern plastic fly lines do not need to be dried after use; in fact, you can leave a line on a reel for years without hurting it. Don't store a fly line where it will receive direct sunlight, as UV rays can deteriorate the finish slightly.

The solvents in aerosol fly sprays and the chemicals in insect repellents can break down the plastic finish on fly lines. When you spray a fly, point the spray away from your fly line. After applying insect repellent,

235

rub your fingertips in the sand for a minute so that you don't get any repellent on your fly line. Mosquitoes don't like fingertips anyway.

Fly lines get dirty, especially in water that has a lot of algae in it. A floating line that is dirty will not float properly; a dirty line of any type will not shoot as smoothly as it should. All lines can be washed in a sink with soap and warm water, then run through a towel.

Floating lines, except the hydrophobic kinds, can also be cleaned with special line cleaner, which also lubricates them. You just rub a felt pad on the cleaner and then run your line through the pad while pinching the outside.

If you can, always practice casting on water. A few minutes of casting on asphalt can ruin a line. If you can't find any water, wet grass is preferable to asphalt or cement.

Fly lines don't last forever. Eventually you'll notice cracks in the finish of your line, which signals that it's time to get a new one. Most fly lines last two to six years, depending on how hard you use them.

LEADERS

Nylon can be hurt by solvents from fly sprays, by insect repellents, and by constant exposure to the UV rays in sunlight. Store leaders and tippet material in the dark. I don't trust the very fine diameters of nylon, 5X and smaller, after they are two years old. There isn't much margin for error in material that tests a pound and a half, so if a spool of tippet material is over two years old (few last that long anyway) I throw it out. Reputable tackle dealers constantly rotate their stock of tippet material, so you don't have to worry about buying old stuff.

WADERS

Most of the maintenance time spent on fly-fishing tackle is spent on waders. They won't last forever. The rubber in waders is gradually broken down by UV rays in sunlight, ozone in the air, barbed wire (not so gradually!), and abrasion when you walk.

Never store waders in direct sunlight, and never near electric motors, which give off small amounts of ozone. Waders should be stored in a cool, dry place. Boot-foot waders should be completely dry when you store them; use a hair dryer on the cool setting if they are wet inside. They should be hung, by the boots, on special wader hangers, or folded loosely and put back in the box they came in. Stocking-foot waders can be folded, rolled up, or thrown in a corner—just keep them away from sunlight and electric motors.

Leather and canvas wading shoes should be dry before you put them away, or they will mildew. The new wading shoes made from artificial leather are mildew-proof and can be stored any old way.

Holes in waders come in three forms: pinhole leaks from abrasion, tears, and seam links. Pinhole leaks and tears can be located with a flashlight in a dark closet. Seam leaks can be found by filling the inside of the waders with water and seeing where it leaks out. Find the leak, mark the spot with a waterproof marking pen, clean the spot with soap and water, and let the waders dry. For tears and seam leaks you will have to use a standard patch kit, similar to an inner-tube repair kit. Follow the directions on the package.

Pinhole leaks don't usually require a patch. Repair by coating the area with the cement that comes in your repair kit, or with silicone tile-sealant. Use two or three thin layers, letting each dry before applying the next.

For all repair jobs, stuff the inside of your waders with newspaper so you don't glue the legs together.

FLIES

I'm a nitpicker about fly care, as are most fly-tiers. Flies should never be put away wet. Put nymphs, streamers, and wet flies on your fleece patch and leave there until dry. Blow the moisture from your dry flies before putting them away.

If the inside of a fly box gets wet, be prepared to remove all the flies as soon as possible and lay them out somewhere to air-dry. Do not put them away until they are perfectly dry. Otherwise, you'll end up with misshapen flies and rusty hooks.

Dry flies should not be stuffed into compartments that are too small or stuffed too many to a compartment. They should never be put into metal clips. Storing them this way will crush their delicate hackles, tails, and wings out of shape.

Flies that have been mashed out of shape can easily be rejuvenated. With a pair of tweezers, hold them near the spout of a boiling teakettle. The feathers will instantly spring back into shape.

Should you throw away flies that are tattered beyond recognition? I don't know. Flies that have been reduced to a few wisps of thread and fur have taken some pretty nice fish. Maybe you should tuck them away in a corner of your fly box where your buddies won't see them.

Essential Reading

General References

McClane, A. J. (ed.). *McClane's New Standard Fishing Encyclopedia*. Holt, Rinehart, and Winston, 1974. The finest general fishing reference ever published. Includes everything from fly tying and casting to the ecology and life history of gamefish. The fly-fishing sections are excellent.

Schwiebert, Ernest. *Trout*. E. P. Dutton, 1978. A massive, two-volume work on all aspects of trout fishing. Especially good on the history and romance of trout fishing with a fly.

Tackle

Keane, Martin J. *Classic Rods and Rodmakers*. Classic, 1976. The most complete and authoritative work on the history of bamboo fly rods. Enjoyable reading.

Kreh, Lefty, and Sosin, Mark. *Practical Fishing Knots*. NLB/Winchester, 1972, 1983. A complete guide to all kinds of fishing knots, especially useful for the saltwater fly rodder.

Trout—Stream Insects

Arbona, Fred. *Mayflies, the Angler, and the Trout*. NLB/Winchester, 1980. A detailed study of mayfly hatches and fishing techniques by a well-traveled fly-fisherman. Contains some excellent advanced tactics for difficult trout.

Caucci, Al and Nastasi, Bob. *Hatches*. Comparahatch, Ltd., 1975. A thorough guide to the mayfly hatches of North America.

Flick, Art. *Art Flick's New Streamside Guide*. NLB/Winchester, 1983. A very practical approach to fishing the mayfly hatches in the eastern United States.

LaFontaine, Gary. *Caddisflies*. NLB/Winchester, 1981. A complete guide to the biology of caddisflies and advanced fishing techniques for their hatches.

Schwiebert, Ernest. *Matching the Hatch*. A guide to fishing all kinds of insect hatches by the man who coined the phrase.

Swisher, Doug and Richards, Carl. *Selective Trout*. NLB/Winchester, 1971. Contains many innovative flies and fishing techniques, mainly on mayflies but with brief sections on caddisflies, stoneflies, midges, and terrestrials.

Whitlock, Dave. *Dave Whitlock's Guide to Aquatic Trout Foods*. NLB/Winchester, 1982. A practical guide to fishing all kinds of imitations, from mayflies to salamanders. Heavy on technique, thankfully light on Latin names and entomology.

Stream and Still-Water Strategies

Atherton, John. *The Fly and the Fish*. Freshet Press, 1951, Macmillan, 1971. One of the most delightful books on fly-fishing ever written. Contains some obsolete material on silk fly lines and gut leaders, but the material on flies and strategy is a valid today as it was in 1951.

Humphreys, Joe. *Joe Humphrey's Trout Tactics*. Stackpole, 1981. All kinds of advice on finding and catching trout on dries, wets, nymphs, and streamers.

Marinaro, Vincent. *A Modern Dry Fly Code*. NLB/Winchester, 1950, 1970, 1983. A timeless study of limestone stream trout fishing. Very enjoyable reading.

Merwin, John (ed.). *Stillwater Trout*. NLB/Winchester, 1980. How to catch trout in lakes and ponds by a host of experts.

Salmon, Saltwater, and Steelhead

Bates, Joseph. *Atlantic Salmon Flies and Fishing*. Stackpole, 1970. A practical reference on the techniques and flies used to catch Atlantic salmon.

Combs, Trey. *Steelhead Fly Fishing and Flies*. Frank Amato Publications, 1976, 1979. A valuable reference on all aspects of steelhead fishing, from tackle to tactics to flies.

Kreh, Lefty. *Fly Fishing in Salt Water*. NLB/Winchester, 1974. The most complete guide to saltwater fly-fishing by a leading authority.

Wulff, Lee. *The Atlantic Salmon*. NLB/Winchester, 1958, 1983. The unchallenged master of Atlantic salmon fishing discusses all aspects of fly-fishing for salmon.

Flies and Fly Tying

Harder, John. *The Index of Orvis Fly Patterns*. Orvis, 1978. Includes patterns for 355 flies, pictured in color, plus tying hints.

McKim, John. *Fly Tying*. Mountain Press, 1982. A good introduction to the basics of tying all kinds of flies. Excellent, helpful line drawings.

Talleur, Richard. *Mastering the Art of Fly Tying*. Stackpole, 1979. A well-rounded book on trout flies, with very sharp black-and-white photographs.

Magazines

Fly Fisherman Magazine. Historical Times, Inc., 2245 Kohn Road, Harrisburg, PA 17105. The largest magazine devoted entirely to fly-fishing and fly-tying. Published six times per year.

Fly Fishing. Frank Amato Publications, P. O. Box 02112, Portland, OR 97202. An informative publication, heavy on the "how to" and "where to." Published six times per year.

Rod & Reel Magazine. Down East Publications, P. O. Box 370, Camden, ME 04843. Classy editorial with lots of features on fly-tying and fly-fishing equipment. Published five times per year.

Fly Fishing Made Easy, Fly Fishing for Trout, Fly Fishing for Bass, Fly Fishing in Salt Water. Aqua-Field Publications, Inc., P. O. Box 721, Point Pleasant, NJ 08742. Published under the editorial guidance of 3M's Scientific Angler's Division, these annuals are valuable sources of fly fishing information.

Organizations

The Atlantic Salmon Federation, 1434 St. Catherine Street W., Suite 109, Montreal, Quebec, Canada H3G 1R4. Dedicated to proper management and study of our dwindling stocks of Atlantic salmon. Members receive *The Atlantic Salmon Journal*, which has both conservation and angling articles.

The Catskill Fly Fishing Center, Roscoe, NY. Dedicated to preserving the history of fly-fishing, both past and present, through educational programs.

The Federation of Fly Fishers, P. O. Box 1088, West Yellowstone, MT 59888. An international organization with local chapters, mainly in the United States, involved with education of the fly-fishing public and conservation of coldwater, warmwater, and saltwater fish species. Runs the International Fly Fishing Center in West Yellowstone and publishes *The Fly Fisher*, a high-quality magazine devoted to fly fishing for all kinds of fish. Members only can receive *The Fly Fisher.*

The Museum of American Fly Fishing, Manchester, VT 05254. Maintains the largest collection of fly-fishing memorabilia in the United States, with exhibits in Manchester, Vermont, and in the International Fly Fishing Center in West Yellowstone, Montana. Publishes *The American Fly Fisher*, a historical journal available to members only.

Trout Unlimited, P. O. Box 1944, Washington, DC 20013. National organization with local chapters; lobbies and educates on preserving coldwater habitat. Embraces all fishing methods, but members are predominately fly fishermen. Publishes *Trout*, a magazine with articles on fishing methods, plus the ecology and natural history of trout and salmon.

Index